A Long Journey Backward

From DARKNESS to LIGHT

Nancee J Soisson

ISBN 979-8-89345-433-8 (paperback)
ISBN 979-8-89345-434-5 (hardcover)
ISBN 979-8-89345-435-2 (digital)

Christian Faith Publishing
832 Park Avenue
Meadville, PA 16335
www.christianfaithpublishing.com

Printed in the United States of America

To my husband, Joby, who so willingly joined me in this adventure. Truly you are the love of my life.

CONTENTS

SYNOPSIS OF BOOK 1

This book is the continuation of Lucinda's story as chronicled in *A Child from the Inside Out.* Lucinda blew into my life on a March day in 1989, upending my comfortable life as a middle-class mom. I was a student counselor, and Lucinda was a young woman with a ferocious anger, seeking help to control her temper with her three young sons. Together we traveled a long road, a road of discovery and healing for Lucinda and a road of learning for me.

The first obstacle we encountered were her "staring spells," trancelike states that would overcome her whenever the material we were discussing was too painful for her to acknowledge. Not knowing what to do about these spells or how to help her, we set out on a quest to find psychiatric help for her. Through a series of doctors, we were able to piece together that these were dissociative states: attempts to escape her present reality, a survival tool she learned in the crucible of trauma.

In time, the staring spells were left behind, but not until another psychological phenomenon surfaced: alter personalities who carried the memories and pains of her traumas. Five-year-old Lucy, the first alter to reveal herself, carried memories of sexual abuse from her father and brothers. Lu, a protector, surfaced next. Lu was filled with rage but became a strong ally of mine as we worked together to help other alters. Then there was Lucia, who did not speak but wrote and drew pictures to tell the stories of what happened. As I listened to their stories and walked though their pain with them, we were cemented by a deep and lasting bond.

In the midst of all the subconscious material that came to light, something very dark and sinister emerged. It began with the memory of a single satanic ritual in a railroad car, but grew to encompass a multigenerational satanic cult led by her grandmother as the high priestess. Lucinda's alter personalities had been groomed to take her grandmother's place. With her grandmother's death, events were set in motion for Lucinda to be initiated as the next priestess. With Lu's help, the initiation was averted. As grateful as we were for this turn of events, we had no idea that Lucinda's work was just beginning.

Another level of alter personalities emerged—and then a third level. The new alters had bone-chilling stories of abuse. Those on the third level were specifically groomed to carry on the work of the satanic cult. In the midst of this array of traumatized alters, one surfaced who was different. Her name was Cinda. Lucinda had split into Lu and Cinda during a dark ritual. Cinda claimed that in the midst of the ritual, she saw a light, and she went to that light. The light was Jesus, and Cinda became a ray of hope in Lucinda's dark inner world.

In the second level of alters, I met Amy. Amy carried memories of abuse from her mother. With Amy's emergence, something new surfaced in Lucinda, a desperate longing for a mother to love her. She called it her sickness. She became totally consumed with wanting a mother, usually focusing that longing on me. I felt the pull and wrestled with myself, knowing I could not be her mother, but wanting so much to make things easier for her. Sometimes her longing for a mother focused on other women, especially a friend named Sheila. That relationship ended very painfully.

Lucinda retreated into a fantasy world she had created and allowed another alter to take over as the host personality. It took me many months to figure this out. Thus began a quest to find the original Lucinda.

When she was finally found, Lucinda revealed her own encounter with the light. She knew for certain it was God who delivered her from the dark place within where she was imprisoned. Now she was eager to begin afresh. But this time, she wanted to be a good mother for her three boys and not be consumed with finding a mother for herself. She was positive and hopeful, ready to move forward.

There was just one problem. For her, moving ahead meant leaving those alter personalities behind. Here our story resumes.

CHAPTER 1

The Boy

Lucinda had just arrived for her session. She was obviously agitated. She dropped down onto my love seat, and words came bursting out of her. "I was walkin' Michael to school this morning. He usually walks with a friend, and sometimes his friend's mother comes too. I never liked his mother, and she never liked me. She was makin' fun of Michael, calling him a sissy. I went after her, told her where she could go. She screamed back at me, 'I'm gonna kick you in the balls.' I don't remember much else, but the cops were at my house that afternoon, wanting to know what happened. They didn't do nothin' but told me I need to watch what I say to people."

My heart sank as I listened to her story. We had worked so hard getting her to control her anger, and now it was back in full force. "Lucinda, it's been a while since your anger was so out of control. What happened?"

She shrugged. "I don't know. When she called Michael a sissy, something inside me exploded. No boy likes to be called a sissy. She's not gonna say them things about my son."

"Lucinda, you said you don't remember what happened after she said she was going to kick you." I intentionally did not repeat the rest of that comment, which I felt was very crude and certainly not appropriate to say to a female. "When did you start to remember things again?" By now I knew the signs that one of Lucinda's alter personalities might have been in control of the body.

Lucinda was now in her early thirties. Her thick brown hair was still a bit untamed. Her ever-expressive eyes were slate blue. It was late summer of 1996, so she was dressed accordingly, in shorts and a T-shirt. Protruding from under her shorts was a pair of glossy gray spandex that reached to just above her knees. This had become her standard way of dressing. I thought of it as her armor. She no longer sported the thick black eye makeup she used to wear when she wanted to appear tough and hard. I realized she had taken on a rather masculine way of dressing. *Another protection.*

She thought for a minute. "I guess I don't remember nothin' until I was back home."

"Then who was out?"

Again, she shrugged. Lucinda fluttered her eyelids, and I was face-to-face with eyes that were very angry and glaring right at me. "Who the hell are you?"

"I'm Lucinda's counselor. I'm here to help her…and you."

"Hell, I don't need no help."

"Were you the one who got into a confrontation with that woman on the way to school?"

"What's it to you? Besides, that woman was a pussy. How dare she say she was gonna kick me in the balls?"

"Especially since you don't have any." I stifled a chuckle over the absurdity of this conversation.

The one that was out glared at me. "What do you mean I ain't got no balls?" The alter looked at me with rageful eyes. "You wanna tangle? I could beat the crap out of you."

"No, I don't want to tangle, and I have no doubt you could beat the crap out of me." By now, I was used to dealing with angry alter personalities. So while I proceeded carefully, I was not concerned for my safety.

The personality continued to glare at me. "I got plenty of balls. And she'd better not kick me there."

I looked at this one who was out and considered the way Lucinda was dressed. An intriguing thought entered my head. "What's your name?"

"None of your business."

"I bet it's a boy's name."

"What's it to you?"

"Well, I'd like to know what to call you."

"I ain't tellin' you my name."

"Well, you can tell me when you're ready. Until then, I'll just call you the Boy."

This alter looked at me with eyes that weren't quite so angry. "Well, I ain't no pussy girl."

With that he was gone, and I was looking at Lucinda.

She rubbed her forehead. She had a slight headache, which often accompanied her switches from one alter to another.

We sat across from each other in my office. I still had my pastel love seat with a lone throw pillow. Lu had once pounded and twisted its mate until the seams burst and nuggets of foam flew all over. That was in my first little office, a dreary basement room. Lucinda had painted me a picture of bright-red birds to bring some color into that room. The bird picture hung in my new office, along with two other paintings of her imaginary world of escape.

I was now a seasoned counselor in a bright new office, with a large window overlooking an undeveloped field between new office buildings. Over the seven and a half rocky years I worked with Lucinda, we had both come a long way.

"Lucinda", I said gently, "I met the one who was out during the confrontation with that woman." I wasn't sure how she would respond to having a boy alter. All the others we had worked with, Lucy and Lu and Lucia and Cinda, Amy and Stacey and Angie, Tara and Tasha and Tiffany, and Dominique who was looking for her star, were feminine alters. How would she feel about having a masculine alter personality? "Lucinda, this one was different."

"Different in what way?"

"Well, it seems you have a boy alter."

Lucinda didn't respond at first. I wondered how she was feeling. Finally, she spoke. "Well, that might be why I've been wanting to buy boy dolls lately. It started with that warrior boy I bought a while ago. Now when I shop for dolls, I'm drawn to the boy dolls. And if I try to wear any clothes that look at all like a girl, I find myself taking them off and dressing like this." She spread her hands to display what she was wearing.

"So...you're okay with having a boy alter?"

"Yeah, boys are tough and don't get hurt as much as girls. Sometimes I wish I was a boy. What was his name?"

"He wouldn't tell me his name, so I just called him 'the Boy'."

I was relieved that having a boy alter did not seem to be a problem for Lucinda. I also realized having a boy alter could be one more way of becoming tough and hard, avoiding her pain and brokenness. "This might explain why you've been so angry and unpliable recently. The Boy was very angry, and that could be affecting you."

Lucinda nodded. "Yeah, that could be, but there's another reason I'm gettin' really hard. It's September and Halloween's comin'. My family's been callin' and talkin' about Halloween stuff. Mom called yesterday just to ask me the name of the snake in *Jungle Book*. That's all she wanted. She called back later and said they wanted me to come down on Halloween. Then I started seein' fire and stuff and people in hoods."

I went to my desk drawer and pulled out the packet of information I received several years earlier from a chaplain in a correctional institution. At the time, I was desperately looking for any information I could find on satanic ritual abuse.

One of the things she sent me was a calendar of the satanic year. I shuffled through the papers until I found the chart, then looked to see what it had to say about Halloween. It said it was one of four major holidays in the satanic year, one in each season. It was called the Great Sabbat and was celebrated with sexual orgies and sex with demons.

That all sounded pretty creepy to me, and I didn't think it would be helpful for Lucinda to hear what the chart said. I turned to her. "This chart verifies what we already know, that Halloween is a very important holiday in the satanic year. It's crucial you don't let your family pull you back into all that. You left it behind when Lu refused to take her place as the next high priestess."

"I know, so I have to be hard to fight 'em. But then I hear Cinda talkin' to me inside."

I was glad she could still hear Cinda, the one who chose the light during a dark ritual when Lucinda had split into Lu and Cinda. Cinda was a force within her toward healing and wholeness, toward God and light. "And what is Cinda saying to you?"

"She's sayin' plenty. She's sayin' the way to healing is to be real, not fake and hard. She's sayin' the more I'm fake, the less I see the truth."

"So to be tough and hard, whether it's you or the Boy, is not going to help you."

"I know. Some days I'm so in tune with Cinda, and some days it's total darkness. Everything out here is fake, so you put on an act for whatever they want, but then you get sicker. But then Cinda told me somethin' that really scared me."

"And what was that?"

Lucinda looked down, and her voice got very quiet. "She said… she said she wouldn't always be with me, that the time would come for her to leave. I thought she'd never leave me."

"Well, if she's one of your alter personalities, she will likely integrate—become one with you."

"I don't think that's what she meant. She's gonna leave me like all them others. Every time someone good comes into my life, they leave."

I was contemplating this when I became aware of a switch in personalities. I knew instantly it was Cinda, clear-eyed and peaceful. "Oh, Cinda," I exclaimed. "I'm so glad you're here. I understand you told Lucinda you wouldn't always be with her. That has her quite upset."

"Yes, I told her that. She needs to know the truth. You need to know it too."

Cinda had been so helpful on our long journey, always filled with truth and wisdom and pointing Lucinda toward wholeness and toward God. "I hope you won't leave soon. We couldn't have done this without you."

"It will all be in God's timing. I want you to call Lucinda back and read to her Matthew 18:10." This was not the first time Cinda had pointed me to the Bible.

"All right, I'll do that." I wondered what that verse had to say. "Lucinda, will you come back, please? We have an assignment."

The switch took place quickly, and Lucinda looked at me with a puzzled expression. "What assignment?"

"Cinda wants us to read something from the Bible." I went to my bookshelf and pulled down my Bible. I sat down and paged through it until I arrived at Matthew 18:10. "'See to it that you do not look down on one of these little ones. For I tell you that their angels in heaven always see the face of my Father in heaven.'"

"What's that mean?" Lucinda seemed genuinely interested.

I tried to explain. "Well, Jesus is talking. And when he says not to look down on little ones, he means children. He says they have angels who are always before God."

"Oh...Did I have an angel as a child?"

"Well, if we believe this verse, you did. It suggests that every child has an angel. Maybe that was the light Cinda went to when she split from Lu."

Lucinda was quiet as she contemplated this.

I was quiet too. A very interesting idea was forming in my mind, but I wasn't ready to go there yet.

CHAPTER 2

Halloween

Summer was behind us, and the air had a chill in it. The warm and brilliant hues of fall started to grace the trees, and I enjoyed this display of beauty as I drove to my new office. I anticipated the view from my office window, knowing the field across the street would be splattered with yellow golds against a clear blue sky.

I now had a full caseload of clients, and my life was very busy. Our first son and our daughter were off to college, but I still had a son at home. I juggled sporting events and church activities with my work and was very glad I could make my own schedule to accommodate all the extracurriculars.

I always tried to schedule Lucinda at the end of the day, just in case her latest crisis (and there were many) demanded extra time.

As Halloween drew closer, Lucinda's family continued to contact her. She reported to me that one evening, her mother invited her to come over. "My father was there, and my mom was bein' real nice. I was confused. What was my dad doin' there? He ain't been with her for years. And why was my mom bein' so nice? But I didn't want to leave. Somehow I felt like I belonged. It was like they was welcoming me back. I tried real hard to hide Cinda 'cause I knew she don't belong there. But she came through anyway. I could hear her, and she told me I needed to leave. I think I lost some time while I was there. I didn't get home until one in the morning, but it didn't seem like I was gone that long."

Later that session, Cinda popped out. "She shouldn't go down to her mother's. She's trying to get answers from her. She's hoping to find out all the satanic stuff didn't really happen. It's very sad she won't listen to what those inside showed her." Cinda shook her head. "When she was at her mother's, the Boy was out. He must know them."

Halloween was a very difficult time for Lucinda. Halloween decorations of ghosts and goblins and skeletons unnerved her. But even worse, she would get flashes of people in hooded robes, and she would hear chanting. She reported visions of seeing herself dead.

I hoped she was not getting suicidal again. Many times I had to hospitalize her because I feared for her life. It had been several years since she was hospitalized, and I certainly did not want to go down that road again.

*****

The day before Halloween, Lucinda arrived for a session. One glance at her and I knew she had hardened herself. She had pushed Cinda away as well as the Child, the part of her that connected her with her emotions.

"I'm seein' fire and stuff." Her voice had a hard edge. "There's a part close. I can feel her every time I see Halloween stuff. Or maybe it's the Boy. I don't know. My mother wants me to come over tomorrow night. I don't know what to do."

I studied Lucinda's face. Just a short few months ago, she had emanated a warm, positive energy as she talked about wanting to be a better mother for her boys. Now she was hard and impenetrable. I struggled with my own feelings of discouragement. I wasn't sure how to proceed, so I shot up a quick prayer. *Lord, help me to direct her back to a positive path.*

Lucinda rolled her eyes, and I was face-to-face with an alter personality who sat very still with a faraway look.

"Who's here?" I asked.

"Kathy."

I had met Kathy before. She was a very dark alter, though not especially angry, as so many of the dark alters were. She had told me about dark rituals she had participated in. She related her stories to me in a monotone voice with absolutely no show of emotion.

"What brings you here today, Kathy?"

"It's the marriage to the beast." She said this with no expression at all. "You lay down with the beast. You become one with the beast. You bring the children to him. The time is near. I'm here to destroy pain."

I remembered how the chart describing the satanic holidays had spoken of sexual orgies and sex with demons. I shuddered a little. How should I proceed?

Lucinda's familiar voice broke the silence. "Who was out? That one felt cold and dark."

I was glad Lucinda was back. "That was the one named Kathy. I think she was pulled forward by it being Halloween. Maybe she heard us talking about it."

"When I felt how frosty and dark she was, it made me feel cold." She shivered a little. "It also made me feel very evil. I don't want to be evil. It's like the only goodness in me is Cinda."

"I agree there is goodness in Cinda, but there's also goodness in you, especially when you allow yourself to be close to the Child. Then you can feel, and you are real."

"But then I'm weak, and people hurt me. There's Cinda again."

"What is she saying?"

"She's sayin' the way to healing is to be real. You know, when I'm real, I can really love my boys, but I also feel all the pain. Now that I know I can be real, part of me really wants that. But most of me is scared of it."

"Well, if you really want to be a good mother, you're going to have to be real. That means being close to Cinda and the Child."

"But I can't do it on Halloween. The only way to get through Halloween is to be fake."

I was very concerned about Lucinda spending Halloween with her family. My great fear was it would open the door for her to become re-involved with the family cult. I advised her again and again not to go to her mother's on Halloween.

"But what if all that stuff about satanism ain't true? What if I go and nothin' happens? Then I can believe them alters made all that stuff up."

"But is it worth the risk of doing some horrible things in a dark and hideous ritual?"

Lucinda left that session unsure of what she would do.

My parting advice to her was to stay close to Cinda and the Child, but I was not at all sure she would heed my words.

*****

When Lucinda arrived for her first session after Halloween, I tried to gauge her emotional state. She sat down and said nothing. My first question was, "What happened on Halloween?" I braced myself for bad news.

"Well, my mom made me really mad. She called that afternoon and said she wanted me to come over that night. She also said she didn't have any money for her blood pressure medication and wanted me to get it for her. That made me really mad. She only wanted my money. I felt used. After that, I didn't want to go over. I dropped the damn money off and then went off with Kurt. I did dissociate later that night, but I don't think I went there. I was just runnin' from Halloween."

While her husband, Kurt, was not my favorite person, I was truly glad he had provided another option.

"But that's not all that happened since Halloween." She reached into the pocket of her blue jeans and pulled out several pieces of paper. "I found these in a drawer while I was lookin' for somethin' else. I had forgotten about 'em, but when I saw 'em, I remembered when my brother Leo sent 'em to me from jail." Lucinda's brother, Leo, had been in jail on drug charges. She handed me the three pieces of folded paper.

"Don't read 'em out loud," she instructed. "Everything inside will go crazy if they hear 'em."

I picked up the first paper. It was handwritten in poetic form. The title was "For Love of Satan." There were nine stanzas of crude poetry describing an axe murder as a sacrifice to Satan. It was written in the first person and ended with instructions to not let the wrong person read it.

My mind raced after reading this gruesome account of a murder. Why would Leo ever send a poem like this to his sister? It was very confusing. I looked at Lucinda, feeling slightly nauseated. "What do you make of it?"

"It tells me all this Satan stuff is really real. You know, there was a murder in the railroad yard. Leo's friend went to jail for it, but they questioned Leo."

I picked up another letter-poem, not sure if I wanted to read it. "Shall I read the others?" I asked. She nodded. The next one was written in the same style with a few misspellings and no punctuation. It was entitled "The Fright." This was a description of the same murder with graphic details of flowing blood and the victim flopping around like a fish out of water. Leo signed it with instructions to let *Mom and them* read it, but no one else. While this poem was not written in the first person and therefore was not as incriminating for Leo, it was still chilling to read.

I looked at Lucinda and wished she had never brought these to me. But she was right about one thing: it seemed to give a lot of credence to her family's deep involvement in satanism.

I picked up the final letter-poem. It was shorter than the other ones and did not have a title. This poem did not describe the murder in detail but focused on the appearing of Satan at the scene of the murder. Leo closed the letter by saying this was one of his favorites.

Again, I looked over at Lucinda who was looking down. I handed her the letter-poems.

"I don't want 'em." She pushed them back toward me.

"What do you want me to do with them?"

"Just keep 'em. They'll be safer with you. Maybe someday we'll need 'em."

I stuck them in the back of her file, not at all sure if I wanted them either. "How do you feel about these poems?" I was well aware of my own repulsion.

"I don't like 'em. When I found 'em, everything inside me was going crazy. I heard yellin' and screamin', and it felt like I was gonna explode inside. But now I know my family really is involved in all this stuff. I guess I was hopin' it wasn't true, that my parts had just made it all up."

I ended that session with a prayer to counter the dark and sinister feelings the poems engendered. I remembered how so often God shed his light into Lucinda's darkness, and I prayed he would do the same for Leo's dark heart.

CHAPTER 3

The Child

With Halloween behind us, I hoped Lucinda would relinquish some of the hardness she had taken on. I remembered what she was like when she first returned from hiding away in her inner world of escape. She thought she had created an idyllic world where she would be forever loved by a mother who was a continuous flow of warm emotion and doting admiration. Instead, she found herself in a dark prison of loneliness. By fastening her gaze on a little speck of light that grew stronger the longer she focused on it, she finally was able to find her way out. She knew the light was God, and she returned to this world with a stronger faith and a determination to be a better wife and mother. She was positive and hopeful and emanated a warmth and love that was hard to resist.

But what had happened to that Lucinda? She had become a hardened shell, angry and abrasive.

She arrived for her next session filled with anger because Cinda had told her that someday she would leave. I challenged her. "Lucinda, where is the one who returned from your world so full of hope and love, the one who regretted having missed so much time with your three boys, the one who wanted to be a better mother and wife?"

Lucinda lowered her eyes. "There's just so much pain in this world. If I'm that Lucinda, everything hurts. You know, I keep having this nightmare. In it I'm runnin', runnin', runnin', always runnin'."

"What are you running from?"

Lucinda thought for a minute. "I'm runnin' from love," she said with certainty. "Part of me wants to learn about love, how to really love, but part of me feels I don't deserve love. If I deserved love, my mother woulda loved me. I try to love people by givin' them things and givin' them time, but I don't give them my heart. That's too scary. What will they do to my heart if I let 'em have it? And them parts, when they come close, I feel all their rage and hatred. The Boy comes close, and then I feel as long as I'm strong and tough, no one can hurt me. Then I think, *Who needs them parts anyway?* All they carry is pain, whether it's angry pain or broken pain. So I put a wall around myself so I don't have to hear them parts."

This sounded all too familiar to me. Once again, Lucinda was finding ways to avoid the pain in her life, whether from internal or external sources. I was feeling very frustrated with her. "Lucinda, when are you going to learn running from your pain is a dead-end street? It's like your dream. The running never ends."

My tone of voice must have betrayed my exasperation, and that quickly, Cinda was present. She shook her head. "It's very sad. She thinks she can go on without all those parts. She don't know how much she needs them to be whole. God wants her to remember where she came from. And he gave her something to help her. The key is the Child."

The Child. I felt an inner smile. She was my ray of light during some very difficult times with Lucinda.

Originally, she was an angry, frightened part of Lucinda, a wretched little urchin Lucinda had to accept as part of herself, both the angry beast and the terrified waif aspects of her. Lucinda worked through all this child represented and received her as her own. The powerful result was that Lucinda began to experience some very positive emotions. And the little waif of a girl became a pretty normal child, enjoying the kinds of experiences most little girls enjoy. She was filled with spontaneity and laughter. Sometimes she was so authentically childlike that I almost didn't see her as having an adult body.

Cinda continued. "The Child is all about love. Lucinda will learn how to hold onto good things from the Child. She don't know how to hold onto good things, so she stores them away in a room. That way she thinks she won't lose them, but then she never feels them."

"Is that why she takes any gifts I give her and stores them away in a storage container, never wears them or uses them?" I thought about the Noah's ark shirt I had given her, a lovely white shirt with Noah's ark and the animals embroidered on the front with brightly colored threads. She wore it one time to let me see it and then stored it away.

"That's right. She feels if she stores them, she won't lose them. But then, she never enjoys using them."

"That's what she does with bad things too. She stores them away in a room inside so she doesn't have to feel them."

"You're right again. But then she's numb. She doesn't feel the good or the bad. And she loses herself. When she's close to the Child, she can find herself. And she can feel the good things, like love. The Child's purpose is love. With her, Lucinda will be able to give back to this world. You need to spend time with the Child again."

I took all this in, and I felt a hope rising within me. Now there was something positive I could do to help Lucinda, and it was something as pleasurable as spending time with the Child.

*****

Lucinda arrived for our next session dressed in her now typically masculine attire. She was the hardened Lucinda. When she was like this, I had to draw on all my internal fortitude to maintain a calm and reassuring presence. I remembered Cinda telling me to spend more time with the Child. That certainly sounded preferable to dealing with the hardened Lucinda.

"Lucinda, remember how I used to spend time with the Child? Cinda feels I need to do that again. Would it be okay to have her out this session?"

Lucinda was not especially happy with this idea. "What about me? Will I get time with you?"

"I've been spending most of my sessions with you lately. The Child needs some time with me too."

"You're right," Lucinda begrudgingly admitted. "But she can't have all the sessions."

"You just need to let me know if you're not getting enough time."

"I will. You can have her out."

So I called the Child out. When she saw me, her eyes lit up, and she threw her arms around me. "I've missed you!"

"I've missed you too. Cinda says we need to spend more time together. What would you like to do today?" I thought of all the things we had done together: drawing and coloring, dancing and singing to children's songs, taking nature walks in the field across the road from my office.

"I don't know. You pick something."

I thought for a moment. An idea popped into my head. *Do I dare?* I thought to myself. A brief internal battle ensued. The more daring part of me won out. "Let's go on a field trip."

"You mean walk in the field like we did before?" She looked out my window. "But it's dark outside."

I laughed aloud. "Not that kind of field trip. A field trip means we're going somewhere." I helped her with her coat. After all, she was only about five years old. I grabbed my own coat, and together we headed to my car. There was a shopping mall a short distance from my office.

On the way there, I wondered how this would play out. The Child had only been out with me. Several times Lucinda let her out to play when she worked in a doll store, but only when they were alone. How would the Child react to a mall filled with people? Would she be her usual exuberant child self, filled with spontaneity and excitement? If so, what would people think?

I gulped, but the fun of going to the mall and exposing the Child to a whole world she didn't know was energizing. We arrived at the mall and entered through one of the anchor stores. She hung back a little.

"It's okay," I reassured her. "I'll be right here with you."

It was November, and the store was decorated with greenery and Christmas trees. Displays of packages tied up with bows stood around every corner. Lots of people were engrossed in racks of clothing.

The Child stood still and took it all in. A particular display caught her attention. Her eyes were riveted on it—a six-foot-high polar bear standing on his rear legs with a red and green knit hat perched jauntily on his head. The tail of the hat flowed down his back with a large pom-pom at the end of it. He was surrounded by mounds of packages wrapped in red and green and gold paper with brightly colored ribbons. A sign reminded customers of the store's free gift-wrapping services. The Child pointed, obviously enthralled. "What's that?"

"That's a polar bear."

I let her take in the scene for a few minutes, then urged her on. As we walked through the store, I felt her pull close to me. When we arrived at the place where the store connected to the mall, we stopped to observe the scene. We were right at the center point of the mall. A huge Christmas tree pointed heavenward, bedecked in shiny red and gold balls with mounds of sparkling, white garland encircling the tree.

Below the tree was a gingerbread house covered with peppermint candies and lollipops. There was a window at one end of the house with the head of a red-nosed reindeer peeking out. The double doors of the house were propped wide open to display an empty throne-like seat where Santa himself would be seated.

The Child looked at it with wide eyes. Again, I felt her pull close to me. The display caught her attention, but then she noticed all the people. There were shoppers and mall wanderers everywhere. Many were carrying bags filled with purchases. Parents pushed children in strollers or held their hands, keeping them close by their sides. Teenagers traveled about in groups, and couples strolled together holding hands.

How overwhelming this must have been for a child who had only ever experienced a single person in the world outside. I took her hand to reassure her, then led her a few stores down the mall to a place I knew she would like: the Disney Store.

The shop was packed with children and parents. The Child stood and watched it all, very subdued. I suppose I was grateful for this. We were able to avoid the stares of people trying to understand why an adult was behaving like all the children running excitedly from one part of the store to another.

I took the Child's hand and led her past the racks of princess dresses and bins of Disney toys to the back of the store. It was not quite so crowded there. A wall was filled with stuffed Disney characters, and I knew she would like it.

When she saw the display, she went right up to it and just stared. I handed her a Mickey Mouse doll. She smiled and held it close. Then she reached for the matching Minnie Mouse. I unhooked it and gave it to her. She held the two mice and laughed. She started to make them dance. "This is neat!" she exclaimed in her child voice.

A little boy standing next to her was reaching for a Goofy doll. He looked up at her, but then grabbed the Goofy, shouting, "Hey, Mom, I want this one."

The Child's eyes followed the little boy as he ran to his mom displaying the Goofy doll. She looked at me. Then she looked at all the parents and children. She smiled. Then she laughed.

"We need to get back to my office so we're there when Kurt comes to pick you up." We replaced the two dolls and left the store. The Child stayed close to me as we made our way among the bustling shoppers, past the Santa display at the center of the mall, through the store with the polar bear display, and back to my car.

Once we were alone in the car, the Child began to bubble over, about the polar bear, about the Santa display, about the Disney Store and the Mickey and Minnie Mouse dolls, about all the shoppers, and about all the children and their mothers. "Them children in the store, they weren't afraid at all."

"Were you afraid?" I asked.

"Not when I knew I was with you." She laughed. "Can we go there again?"

I laughed too. "That was fun." I felt alive and energized after our excursion. "Yes, and we can take more field trips together."

CHAPTER 4

Spiritual Mother

I was still energized by our trip to the mall when Lucinda arrived for her next session. But my enthusiasm was short-lived. I felt the joy of our excursion draining out of me as Lucinda sat across from me, arms folded with an empty stare.

"So, Lucinda, what's on your mind? You don't look very happy."

"You never done that for me. You never took me to the mall. And when you called me back and told me what you done, that you took the Child to the mall, I could feel how happy you were. You ain't ever been happy like that with me. I guess I just don't matter. Not like the Child does."

"Lucinda, the Child is you. And you do matter to me. Why would I have stuck with you this long if you didn't matter?"

Lucinda was silent for a minute. Finally, she spoke. "I know you've stuck with us. But everything is so heavy. I wanted to come back to this world, and everything would be easy. But all them parts make it so hard. The new Lucinda, the one who took my place while I was away in my world, is mad she's not out all the time now. She fights with me to come out. She says she hates me." Lucinda let out a long sigh. "Them parts…it would be so much easier if they weren't there. And even though I don't feel like I need to have a mother like I used to, it hasn't left them others. The children inside still cry for a mommy. You know, even though I went away, my problems didn't. They waited for me. I'm trying to be a good wife and mother, but I don't always know how. It's like God's put me at a standstill with all these problems around me. When I was away, I didn't have these problems."

"Lucinda!" My voice must have sounded exasperated. "Do you remember what it was like when you were away?"

Lucinda sighed again. "I know. It was all darkness, and I was all alone with just a little speck of light to look at."

"And what happened as you looked at that light?"

Lucinda lowered her eyes. "I know. God brought me out of that dark prison. But I'm findin' it so confusing being here. I go to see my mom, and I see she's gettin' older. She has kidney disease, and the doctors say she might have to go on dialysis. I see she's growing old, but I feel like she left me behind as a child in a room. She got older, but I didn't. It don't match."

I was contemplating what Lucinda was telling me when Cinda suddenly emerged. She looked at me with her clear, peaceful eyes. "Don't be confused by what she's saying. What she is telling you is very important. She's afraid of being left behind. She sees herself as a child left behind. God wants to bring her out of that."

"But I thought when she came back from her world, she had left all the desperate desire for a mother behind her. I thought she had grown beyond all that."

"In some ways she has. But she is very influenced by all the others inside. And they still want a mother."

"Oh great. I still have to contend with her wanting me to be her mother."

"Don't get discouraged. She knows God healed her from that desperate need. But she's gone too far with it. God healed her so she could help the others. Instead, she wants to leave them behind. If she denies the parts, it will only get worse. She needs to listen to them. They watch her. She needs to show them a new way. God wants her to remember where she came from and what he's done for her."

"So how do I help her?"

"Don't let her forget where she came from, and keep reminding her of what God did for her."

Cinda was gone. Lucinda was looking back at me. "Who was out?"

"It was Cinda."

"Why was she out?" I detected a bit of resentment in her voice.

"I suppose she knew I needed some encouragement. Have you been hearing from her lately?"

"Yeah, I hear her."

"What has she been saying to you?"

"She says I need to remember where I came from. I'm not sure what she means by that."

"She told me the same thing. I think she means you need to remember you were no different from the others inside. You may have acted big and tough and strong, but on the inside, you were just a broken child who longed for a mother to love you. The only reason you are any different now is because God healed you. And he healed you for a reason—to help the others."

"You know, sometimes I feel smothered by all the dolls in the house, all them dolls I got when I worked at the doll store. They remind me of all the broken children, what I used to be. The dolls remind me of what I was and what I can't have. I can't just start over and be a child. I realize now how much children need the love of a mother. I can't have that." She paused for a minute as if considering something. "But I guess I can do that for my boys. I'm findin' I want to go to their games. Before, I was too busy lookin' for a mother to care about what they needed. I think God is helping me be a mother by changin' me on the inside."

"That's wonderful, Lucinda."

"But he's also showing me somethin' else. I'm seein' my mother differently. I think he wants me to forgive her for all she done to me. I think he's sayin' when I forgive her, I'll be better able to be a mom. She did so many evil things to me, but I think she was just seekin' things in her life…like power. But Satan fooled her. She ain't got no power. I look at my family, and all I can see is how broken they all are. That's what you get for servin' Satan. She's just a sick, old broken-down woman. That's what Satan leaves you with."

I sat there amazed at how the tone of our session had changed. Perhaps God really was at work.

*****

With Cinda as our guide, our sessions began to take a new path. The start of each session began with Cinda coming out and saying Lucinda needed to take down the wall she had erected between her and the other parts. "The wall don't just separate her from the parts. It also separates her from God. The wall must come down."

When I explained to Lucinda she needed to take the wall down, she nodded. "Yeah…I'm building a wall with them parts. Without the wall, I feel all the pain of them children. I feel like a child, and a child can get hurt really bad. So I push them all away. I even push the Child away. She ain't got no pain, but when she's close, I'm nothin' but a child. How can I be a mother for my boys if I'm just a child myself?

"Lucinda, I'm not asking you to take the wall down when you're home with your boys. This is for your time with me so the ones inside can find some healing."

Reluctantly, Lucinda agreed to let the wall down in our sessions. The first time we did this, the new Lucinda, the one who had been present while Lucinda had escaped into her imaginary world, came to the surface. When she saw me, she reached out her hands and simply said, "Heart." Then she began to weep, quietly at first, but then with more intensity until she was sobbing with tears streaming down her cheeks. "Mommy, Mommy, want Mommy," she gasped out between sobs.

"That was good," Cinda observed. "She found her pain. And darkness's hold on her is loosening."

The next time Lucinda let the wall down, a succession of personalities came to the surface. It began with the new Lucinda surfacing. Again, she looked at me, reached for me and said, "Heart." Then the tears came, with weeping and crying out for mommy.

Tara surfaced. Crazy Tara who was so out of touch with reality she could not even string together coherent sentences. But this time she was not crying out her typical disconnected words and phrases, like *bad man, hook, hook, fly, fly*. Instead, she wept quietly and peacefully, saying only, "Mommy, Mommy, Mommy."

The following session, Cinda had a new directive. "This time Lucinda needs to let the wall down and go inside with the Child close. She needs to go to the parts as a child."

When I explained this to Lucinda, she was hesitant. "Them parts are mean. If I go as a child, they can hurt me."

I agreed with her that this sounded pretty risky, but I added, "We've got to trust Cinda. She's never steered us wrong."

So Lucinda complied. She let the wall down, allowing others to surface, and then she went inside with the Child close. The first one out was the new Lucinda. She looked directly at me and said, "Heart." Then she added, "Come inside with us."

This was not the first time I had been asked to go inside. I considered this. How I was ever supposed to get inside?

I noticed a vile look. That indicated it was not an alter personality who was out, but a demonic spirit.

The first time I had seen that in her eyes, it had literally taken my breath away. That was over five years ago, and since then I had been schooled in spiritual warfare. I knew the power of the name of Jesus, so I wasn't intimidated.

The spirit glared at me, lifted its lip, and growled.

"In the name of Jesus, you may not interfere with God's work in Lucinda. Now get down."

The vile look disappeared, and Lucinda, the new one, was back. "Come inside with us."

"I don't know how to do that." How do you get inside another person? There had been one time, many months ago, when the alters all cried together, and they later told me I had been inside with them. That had puzzled me. I had no idea how I'd gotten inside.

The new Lucinda wept, expressing the deep grief she felt over the loss of the doll store, the place where she worked for the several years, when Lucinda was in her imaginary world. She wept over missing the store, over feeling like she had a place to be and a contribution to make. She also wept over missing Katherine, the owner of the store, who switched back and forth between being her boss, being her friend, and mothering her. She cried until she slumped over, exhausted.

At that point, the old Lucinda returned. Her eyes were wide. "I went in as a child. I was really scared. But when them others saw me, they all got little, even the mean ones, and they all cried. Some were missin' Katherine, and some, like Tara, were missin' Sheila."

I remembered how Sheila had sought to mother Lucinda, only to have the relationship end very painfully.

Lucinda continued. "But most of 'em were cryin' about my mom. They all cried, really cried." Then she looked right at me. "But that's not all. They didn't cry alone. You was in there with 'em. We weren't alone. And when you was there, I saw some darkness leave. They were really mad you got in there. How'd you get in there?"

"I have no idea how I got in there. As far as I'm concerned, I was sitting right here the entire time."

I remembered how Lucinda's own mother had at one time been part of her inner world. I assumed her own mother within was an introject, a psychological construct where one internalizes an external reality.

Was I now an introject in Lucinda's inner world? I mulled this over, trying to reassure myself that being in her inner world was probably positive. It would provide a sense of safety and comfort for all her broken parts. They would not feel so alone. And it sounded as if my presence in her inner world was a force against all the dark demonic presences that lurked within.

Instead of trying to explain all of this, I decided to simplify it. "Maybe I got in because you were willing to go in as a child. That was an act of obedience and trust. Maybe God honored that."

Before Lucinda had a chance to respond, I was aware of a switch in personalities. Her posture was very erect, hands folded neatly on her lap. I knew at once who this was. Lucia. Her role in the system was to tell the story of what had happened in Lucinda's life. She didn't speak, only wrote and drew pictures. She had drawn many very sad and tragic pictures for me. But it was with her help that Lucinda was able to circumvent replacing her grandmother as the head of the satanic cult that permeated her family for generations.

"It's so good to see you, Lucia." Indeed, it had been quite a while since I had seen her.

Lucia pointed to the tablet on my lap.

I got her a clean sheet of paper, put it on a clipboard, and handed her a pencil.

Lucia took the pencil and began to write. She wrote slowly and carefully, very intent upon what she was doing. She carefully printed the word SPIRITUAL, all in capital letters. She showed it to me and then she began to write again. This time she wrote the word MOTHER.

"Spiritual mother," I said aloud.

Lucia nodded eagerly. Then she pointed at me.

I considered what this might mean. I was lost in my own thoughts when I was drawn back to the present by the sound of growling, that low, guttural growl I had come to associate with darkness. I focused on Lucinda.

There was that vile look of pure evil in her eyes.

"In the name of the Lord Jesus Christ you are to get down and not interfere with God's work here."

That quickly, Lucia was back, hammering the words she had written with the tip of the pencil. Then she pointed at me again.

I was not comfortable with where this was going. I thought of all the times I had told Lucinda I could not be her mother, but it seemed as if Lucia was telling me to be her spiritual mother. What exactly was a spiritual mother? If I told Lucinda I was her spiritual mother, would she be able to differentiate that from being a mother?

Finally, I said, "You want me to be her spiritual mother."

Again, she nodded eagerly.

"I'll have to think about this. I'm not even sure what a spiritual mother is."

Lucia looked at me again, pointed to her written words, then pointed at me. Then she put the pencil down, folded her hands and was gone.

I quickly grabbed the clipboard from her lap. I did not want Lucinda to know what Lucia had written.

Fortunately, it took her several seconds to reorient to the present. She was not aware I had grabbed the clipboard. “Boy, darkness was really mad in there. They didn’t like what happened here today.”

“Then you’ll go in again with the Child?” I asked.

“Yeah, I’ll do it. As long as I don’t have to be with the Child at home.”

*****

The sessions with Lucinda taking the wall down and going in as a child proved very productive. Typically, different alter personalities would surface and weep and cry about not having a mother. Little child voices would cry out for mommy. And very often, I was aware of dark spirits leaving her through long exhales as these children received healing through their tears. Sometimes I would be unaware of darkness fleeing, but Lucinda would report to me that she had seen darkness leaving as she cried inside with the other alters.

One particular session, Lucinda had gone inside with the Child. The first one to surface was the Boy. His first words were, “Boys don’t cry. I’m not one of them pussy girls.”

“You must be the Boy. It’s good to see you again.”

He glared back at me. Again, he said, “Boys don’t cry.” He held his head erect and had a steely expression on his face. He was determined not to cry.

“If you could cry, what would you want to cry about?”

“Boys don’t cry,” he asserted, but his voice seemed to soften.

“No one can make you cry outwardly, but I bet you have some inside tears.”

“How did you get inside? I saw you when you were in there.”

“I’m not sure how I got inside, but I’m glad you all weren’t alone when you were hurting so bad.”

“All them little ones just want a mommy. Boys don’t need mommies.”

"Sure they do. All children need mommies." By now his voice had softened, so I decided to ask him his name. "What's your name?"

He hesitated. "If I tell you, you can use it against me."

"You're right. You have to believe I won't hurt you. That's called trust. You have to trust me."

"I ain't ever trusted anyone. Why should I trust you?"

"I didn't hurt any of those little ones who were crying inside. They trusted me to cry with me."

He was silent for a moment. Then he said, in a barely audible whisper, "Steven."

"Steven. That's a great name. There was a very strong and courageous man in the Bible whose name was Steven."

Steven looked at me. The steely look was gone. He smiled slightly. Then he added, "You'd better not use my name against me."

I smiled back at him. "Thank you for trusting me with your name."

This course we were on seemed a good one. Being inside with the broken children while they cried seemed to have won Steven over. He was starting to trust me.

*****

Meanwhile, I kept mulling over Lucia's written words: spiritual mother. What indeed was a spiritual mother? Perhaps a spiritual mother was someone who nurtured someone else in the faith, helped them grow in understanding and trusting God. If that was the case, I certainly qualified as a spiritual mother in Lucinda's life. Dare I use this term with her? Would she be confused and think I would be her mother? I trusted Lucia was a force for good in Lucinda's life. Did I trust that what she was asking me to do would be for good and not harm? I certainly did not want to lead Lucinda into expecting more from me than I could deliver. Silently, I prayed. *Help, Lord. I need your wisdom for this one.*

CHAPTER 5

Heartbeat

I was feeling very hopeful about our work together. When Lucinda let the wall down and went inside with the Child close, Lucinda herself became a child. For reasons I did not understand, seeing Lucinda as a child affected the inside alter personalities in a very profound way. Seeing Lucinda shed her tough outer shell and be the broken child she really was freed the others to do the same. Even the toughest and nastiest of her alters would soften, much as the Boy, Steven, had done with me. Lucinda was convinced the Child was the key to all this, that it was the Child who connected Lucinda, and all the others, to their true emotions. Together they could cry and express the deep pain they all carried.

But as so often happened with Lucinda, this positive direction got derailed. She arrived for a session in an obviously agitated state. Her oldest brother, Leo, the author of the gruesome poems about an axe murder, was in the hospital. He had been threatening to kill himself because he was addicted to heroin and felt powerless to conquer this addiction. He had been admitted to the local hospital for detox but was to be sent to a rehab in a neighboring county.

"I got a call from Mom to come down right away, that Leo was in trouble, and we needed to stick together. So I went down to her house, and everyone was there, my sister Janet, my other brother, even my dad. They told me Leo needed us now and we needed to be family for him. They said blood is thicker than water. You know, my Gram used to say that a lot. But what really got me mad was seein' my mom cry about Leo. They was real tears, not fake tears. That did damage to me. All them times I was in the hospital, and the family never came together for me. The only time she came to see me in the hospital was when the doctor told her to come. And she never shed no tears for me. Now everyone wants to run and help Leo, but no one ever came to help me. I was afraid her tears for Leo would kill me. The pain was so bad. So I thought, if I don't feel 'em, them tears can't kill me. So I got fake. It's the only way I can be with my family. I used to think she couldn't love anyone, but then I saw her tears. As her tears fell, I wanted to die. I felt connected to nothin'."

I looked at Lucinda. She had on thick black eyeliner. She was dressed in black jeans and a black sweatshirt. Her jaw was set, and her eyes lacked any life. "Lucinda, where is the Child?"

"I pushed her away. If she's close, I can't be tough. And I told Cinda I didn't need her anymore either. That I had God, and we would handle this without her."

"And how did Cinda respond to that?"

"She said that I lie, and the truth ain't in me."

"Lucinda, I know it was very difficult for you to experience this with your family, but you're not with them right now. When you are here with me, you can let the Child come close. Then I can help you with what's really going on inside you."

Lucinda looked at me and shook her head. "I can't do that. There's too much pain. Besides, I have to hide her and protect her. They want to lock her in a cage."

That last comment caught my attention. I had seen times before when the pain she carried was so great she would lose touch with reality. Was she becoming psychotic? "Lucinda, who wants to lock the Child in a cage?"

"Them monsters inside. They don't like her."

"Of course, they don't like her. She's your path to wholeness. But I'm not an inside monster. I think you know she's safe with me."

So Lucinda reluctantly agreed to bring the Child close. She was quiet at first, but then she began to weep. She began with gentle tears, but then she began to let out huge sobs that were interspersed with cries for "Mommy, Mommy, Mommy." The longer she cried, the faster the tears came, huge tears flooding down her cheeks and dampening her sweatshirt. Then there were cries of, "Wanna go home, wanna go home, home, home, home."

My own heart was wrenched as I observed this outpouring of pain, coming not from an adult but from a small child. I sat down next to her on the couch and let her lay her head on my chest as she poured forth the cries of a lost little child. Gradually, the sobs and the cries subsided until she was softly whimpering. Then the whimpering ceased, and she fell sound asleep. She slept peacefully for a few minutes.

When she opened her eyes, she looked at me and said, in a small child voice, "Heart."

I remembered the new Lucinda saying the same word to me. What was the meaning of this? "What do you mean by 'heart'?"

She just looked back at me, gave a little half smile, and laid her head back on my chest.

In a few minutes' time, Lucinda sat straight up, looked at me, and said, "That was very strange. I was in every way a child. I felt like a child. I sounded like a child. It even seemed like I had a little body. Yet it was me, not one of them alters. When the Child gets real close, it's like I become her, but I still have all the pain of being me. You know, I thought God had taken away all the pain of not having a mother, but I guess there's still some there. And it's not just the pain of not havin' a mother. It's the pain of not havin' a home. It's like I'm in a waitin' place. I'm waitin', always waitin', waitin' for my mom to come get me. And when you were holdin' me there at the end, I felt somethin' really different. I had my head on your chest, and I could hear your heart beating…and it was like I'd heard it before. And I could feel they was all gettin' close, and they was all listenin' to your heartbeat. And then we all fell asleep.

"You know, I was eight years old when my mom gave me away the first time. That was when I went to live with the couple next door. At night I could hear my mom's voice through the wall between the houses. I just wanted her to come get me and take me home, but she never did. That's why I'm so scared about losin' you. In March it will be eight years since I first came to you. If she gave me away after eight years, why won't you?

"You know, when I was little and lived with the couple next door, I drew a picture. It was a house with a lady inside the house. It was a mother, a good mother. I hid the picture so no one could find it, but everyone inside knew I drew it. Some want that good mother. Others say we can never have her. We can never have a good mother, and we're never goin' home. They say we don't need love or a mother, that we've learned to live without it, and we're just fine. They say there's no such thing as a good mother, and we're givin' the children false hope.

"When I go down to my mom's, some of them inside, the little ones, think we're goin' home, but then they see she don't want us. She'll say we're family, and family sticks together, and then she cries about Leo, but I don't do nothin' to comfort her. Something's missin' inside. I don't know how to take care of her. And my whole family fights with each other. They want to rip each other's throats out. Then when they make up, they remember what you said and turn it on you. I'm still tryin' to find what I lost, but I don't think it's with them. Part of me wants to shut the door and leave them all there. I'm trying to figure out where I belong. Sometimes they act like they want me there. But when they fight, they try to pull me in. They play games with each other, and then they use me. When my mom's mad at Janet, she'll call me to get Janet jealous. If I play the game, I just get hurt again. She gives me false hope, and if I grab it, she's got me to hurt me."

I had long since learned that when Lucinda processed things verbally, it was best to just listen. My questions would be intrusive and would interrupt her train of thought. So I let her ramble on and tried to discern what was going on in her inner world. It seemed she was beginning to see her family in a new way. She was able to be removed enough from their interactions to objectively observe the way they behaved with each other. As she observed this, she saw the futility of trying to find love and acceptance with them.

Finally, I spoke. "Lucinda, I think you are being very realistic about what your family can and can't do for you. They are so broken themselves that they are unable to give you the kind of love and acceptance you crave. They can't give what they've never gotten themselves."

"I know you're right, but I can't get all them parts to let go of the mother dream. Even the ones inside who say they don't need a mother are just acting tough. Every one of us wants the good mother we drew in the picture, even if they say they don't."

Cinda emerged, her eyes especially clear and as peaceful as ever. She was such a positive presence, very even-keeled, never shaken by the events of Lucinda's chaotic life. Her voice sounded less childlike than I remembered. "It's good Lucinda can see the truth about her family. It's the truth that will set her free."

I nodded.

"It's time for you to know something. I want you to listen carefully and consider what I say."

I gulped, wondering what she had to say.

"Do you remember when Lucinda told you the story about the old lady with the mop?"

I certainly did remember. Lucinda told the story to me several years earlier after she tried to force an integration with Cinda.

> I was in a dark place. I couldn't see very much of what was around me. I was cold and alone. And I was feelin' scared. I was curled up in a ball on a hard floor, and it felt like I was waiting for somethin' terrible to happen. I was so scared. And then, somethin' very strange happened. It was as if a little bit of light came into the dark. Where I was seemed to lighten up a little bit. Then I could see where I was.
>
> I was in a pretty big room that looked like a basement, and all along the wall on the other side of the room were cages, like you'd use for a

dog. Then I realized that I was in one of them cages, and I couldn't get out. That really scared me. Then I heard a noise...it sounded like footsteps. When I heard it, everything in me froze. I was even more scared.

Then I heard a soft voice singing, a lady's voice. It was soft and gentle and not at all scary. I looked to see if I could see her, and there she was with a mop in her hand.

She was moppin' the floor and singing. She was workin' her way toward me. When she got close, she stopped moppin' and looked at me. It was still pretty dark, and it was hard to see her face real good, but I knew she was kind, and I didn't have to be afraid.

She leaned on her mop and looked at me for a few minutes. Then she stooped down so she could see me better. She was old and wrinkled; her hair was gray and pulled back from her face, but now I could see her eyes. They were soft, and again, I knew she was kind.

She talked to me, very quietly, like she didn't want anyone to hear. "My dear girl, what an awful place to be. But you know you're not alone in there. There's one who loves you with a love that will never end. His name is Jesus. He knows how much you've been hurt, but he will never hurt you. He's there to help you. He's right there with you. Find your heart. It's in your heart that you'll know that he's there."

When she talked, I felt this calm feelin' come over me, and the fear went away. I didn't say nothin'. She talked some more, told a few stories about Jesus, how he wanted little children to come to him, how he made a sick little girl all

> better. The last thing she said was, "In the end, he makes everything right." Then she was gone.

I remembered how amazed I was when she first related this story to me, that some old washerwoman came to her in some horrible, godforsaken place and told her about Jesus. Then I wondered, *Was it really so godforsaken?*

I responded to Cinda, "I sure do remember that story. It filled me with great wonder that such a thing happened to her in such a dark place. But I also had so many unanswered questions. Who was this woman? What was she doing there? And where was Lucinda?"

Cinda looked at me with her clear, peaceful eyes. "There's more to the story."

"Oh?" I was truly interested in what more Cinda had to say.

"That night, Lucinda slept, slept really long and really peacefully, even on the hard floor. That was because she heard something."

"What did she hear?" I was hanging on Cinda's every word.

"She heard a heartbeat."

My thoughts stopped in their tracks. "A heartbeat?' My own heart pounded.

"That's right. But not just any heartbeat. It was a heartbeat that brought them great comfort and great hope. It was a heartbeat that reassured them they wouldn't always be alone without anyone to love them. It was a heartbeat they would have recognized again anywhere. And now they've heard it again. It's your heartbeat."

"My heartbeat? How is my heartbeat different from anyone else's heartbeat?"

"Oh, it's different. They've been waiting to hear it again all them years, and now they've heard it."

I truly did not know what to say. My heartbeat? They heard it all those years ago, before I had ever laid eyes on her? On the one hand, I found this very exciting, that God had done something like this for her. On the other hand, I found it frightening. My heartbeat had been in that horrible place. What was the meaning of this? What did this mean for me? Or was this one more way Lucinda was seeking to draw me in and connect me to her in unhealthy ways?

I looked into Cinda's clear, peaceful eyes. She was truly guileless. Perhaps Lucinda would seek to pull me in by playing on my emotions, but not Cinda. She was straightforward and uncomplicated. I had never known her to speak anything but truth.

"But that's not all that happened that night." I wasn't sure I wanted to hear more, but Cinda continued. "That was the night things got scrambled."

"Things got scrambled?" My voice was weak and quavering.

"Yes, God allowed things to get scrambled."

I remembered how Lu, one of the first alter personalities I had worked with, had mentioned several times that things got scrambled. She also said it wasn't yet time for me to know what she meant. "How did things get scrambled?"

"God allowed the rigid walls separating the cult alters from the other alters to come down. That way, Lu was able to find her way out at school. And she was able to find her way out with you. Lu knew who you were. She knew you had the heartbeat. And later, others found their way out with you too. Your heartbeat is very powerful. All them who heard it know it's what they've been waiting for."

"Cinda," I said rather weakly, "I need time to process all this. On the one hand, I'm thrilled if my heartbeat can help them. On the other hand, what does this mean for me? It sounds like I'm much more than just their counselor."

"The answer," Cinda replied, "is in your heart. Search your heart." And with that, she was gone.

CHAPTER 6

Miss Kindle

The Christmas season was behind us, and we were now into the heart of winter, those long stretches of January and February when everything is cold and bleak. I took all my questions and concerns about spiritual mothers and heartbeats and put them in the back of my mind. My work with Lucinda had been derailed from the hopeful times when she would take down the wall and go to the parts as a child, allowing them to be the broken children they really were.

The external events of her life were too pressing, and processing these events seemed to occupy our sessions. Her brother, Leo, had been released from rehab and seemed to be on a better path in his personal life. Lucinda's mother gushed over him when he came home and was clearly delighted to have him around again. Lucinda was painfully aware she had never received such warm receptions when she was released from her various mental health hospitalizations. She struggled daily with a deep sense of rejection.

Then, to add to her already difficult circumstances, she began to retrieve some memories. Some of it came to her while she was in session with me; some of it came to her at home. At first, she received images of "bad hands" and "cold eyes." She didn't understand why these images impinged on her consciousness. Then she began to clearly see the face of a person, a man, who "came a long way to get us."

"Did he come to take you away?" I asked her.

She didn't know the answer to this question. "He came that he might find us."

This made no sense to me. It didn't make much sense to her, either.

Over the weeks, Lucinda began to retrieve more images, images of dark rituals with candles and chanting and the shedding of blood. Fragments of the memory started coming to the surface from other alters. The things they described to me in bits and pieces were almost too much to take in.

I began to piece together that Lucinda had been systematically tortured under the instruction of this man who had "come a long way." The purpose of the torture, often done in a ritual setting, was to find something—something within Lucinda. When all attempts to find this something failed, they tried a new tactic. Something was released into Lucinda during a very dark and frightening ritual, a dark spirit named Ziro, whose mission was to uncover the missing something.

This was not the first time I heard the name Ziro. Lucinda had described an inner monster named Ziro to me a number of years earlier. By now, Lucinda was a veteran of deliverance ministry. We had made numerous trips to visit with Paul and Adele who would skillfully ferret out dark spirits hiding among her alters, sending them away in the name of Jesus.

It was also not the first time I heard about others looking for something within Lucinda. Her grandmother wanted Lucinda to find something inside and tried various tactics to have her find this unknown something. Lucinda, or whichever alter was being challenged with this mission, would dutifully go within and look for something, but without any idea of what they were to find. This obviously frustrated her grandmother.

It now sounded like she had sought help in this mission, help from the man who had "come a long way."

What did they want to find within Lucinda?

Lucinda considered different possibilities of what her grandmother may have been seeking. Was it the original Lucinda, the innocent baby who had been born and was protected from trauma by a whole system of protective alters? Or was it the Child, who seemed to be so important in connecting Lucinda and the other parts to their emotions so they could heal? Or was it Cinda, the one who had gone to Jesus during a dark ritual and now was a force for light and truth within Lucinda?

"All I know was she wanted somethin' inside that kept them from fully having me."

I listened, wondering what they wanted. I was sure of one thing. "I know they never fully got you. Or things wouldn't have gotten scrambled, and Lu would not have found her way out with me. Even with the help of this man who 'came a long way' and a dark spirit named Ziro, they couldn't fully get you. You know why? Because light is stronger than darkness."

Lucinda tried to draw some hope from this, but then she said, "Even though they never fully got me, it sometimes feels as if they never let go of me either. I live every day with the pain of bein' part of that cult. Sometimes I wonder if I'll ever be free of them parts and what was done to them."

*****

Late in February, as the winter snow turned slushy and above-freezing temperatures offered tantalizing hints of spring to come, I had an unexpected surprise in one of our sessions. After processing a gut-wrenching abreaction of a man with a scar on his face having oral sex with a young alter, I felt totally spent.

It was a huge relief when the alter, who so graphically played this out before my eyes, fell asleep in total exhaustion.

I took a deep breath and prayed inwardly for the healing of this alter. I still could not witness such atrocities being played out before me without it affecting me on a personal level. Even though I knew there was healing when these long-hidden secrets came to light, to watch it unfold before my eyes took an emotional toll. So I prayed for myself as well, that God would help me to come to terms with what I had just witnessed. I felt totally spent and asked God to renew me.

After a few minutes of silence, Lucinda sat up, rubbed her eyes, looked at me, and smiled. "I missed you," she said in a small child voice. I looked at this child alter and wondered who she was. The child smiled again. "I've been in the light with Cinda." Lucinda's inner world had a dark side and a light side. The light side had a place where the light of God was very strong and very healing. For this one to have spent time in the light indicated she was willing to yield to God and his very powerful healing presence.

"That's wonderful. I'm sure your time in the light helped you a lot. But I'm not sure who you are. Maybe your time in the light changed you so much that I don't recognize you."

The child laughed. "It's me…Angie."

"Angie! You look great. Your time in the light has changed you." It had been several years since I had seen Angie. I was reading *The Velveteen Rabbit* to Lucinda as a reward for some hard work she had done in session. After closing the book, Lucinda reported to me that Angie had quietly moved into the light. I hadn't seen her since.

My times with Angie had not always been easy. She was a broken little waif of a girl, maybe four or five years old, who was often very demanding and very needy. A number of times I lost my patience with her. I remembered telling her she was acting like a brat and then feeling so remorseful.

I looked at Angie. Her eyes were sparkling. Her laugh was infectious.

"Cinda told me to come see you."

"I'm so glad she did. Would you like to color with me?"

Angie nodded her head eagerly. Out came the crayons and the paper. So often these crayons had drawn dark and tragic pictures. They had also drawn the Mickey Mouse that helped me bring Lucinda back after being trapped in her imaginary world.

I handed Angie a piece of paper. "What color crayon would you like?"

"What do you mean?"

"What color do you want?" I repeated.

She just looked at me.

"Do you want the red one or the blue one?" I held them up.

She pointed to the red one.

"You want the red one." I handed her the crayon. "Angie, do you know your colors?"

She looked at me with a blank expression.

"Would you like to learn the colors?"

She smiled shyly and nodded.

"Okay. This is the red crayon. See what color it makes."

She scribbled on the paper.

"That's red. What else in the room is red?"

She looked at me with a puzzled expression.

I looked around the office and spotted a book with a red cover. "Look Angie, this book is red too." I placed the book next to her red scribbles. "See, they are the same color. Do you see anything else that is red?"

She looked around the room and then squealed with delight. She ran to my bookshelf and pulled down a figurine of a Scottish terrier with a red bow around its neck. She pointed to the bow.

"That's right, Angie. The dog's bow is red."

Angie looked around the room again. She spotted a picture on my wall, one that Lucinda had painted for me, with bright-red birds. She ran to the picture and pointed to the birds. She laughed with delight.

I laughed with her. "That's right, the birds are red."

Then she picked up the blue crayon.

"That crayon is blue. See how it looks when you draw with it."

"Blue," she said as she scribbled on the paper.

Together we found things in the office that were blue—the jeans she was wearing and another book. She laughed with delight each time we found something blue.

"You're learning your colors, Angie." I truly regretted time had come for the session to end. "Next time you come out with me, I'll teach you more colors."

She nodded. "More colors."

I reluctantly called for Lucinda to come back.

There was a slight pause, a few eye movements, and Lucinda was back. She looked at me for a few seconds, then blurted out, "What happened? You seem to be glowing. Cinda must have been out with you."

"No, it wasn't Cinda. It was Angie."

"Angie? The one you called a brat?"

"Well, she's not a brat anymore. It seems she's been basking in the light for several years. All the clinginess and neediness is gone. She is just a delightful little child. It seems her time in the light healed all her brokenness and pain. It was truly amazing."

Lucinda looked at me a little suspiciously. "Kinda like the Child. You get all excited when you're with her too. I wish you'd get that excited about bein' with me."

"Well, there is something special about being with a child who is filled with life and spontaneity. I was feeling pretty depleted, but being with Angie restored me."

Lucinda left muttering to herself, "I don't see why God don't restore me like that."

"Maybe he will," I called after her as she left.

*****

The next time Lucinda arrived for a session, her face looked brighter. She reached into her jeans pocket and pulled out a piece of paper. "You'll never guess who I saw. I was in the grocery store with Kurt, and when we turned the corner at the end of the aisle, there she was. It was Miss Kindle. Remember I told you about her. She was the teacher in junior high who really liked me and wanted to help me. She even offered to have me come live with her, but I got sent to my gram's instead."

I did indeed remember her telling me about Miss Kindle. She always spoke about this teacher in a very positive way.

"Anyway, we talked for a while. I told her about you and all the work we done together. I also told her I have parts. She didn't understand what I meant at first, but when I said I had multiple personalities, she just stared at me and said it made so much sense. She gave me her phone number, and I asked if it would be okay if you called her, that maybe you could explain things to her better than I could." She handed me the paper.

I unfolded it and saw a phone number written in neat numerals.

"She said it would be okay for you to call her. I think it would be good for you to talk to her."

"I'll be glad to call her, Lucinda. I am very curious to hear what she might have to say."

So later that week, on a mild day early in March, after all my sessions for the day were finished, I gave this teacher, who had befriended Lucinda almost twenty years earlier, a phone call. When she answered the phone, I told her my name and that I was Lucinda's counselor.

"Oh yes, she said she would have you call me. Anything I can do to help Lu...any way I can be of assistance, please let me know."

I noted she called her *Lu*. These were the years after things became scrambled and Lu found her way out in school. "I'd be really interested to know your impressions of her, your experiences with her and her family, anything you think might help me understand her better."

Miss Kindle gave a laugh. "I could give you a boatload of information. I spent a lot of time with her. I really wanted to help her, but I always knew I was in way over my head. I would tell her I couldn't be her mother and I was not the one who could help her. She didn't like hearing that."

"You mentioned you couldn't be her mother. Did you ever feel a pull in that direction?"

"No, not really. I knew it couldn't be. I had considered taking her into my home when the abuse from her brother came to light. I reported the abuse, wanting to be anonymous, but they released my name to her brother. That did not go well. Her family moved in to block her coming to stay with me. She went to live with her grandmother instead. In some ways, I felt that was best because, as I said, I knew she needed help that I couldn't give."

"What was she like as a young teenager?"

Miss Kindle gave a low whistle. Then she laughed. "She was a handful—a tomboy, a tough cookie. I think she lived in the shadow of her brother's bad legacy. He left his mark in the school as a hellion. People expected the same of her, and sometimes she lived up to that. She could be extremely violent. But …" Miss Kindle's voice trailed off.

"But what?"

"Well, I always got the sense that underneath it all, she was a just little girl who wanted a loving family and didn't understand why she didn't have one."

Now it was my turn to laugh. "You got that one right. That is the exact truth."

"She just wanted to please. She would buy me gifts. She also spent a lot of time on the phone with me. She was very artistic. She got along well with the art teacher. She generally connected well with female teachers. But she did not get along with the male teachers, especially if they were overbearing."

So far, everything Miss Kindle had shared with me was right on the mark. Her experiences with Lucinda as a young teen lined up amazingly well with the young adult I had come to know so well.

"What about her family? What were your experiences with them?"

"Her family were all losers." Miss Kindle's abruptness surprised me. "Her mom is a taker. Her sister is also a taker, and she is lazy. Her family will take anything Lu gives, but they aren't there for her. When I was involved with Lu, she made a few veiled allusions that her family was involved in satanism. I didn't know what to make of that, but when I saw her at the store the other day, she told me outright they were satanists.

"She said she has nothing to do with it anymore. That didn't surprise me. Underneath it all, she has an incredible sense of right and wrong. Sometimes that got her in trouble. She would get enraged at injustice. She also told me she has multiple personalities. That explains so much. I wish I had known that back then. Maybe I could have helped her more."

"Miss Kindle, thank you so much for being so forthright with me. The things you shared align so well with my experiences with Lucinda. And somehow, to hear all this from you gives credence to all the things she told me over the last eight years. Everything you said validates what she told me. Her stories match your stories. Your impressions match my impressions. In a new and deeper way, I believe that all she revealed to me can be trusted. It is all really true."

After ending the call, I looked out my office window at the melting snow in the field across the road. The late afternoon sun glistened as it reflected off the snow. I heard the steady drip, drip, drip of a melting icicle that hung just above my window. Signs of waning winter.

I felt at peace as I prayed, thanking God for Miss Kindle, for the role she had played in Lucinda's teenage years, for her genuine concern for a broken young girl, for her penetrating insight that could see beyond the tough city chick to a hurting little girl who just wanted to be loved.

And I thanked God that he had, through this phone call, validated the reality of Lucinda's tragic story.

CHAPTER 7

Angie and Steven

Now I had two delightful children to interact with, the Child and Angie. I would try to take time each session to be with one or the other of them. Angie was the one I spent the most time with that spring, perhaps because she had so much catching up to do. I also suspect it had to do with the role she was to play in the months to come.

It was a sheer delight to teach her all the colors, and then we moved on to the alphabet. I read to her and took her for walks in a nearby park. As we walked, I showed her things, like birds and flowers and other children playing.

She would squeal with excitement when I found something especially interesting, a bird feather or a dandelion gone to seed that was just waiting for someone to blow gently upon it so that the seeds could be wafted on the breeze.

"Make a wish before you blow," I instructed.

"What's a wish?"

"It's something you really want to happen. I wish for all those inside Lucinda to be as happy and carefree as Angie. Now you make a wish."

Angie thought for a minute. "I know. I wish for Steven to be my friend and that I could show him things like you show me things."

"That's a great wish, Angie. Now blow." I demonstrated how to gently blow on the dandelion.

Angie puckered up her lips then let out a big puff of air that sent every last seed wafting away on the breeze. She laughed and then went chasing after the seeds as they drifted away.

We continued walking. "You said you wanted to be Steven's friend. Do you see him when you're inside?"

"Sometimes I do. Sometimes he's big and mean, but sometimes he's just a little boy. When he's like that, I want to play with him, but he acts afraid of me. I won't hurt him."

"I know you won't, Angie. But I think that when he's a little boy, he gets afraid easily. I don't know if you remember what it was like before you spent all that time in the light with Cinda, but you were afraid back then."

Angie squinched up her face. "No, I don't remember before the light. The only thing I remember from back then was you reading the rabbit book, and I was inside listening."

"I remember that too. God has done an amazing job of healing you from the inside out. Maybe he can do that for Steven too."

*****

The next time I called Angie out, I knew instantly that something was wrong. There was no sparkle in her eyes. She looked at me with a doleful expression.

"What's wrong, Angie?" I was truly concerned.

She said nothing but hung her head.

"It's okay, Angie. You can tell me why you're so unhappy."

She shook her head.

I continued to reassure her that she could tell me what upset her. "I'm a safe person, Angie. You need to know that it's okay to talk to people who are safe and will listen and won't hurt you."

She looked at me. A tear was forming on her lower eyelid. She was silent for a long time.

I reached over and took her hand.

Finally, she said in a voice that I could barely hear, "He hurt me."

"Who hurt you, Angie?"

"I just found myself out. It kinda felt like someone inside had pushed me out. He was on top of me…" Her voice trailed off.

I did not like the way this sounded. I put my arm around her and pulled her in close. "Was it Kurt?"

Again, she nodded.

Indignation rose up within me. I reminded myself not to jump to conclusions. "He wouldn't get off me. I started crying and saying, 'Stop, it hurts.' But he didn't stop. Then he said, 'Call me Daddy.' I just cried and said 'Stop.' When he was done, he said, 'You like it when Daddy does that to you.'" Her lip started to quiver, and then the tears came. Buckets of tears.

I felt enraged. It sounded like Kurt had full awareness that a child alter was out, and yet he felt it was perfectly acceptable to have sex with her.

Now I knew that in a court of law, Kurt would never be charged with sexually abusing a child. But Angie was authentically a child in all her ways—developmentally she was very young. To me it felt like he had indeed preyed on a child. I looked at her and saw a broken little girl sobbing her eyes out.

Jesus, this isn't right. A child should not have to endure this. How do I help Angie?

I held her close and had her lay her head on my chest. "Angie, Jesus is here with us. Let's ask him to help you. Jesus, please help Angie. Heal her from the inside out. She needs you to take away all the pain she had to endure. Jesus is right here, Angie. Allow him to heal you from the inside out."

She nodded, her head lying on my chest. Gradually the sobs subsided, and the tears slowed down to a trickle. "He is here. It feels good and warm, like when I'm with Cinda in the light. And I can hear your heartbeat. It makes me feel loved." She looked up at me, a slight smile on her lips. "You care. I don't think anyone else ever cared."

After a few minutes of silence, I pulled *The Velveteen Rabbit* off my bookshelf. I held it up for her to see. "Do you remember this book, Angie? I was reading it to Lucinda when you went into the light."

Her eyes brightened a bit. "Can you read it to me now?"

"I sure can. It's a pretty long book for one sitting, but we'll get started on it today." So with Angie snuggled up next to me, I began the story about a velveteen rabbit who longed to be real.

When I closed the book, Angie smiled at me. The doleful expression was gone.

"How do you feel now, Angie?"

"I feel warm inside. It's like it don't matter that Kurt done that to me."

"I believe that Jesus brought you some healing. He didn't want you to feel all that hurt. Maybe when you go in, you can be in the light for a while. Jesus just wants you to be a whole and happy little girl."

The next moment, Cinda appeared. She sat straight up and looked me in the eye. She looked very serious. "There's a real battle going on inside. Angie has become real. You know, all them parts are really just broken children, but most of them pretend that they are big and tough. They are too scared to be little, so they pretend. When they see Angie being little and real while she's out here, just being a child, they get afraid. So they want to stop her. That's why they pushed her out to be with Kurt, to teach her that it is dangerous to be a child. But God is pleased that she is being real. That's why he healed her so quickly. Angie needs to stay real. She will show the others a different way."

"I know she needs to be real, but it was so hard to see her hurting like that."

"You did the right thing. You let her hear your heartbeat. And you asked Jesus to heal her. That was good."

I looked at Cinda. When I had first encountered her, she had been a child who spoke in a child voice and said childlike things. Now her voice and her conversation seemed more mature. I considered this for a minute. Then I asked her, "Cinda, are you growing up? You don't seem like a child anymore."

Cinda smiled. "Many things are changing."

*****

Angie did indeed bounce back from her ordeal. She continued to be the child that she really was, and like any child, she wanted a friend. When I spent time with her, she would often talk about Steven. "I want to show him things, like you show me things, but he gets mean and tells me to go away. I tell him about colors and letters and that he can learn them things too. But he says that's sissy stuff."

"Why don't I have Steven out with me? Maybe if he spends time with me, he'll feel safe enough to be the little boy that he really is." As I said this, I realized the irony of saying he was a little boy when his body was fully female. I reminded myself that I considered Angie to be a child in every way despite her adult body. *What is the reality in all this?*

Angie nodded eagerly, so I called Steven out. After a short pause, I saw a switch take place. "Steven?"

"You better not use my name against me." His voice was harsh and accusing.

"I don't intend to. I just thought you might like to spend some time with me. We can do something you like."

"Like what?"

"Angie likes it when I read to her. Would you like to hear a story?"

"That's sissy stuff."

"What would you enjoy doing?"

Steven looked at me suspiciously. "I enjoy taking all my pain and dumping it on Angie. She's such a little wuss. We're all gonna give her all our pain. That way she'll stop being little. When you're little, you get hurt."

"Steven, you said you have pain. What's your pain about?"

"None of your business!" he shouted.

I decided to try another track. "Steven, do you remember when I was inside with all of you while you all cried. You cried too. And I didn't hurt any of you."

"Yeah, I remember. But boys aren't supposed to cry."

"That's a silly rule. Without tears, our pain doesn't heal. Did you feel better after you cried?"

"What's it to you?"

"Hey, Steven, I have something I think you'd enjoy." I had just remembered a crazy spinning top that was in one of my desk drawers. I pulled out the top. It had a flat shiny plate that the top would spin on, and it would go for long periods of time since the surface was so smooth. "Watch this." I spun the top for him. He watched what I did, and he watched as the top spun and spun and spun.

"Hey, can I try?"

"Sure." I handed him the top.

The first time he tried, the top spun wildly off the plate, and we laughed together. After several tries, he got it spinning, and then he watched it with interest. "That's neat. What's it called?"

"It's called a top. It's something children like to play with."

"Is this what Angie means when she talks about you showing her things?"

"Yes, it is." I put the top away and sat down on the couch next to him. I truly was not prepared for what happened next.

Steven's tough outer shell melted away. He put his thumb in his mouth, closed his eyes, and began to cry. He sobbed and sobbed. The only words he said were, "Hurt, hurt, hurt." He was a small boy, maybe four years old, with tears running down his face and a runny nose mixing with the tears.

I put my arm around him and held him close.

When the tears finally began to subside, I wiped his face with a tissue and then laid his head on my chest and let him hear my heartbeat. In a few minutes, he was sound asleep. As he slept, I thought about the many, many months it had taken for Lu to shed her hard exterior and begin to trust me. After only a handful of encounters with Steven, he was already broken. Was it because I had gotten inside when they had cried? Was it because of the example that Angie was setting? Was it the heartbeat? What was different?

While I didn't have an answer to this question, I found myself agreeing with Cinda. Many things were changing.

*****

Fortunately, Angie was compliant about Steven taking up my time. I would spend a few minutes with her, then ask if it would be okay to have Steven out. She would eagerly nod her head. She seemed determined to help Steven so he could be her friend.

Steven would typically emerge acting big and tough and very much a boy. Then I would get the top out and spin it. Steven would watch it spin and then spin it himself. After that, he would melt, shedding the tough-boy skin and become a weeping little child.

After several sessions of playing with the top, I decided to introduce Steven to something else. I got out the crayons and paper. I took my own sheet of paper and began to draw a house. Steven watched with curiosity. Then he picked up a red crayon and a black crayon and began to draw. I suppose I should have been prepared for the picture he drew. But my heart sank as I watched him work.

He began by drawing a figure lying down with someone or something on top of the figure. Then he drew a hook suspending down from the top of the page.

I remembered all the hooks Tara drew and the horrific memory attached to that hook.

Then he drew two figures wearing black hoods. One had a pentagram on his chest. Both figures were holding knives. As the fairly well-drawn shapes emerged, Steven began to whimper. As he did, his drawing skills regressed until he was scribbling like a two-year-old.

He scribbled, and he cried. The more he scribbled, the harder he cried. Tears ran down his cheeks and mixed with his runny nose. I noted that he had done the entire drawing in red and black.

Now he picked up a green crayon and cried as he scribbled. Then he took a purple crayon and scribbled away. By now he was choking on his sobs.

Steven's first drawing.

I took the crayon from him and pulled him close. "You're telling me what happened, aren't you? I'm sorry you have such an awful story to tell."

Steven continued to sob, then he laid his head on my chest. After several minutes, the sobs subsided, and he fell asleep.

As he slept, I studied his picture. It sickened me to know that he, too, had memories of hideous satanic rituals. My heart cried out to God. *When will it all end?*

It was Lucinda who emerged upon waking. She saw the picture. "Them parts. When are they going to just let me go on with my life? I'm tired of pictures and memories." Her voice was hard and her jaw was set.

"I know, Lucinda. I'm tired of it all too. But all those inside need to tell their stories, just like Lucy and Lu and Amy and all the others. You'll never be whole unless they have their turn too."

Lucinda stood up to leave. She marched out of the room with a parting shot. "All you do is spend time with all them others. When is there time for me?"

She's right. I need to make time for Lucinda too.

*****

It seemed as if Steven was being a child more often when he was inside, and Angie would tag along after him. Occasionally, he would talk about the top I had shown him.

"What's a top?" she asked with genuine interest.

"You don't know what a top is? That's because tops are for boys."

So Angie asked me to show her the top, which I did, but Angie was much more interested in coloring and books.

I tried to divide Lucinda's sessions into three segments: time for Lucinda, time for Angie, and time for Steven. Trying to keep this balance did not always work. Steven needed a lot of attention, so I would see him last so that he did not usurp the entire session.

He continued to draw pictures for me, most of them similar to the original one he had done. After one particularly gruesome picture, Steven began to rant about fire. He wanted to burn the picture up. As long as he focused on fire, he did not get little, but remained hard and impenetrable.

Cinda emerged that session. She explained that when Steven was consumed with thinking about fire, it distracted him from his pain and kept him from becoming the child he really was. "He needs to choose between fire and you."

I tried to get Steven to focus on me. I even spun the top for him, but nothing seemed to break his hardness. After that session, he went inside, took the pain that he had refused to look at, and transferred it all to Angie.

Our next session was particularly difficult. Steven came out as the session began, as hard as I had ever seen him. "It's time for war. There's a bloody war going on, and there will be killin'. I gotta kill them first. The whole world is in a war, and they're comin' for me. I need guns and knives. I need to fight them. Where do you keep your guns? I need them. I need to be strong. This is no time for pain. I took all my pain and put it on Angie. That way I can be strong for war. You kill first or be killed." His voice was harsh.

I tried to talk rationally to him, to reason with him that there was not a war going on; but when people are delusional, all the sane reasoning in the world cannot change their perspective. What happened to the broken little boy who would cry with me? It felt as if all the progress Steven had made was lost. He was hard, paranoid, and delusional. I felt emotionally drained and at a loss for how to proceed.

"He has a lot of pain, and he's running from it." It was Cinda. I felt like throwing my arms around her and sobbing. "The pain was too much for him, and it made him crazy." She was totally unruffled, a breath of sanity in the midst of the craziness. "He is putting all his pain on Angie. That's not fair to Angie. She needs to let him go. When she is so attached to him, he can easily transfer his pain to her. Call Angie out and tell her let him loose." Cinda sounded deadly serious. She spoke with certainty and authority.

I had learned to trust her wisdom, so I called Angie out.

When Angie appeared, she was crying and quaking. She looked at me with pain-ridden eyes and grabbed my arm.

"Angie, Cinda says that you must let Steven loose. He is dumping all his pain on you, and that's not fair to you. I know you like him and want to be his friend, but right now, that is not possible. Please try to let him go."

Angie nodded. "I'll try," she said in a quavering child voice.

I waited a minute and then asked, "What's happening, Angie?"

"He's fighting me. He won't go away." Angie was crying hysterically.

My head was throbbing, and I felt totally spent.

Cinda's calm voice broke the hysteria. "He has been removed from Angie, and he has his pain again. He had been getting close to his child, but now he's pushed that child away. So he's the hard warrior boy right now. Pray that God seals him off so that he won't be able to come out. Now call Angie and check on how she's doing."

When Angie reemerged, she grabbed my arm and whimpered. Between whimpers, she said, "There's something wrong with you. I can feel it." She clung to me all the more tenaciously. She clung, and she whimpered, and she kept saying, "What's wrong, what's wrong?"

This felt like the old, needy, clingy Angie that would drain the life out of me. I was totally exhausted and discouraged. I felt like I had no inner resources to help Angie. All I could think was that I wanted this session to be over. I just wanted to go home. "Angie, I'm just worn out. It's hard to see that all the progress Steven made is gone. We need to pray for Steven, that God will keep him from coming out because right now, he does not know what's real." I said a simple prayer asking God to keep Steven inside. Then I called Lucinda out to take them all home.

"Boy, you don't look too good. What happened?"

I gave Lucinda the *Reader's Digest* version of our session. "I'm sorry there was no time for you. The next session will be yours."

Lucinda must have sensed I was emotionally spent. She compliantly left.

*****

The next time I saw Steven, the paranoia and the talk of war was gone. He was subdued, with no talk of being big and tough and strong.

"You seem different, Steven. Has something changed?"

He smiled slightly. "Yeah, something's changed. I decided I didn't really want to go to war. I decided I liked it when we play with the top and when I fall asleep to your heartbeat. So I took that little boy part of me."

I wanted to let out a shout. "That is super great news, Steven. I'm so glad you did that!"

"But I'm feeling different kinds of things now. Sometimes I want to play. And sometimes I find myself sucking my thumb. Angie said maybe I need a room of my own where I can feel safe. So she went down to her mother's and asked if I, we, had a room when we were little. She thought maybe it would help if we knew we had a room. I just got mad at her for taking us down there. My mother can't see me as a child. She'll hurt me for sure. She told Angie to grow up. Then Cinda told us that the room we need is not with our mother but with you. Do we have a room with you?"

"Maybe my office is your room, a place where you can feel safe."

Steven seemed to consider this.

I went to my desk and pulled out the paper and crayons. I was curious to see if his drawing would be any different now that he had taken the little boy. He picked up a red crayon and began to draw.

He drew hooded figures with pentagrams on their chests and blacked-out faces, one holding a knife. They hovered around a table with a body on it. There was another table with a knife on it. The blade of the knife he scribbled with red. The always present hook hung from the ceiling, and a door with a window was in the upper left-hand corner.

Above the hooded figures was the face of a creature. Somehow it looked like a cow to me, but I suspect he wanted it to look much scarier. There was a second group of hooded figures with what appeared to be a baby in front of them. There was a knife pointing into the baby.

Another gruesome ritual.

He was working on flames in the bottom right-hand corner when his drawing ability began to regress. He finished with scribbles all along the bottom of the paper.

Steven's drawing after taking his child.

Something caught my attention. Steven changed positions, sat up more erectly, took the crayon, put it in his left hand, and continued the scribbles. Whoever was out was quite at home using the left hand. Was Steven ambidextrous or was another one out?

"Who are you?" I asked.

There was no response. Then the crayon went back to his right hand.

"Steven, were you drawing with your left hand or was someone else out?"

"Someone else came out"—he sniffled—"a girl. But I didn't want her messin' up my picture." He looked at his picture, and the tears began to flow.

I asked Steven if he wanted to tell me about his picture. He shook his head vehemently. So I let him cry for a few minutes. As he wept, I considered what I had seen. I had never been aware of a left-handed alter before.

I never ceased to be amazed at the complexity of Lucinda's system of alters. I marveled at the capabilities of the human mind. The alters can be so separate from each other that even their dominant hands are different.

Unlike other times when Steven cried, this time his tears tapered off quickly. It wasn't the gut-wrenching display of pain I had seen before. His sniffling ceased, and he reached for another piece of paper. This time, he reached for a blue crayon and began to fill in the bottom part of the paper with blue. Then he added some green to the top of it. I assumed that he was trying to portray a lake or ocean next to some grass. He then drew two stick figures. One had a slight smile. Next, he drew a rectangle in the upper left part of the paper. He drew a door in the rectangle. Then he took a yellow crayon and put yellow around the house and one of the stick figures. He seemed to be finished and put his crayon down. This was truly a child's work.

"That's a wonderful picture. Steven. It's a happy picture. Tell me about it."

Steven's happy picture, with help from the left-handed girl.

Before Steven could speak, he reached, with his left hand, for the orange crayon he had used to draw the house. He—perhaps I should say she—carefully drew two crosses on the house, one on either side of the door.

"Who are you?" I asked again, but that fast, she was gone, and the mystery of the left-handed girl was never solved. But it was reassuring to know that there was another one inside who willingly identified herself with the cross of Jesus.

I turned my attention to Steven again. "Tell me about your picture."

"It's a lake," he blurted, in a childlike voice.

"Who are these people?" I asked.

"It's me and you. And you have a light."

"It looks like the house has a light too."

"That's because you live there." I remembered the house picture Lucinda had drawn, the one with the good mother in the house.

"I think it's a wonderful picture, Steven. It looks like we're having fun together."

"Yes, we are. You're showin' me things." We laughed together.

Needless to say, that was a very renewing session. Steven had taken his child, he had drawn a happy picture, and a mysterious left-handed girl alter had drawn crosses on his picture. What a contrast to the last session with Steven, when he had been the hard warrior.

This truly is a roller-coaster ride.

*****

The next time we were together, I decided to give the two children, Angie and Steven, a positive experience. I explained to Lucinda that we were going to the park, that Lucinda and I could walk around together and talk, and then I would have Angie and Steven out for a bit. It was the kind of spring day that beckoned you to come outside, so Lucinda was all in on the idea. We walked among the many flowering trees, taking in the warm air and sunshine and discussing the importance of Lucinda accepting the parts as her own.

"I just want to be normal," she lamented. "As long as them parts are there, I'll never be normal."

"The parts aren't going away," I reminded her. "They are part of you. You don't want to forget where you came from."

"It just ain't fair that I don't get to be normal."

"I agree. It's not fair. But it's truth. And it's the truth that will set you free."

When the time came for Angie to be out, I expected her to be delighted to be outside in the park. Angie emerged, looked at me, looked at the ground, and said nothing.

"We're in the park, Angie. Maybe I can show you some neat things. Look at the flowering trees. Aren't they beautiful?"

Angie stared at the ground and said nothing.

"Okay, Angie, what's wrong?"

After several attempts to get her to speak, a tear began to form in the corner of Angie's eye. She hung her head.

"Did something happen that hurt you?"'

Angie nodded, ever so slightly.

"Well, tell me what happened."

"There was a lady at church. I was out because the children were singin' a song, and I wanted to hear it. I was still out when we were leavin'. There were lots of children there, and it was so fun to see them all. I wanted to play with them. I was skippin' along singin' the song they had been singin'. But there was this lady there, and she was watchin' me. I smiled at her, but she looked at me funny and said, 'Act your age. You're not four years old.'" The tear made its way down her cheek.

My heart hurt for Angie. "I'm sorry that happened. That lady simply did not know that you were doing exactly the right thing, exactly what Jesus wanted you to do. You were being real." I gave her a hug. "Why don't you go inside and spend some time in the light so that Jesus can heal you."

She nodded.

I silently prayed for Jesus to heal her and restore that wonderful, spontaneous little girl that Angie had become. Then I called Steven out.

Steven burst onto the scene. He looked around and exclaimed, "Where are we?"

"We're at the park."

"Hey, look at that. Why's that man riding in that chair?" Steven had spotted a man in an electric wheelchair, enjoying the park on this beautiful spring day.

"That man can't walk, Steven, so he gets around by riding in a wheelchair."

"Why can't he walk?"

"There's something wrong with his legs. I don't know exactly what. But isn't it good that he still has a way to get around?"

Steven watched him for a bit. "Will his legs get better?"

"I don't know. But we can pray for him. Jesus loves him too."

Then Steven spotted something else. "Hey, how come the ground is all pink?" He pointed at a flowering tree that had dropped all of its blossoms. The ground under the tree was a carpet of soft pink petals. He ran toward the tree. I followed.

Child Steven dove into those blossoms, throwing them about and kicking them with his feet. I joined him in the carpet of pink, and we had a blossom fight, throwing the soft, pink petals back and forth at each other. Then we lay down in the bed of blossoms and laughed. I wondered if anybody was watching these two grown ladies playing like two children. I decided not to look around to see, but just to enjoy the delight of the moment.

*****

Despite the hope of Steven starting to be real, the roller-coaster ride was not over. Lucinda was getting set in her hard outer exterior. She complained about the parts, about the pain they all carried with them, which would occasionally filter through to her, and about the amount of my time they were usurping. She complained that she couldn't be normal like other people, that even though she was no longer obsessed with having a mother, the longing the others felt would sometimes come through to her.

She was getting hard and impenetrable, and I wondered if the progress of Angie and Steven was helping things or making them worse.

"Normal people don't have children inside them, and they don't get told to act their age. I just want to be a normal adult."

"But remember that underneath it all, you're just a wounded child too. Most of your parts act big and strong and tough to hide what they really are. Steven was a warrior boy to hide it. And when you get like this, you are doing the same thing. Jesus wants you to be real, not fake. Where is the Child? Are you allowing her to be close to you?"

"I pushed her away. How can I be a good mother for my boys if I'm just a little child?"

I didn't have an answer for that question. "Maybe you don't have to be little like Angie and Steven, but you need to remember where you've been and that all your parts are an important part of you. You need to receive them, not push them away. And you shouldn't push the Child away. She connects you to your true feelings. When she is close, you can be real."

Spending time with Lucinda was emotionally draining—such a contrast to Angie and Steven, who were fun and spontaneous and full of life despite the incongruity of their adult body.

Finally, at the end of one of our sessions, Lucinda made a concession. "I don't like being hard like this. I remember what it was like when I first came back from my world, when I felt alive and filled with love for my boys. Now I don't feel nothin'. I'm numb all the time. I feel half dead."

"Well, I think the key to feeling alive again is to embrace the Child and to embrace the others inside."

That session, Kurt was unable to pick Lucinda up, so I had volunteered to give her a ride home. We left the office and had no sooner climbed into my car when Angie emerged. She squealed with delight when she saw me.

I helped her with her seat belt. She could barely sit still for me. She was especially elated that evening. She was beyond elated. Her eyes were alive with light and sparkle. She bubbled on and on about playing with Steven. He had shared with her our escapades under the tree playing in the blossom petals. She was filled with questions about what it was like to lie in the petals and to have a blossom fight. Energy was pouring off her, a good energy that filled the car with warmth and excitement.

I had never experienced such pure, positive vibes coming from a person. I could not help but to laugh with her, and I felt my spirits being lifted, not just out of the doldrums of Lucinda's despair but to new heights of joy and excitement. The whole ride to Lucinda's house, about ten minutes, I felt myself riding the wave of her exuberance. When we arrived at her city row home, I didn't want her to leave. I wanted to soak in every last moment of all her positive energy. "Angie, it's been so good to be with you. I hate to see you go."

She laughed her contagious laugh, her eyes filled with sparkle and joy and light. It seemed as if Angie was emanating pure light. To this day, my experience with Angie that evening is one of the highlights of my decades-long relationship with Lucinda. I wondered if she was reflecting what it's like to be in the light, in God's presence, to be a true child of God. I thought of how far she had come, from being a broken, needy, whiny, demanding waif, to being a child of pure light, or so she seemed that evening.

It was with great reluctance that I called Lucinda back. When Lucinda emerged, she took one look at me and said, "What happened to you? You look different."

"Angie's filled with light right now. I guess it rubbed off on me." I laughed aloud.

Lucinda looked at me out of the corner of her eye. I could see that she was quite taken aback by my presence, as I had been with Angie's.

"It's all right, Lucinda. I don't know what happened to her, but she is filled with God's light right now. It's contagious."

Lucinda climbed out of the car and waved goodbye, still not sure what to make of my presence.

*****

The next morning, I received an excited phone call from Lucinda. "Last night, Angie integrated into me, became part of me. You're right. She did have light. That little girl has given me life again."

As excited as I was about the integration and the positive effect it was bound to have on Lucinda, I would truly miss Angie. I regretted I didn't get to say goodbye to her, as I had with Lu a number of years earlier. But I consoled myself with knowing that my last experience with Angie was a wonderful parting gift.

CHAPTER 8

Who Is Cinda?

I eagerly anticipated my next session with Lucinda. What would she be like now that she had become one with Angie? Would any of that life-giving energy Angie had displayed be part of her now? Would she be less hard and resistant to accepting the parts? I could not imagine anything negative coming from this integration.

Perhaps I was naive to have my hopes so high. When had anything ever gone smoothly in this process with Lucinda? I knew the second I laid eyes on her this was the hard, resistant Lucinda.

Her first words were, “I just want to be normal. I don’t want them parts or their memories. And I’m tired of that Steven. He keeps asking me where Angie is. I told him to shut up and leave me alone.”

I winced at her words. I felt my emotions crashing as I reached within myself for the fortitude I needed. I took a deep breath and tried to sound as level as possible. “Lucinda, you sounded so positive on the phone the other morning. I believe you even said that taking Angie had given you new life. What happened?”

She cast her eyes downward and was silent for a moment. Then she shook her head. At last, she spoke. “When I first took her, I felt so alive. The whole world looked brighter, and everything seemed to be new and interesting. I found myself being drawn to things a child would like, like all my dolls. Then I found myself taking them out of the cabinet and playing with them. The whole morning went by, and all I did was play with them dolls. Then I realized what was happening. I was becoming a child. It was like integrating Angie was all a trick, a way to have me become a child. Then I got really mad. I wasn't gonna be no child. How can I be a mother for my boys if I spend all my time playing with dolls? Besides, being a child in an adult body will make me like a freak. Look what happened to Angie when she was a child at church."

I understood Lucinda's dilemma. But my last encounter with Angie had been so powerful. That positive energy that poured from her, the light and exuberance she displayed, had to be from God. Surely, God would not have allowed the integration if it hadn't been the right time. I truly did not know how to proceed.

Finally, I said, "Lucinda, the integration would not have happened if it wasn't the right time. I think we need to trust God. You're not pushing Angie away, are you?"

Lucinda stared at her hands. She said nothing. Finally, she murmured, "She's still there."

"Don't be discouraged." It was Cinda, with her clear, peaceful eyes. "You're right. It was God's time. But when Lucinda realized that she was learning to be a child from Angie, it scared her. She jumped in front of Angie. Angie was supposed to be in front. Angie was to lead her, to teach her how to be a child. She doesn't know how to be little. Angie was going to teach her to be little."

"But she's right. She needs to be an adult to parent her boys. How can she do that if she's five years old?"

"You need to trust God's plan." Cinda vanished, and Lucinda was back.

"Lucinda, I understand you jumped in front of Angie." I wasn't even sure what that meant or how Lucinda could have jumped in front of Angie. But Lucinda seemed to understand what I was talking about.

"I'm protecting myself." Lucinda's voice was loud and harsh. "I can't be a child. I pushed the Child away because she was trying to get me to be a child too. Now if I approach her, she's scared of me. It's like everyone wants me to be a child. I can't be a child!"

Lucinda's eye makeup was thick and dark. She was dressed in black jeans and a ragged green T-shirt. She wore heavy boots despite the warm weather of late spring. Her hair was uncombed. Something about her felt wretched. Nothing about her was appealing. I prayed inwardly. *Lord, she is truly lost. Help her find herself.*

After a moment of silence, Lucinda spoke, her voice softened a bit. "I guess part of me is afraid of the Child…and of Angie being part of me. This world is just too scary and too cruel to be a child. I don't see why God would do that to me. We got hurt so much when we really was a child. Why would he want me to be a child again?"

"Lucinda, I don't have the answers, so I suggest that we pray together and ask God to help us."

We ended that session with a prayer. When Lucinda left, she had softened a bit, and I was not quite as discouraged.

*****

Lucinda arrived for our next session with thick black eyeliner caking her eyes. She dropped down onto the pastel love seat and folded her arms. "I feel distanced from everything. I don't want to be around nobody. I'm not being nice to people. I feel like a bomb ready to explode. And Steven isn't helping. He wants Angie. I told him I hate him. Then we fought. I'm fake more and more. I don't even know how to be real. There's a rage inside, a pain over not bein' picked. I went to my mom's today. I snapped at her, but she's sick and ain't gonna live long anyway."

Listening to Lucinda was draining the life out of me. I found myself wishing I could have Angie back, that winsome little girl who was so full of life. I decided to just let Lucinda vent all her unhappiness, perhaps because that was the path of least resistance. After nearly half an hour of angry monologue, I asked Lucinda if pushing the Child away and jumping in front of Angie was helpful for her.

My question must have caught her off guard. She stopped talking for a moment and then hung her head. "No, it ain't working. I'm just miserable."

"You are miserable. What can you do differently?"

She paused for a moment, and then she said rather defiantly, "I'm willing to let Angie in front, but I ain't willing to accept them parts."

"That's a good first step, Lucinda."

"Next week is your birthday. I know it would make you really happy if I let Angie in front." Her voice had softened. "I bought you a gift, and I don't want to give it to you when I'm really miserable like this. What if I let Angie be in front for your birthday?"

"That would be a wonderful gift, Lucinda. I'm already looking forward to it."

Lucinda gave me a half smile. "I want your birthday to be nice."

Lucinda arrived for her session on my birthday with a bag filled with gifts, a small cake, paper plates and napkins, and plastic forks. "I want to make your birthday nice for you. You know, you done a lot for me. I'm gonna to give you your gifts with Angie, but first, we'll have cake." She pulled the store-bought cake out of the box and cut two pieces. The cake was decorated with pink and blue flowers. *Happy Birthday* was sprawled across the cake in blue gel icing.

"This is very nice, Lucinda. Thank you so much."

"I know I haven't been doin' what God wants lately. I'm just so scared to be a child. But I know it will make you happy if I let Angie in front, so I'll try."

When we had finished eating our cake, Lucinda reached into the brown paper bag and pulled out several gifts. She picked up the first one and held onto it. "I don't know if I can do this," she whispered. "I'm afraid I won't be picked. You'll pick Angie, but not me."

"Lucinda, I'll pick both of you."

I watched as an internal battle raged within Lucinda. She held onto the gift, a small box wrapped in brightly colored wrapping paper with a premade bow taped to the top. Several times she reached toward me with the gift, each time pulling it back.

I watched her struggle but said nothing.

Finally, she placed the gift back in the bag. "I can't do it. But I won't give you the gifts until I can."

"Then I'll wait until you are ready to do it with Angie in front."

"But I do have something good to tell you. I told God I will give up the right to kill myself. I know he don't want that for me. Steven's really mad about it. He afraid he can't face all the memories without that as a back door, but I told him we have you to help us."

"Lucinda, that is a wonderful birthday gift. It's a great relief to know I'll never have to worry about you killing yourself again."

"Well, I don't know what them parts might do, but I think that all of us that are in the light have agreed to this."

So Lucinda left with her brown bag of gifts, but she did leave one gift behind for me, the reassurance that at least those in the light were committed to life.

*****

The next session, Lucinda arrived with her brown bag of gifts. She placed the bag next to her on the couch and proceeded to tell me about some very unhappy interactions with her mother. "She called and told me I never come see her, that I used to come a lot and that I would get her whatever she wanted. She said she knew how to use me to get what she wanted. Boy, did that make me mad. She also said that if I start acting little, she'd hurt me, and that you won't want me after she's done with me. I was so mad that I almost took back the right to kill myself, but then I figured God wanted me to give it up for a reason. And I saw how relieved you was when I told you I gave it up. I know it would hurt you if I did it, so I told God I wouldn't take it back. But now I have all this rage at my mom, and I don't know what to do with it." Lucinda spent the entire session venting her anger at her mother. The more she vented, the harder she became. At the end of the hour, she picked up the bag of gifts and left.

*****

It was eleven days after my birthday when Lucinda ambled into my office like a little lost child. She carried the brown bag of gifts.

She spoke in a child voice. She looked around my office as if she was taking it in for the first time. "I put Angie in front."

"That's good news, Lucinda. How has it been for you with Angie in front?"

"It's scary. But when Steven saw me like this, he came over into the light."

"He did?"

"Yeah, I don't know why, but he's been hanging close to me since. Maybe he can tell that Angie's in me. And then, there's one named Brandy who came out of the darkness. She knew Steven and says she wants what he has. He told her to talk to you, that you could help her."

"Lucinda, it sounds like your decision to put Angie in front is having a very positive effect."

"I guess so, but it's so scary with Angie in front. It's like I can't stop myself from being little. But we can give you your gifts now." She pulled the top one out of the bag, the same little gift wrapped in brightly colored paper that she had tried to give me before. She held onto the gift. "I'm starting to feel sick. I don't know if I can do this."

I watched Lucinda as she made contorted faces. What was happening? She had never behaved like this before. Then suddenly, she burst into an infectious child's laugh. "Happy birthday! It's me… Angie."

"Angie, what are you doing here? I thought you were part of Lucinda now."

"Cinda separated me out. She told me to say goodbye to you." I remembered when Lu had gone through a similar process, breaking out of an integration to say goodbye to me. But that was Lu's own doing.

"How could Cinda separate you out?"

"I don't know, but she did. Open your gift." She was clapping her hands together in excitement. So I took the package and opened it. It was a lovely ring with a light-blue stone. "Lucinda and me picked it out together. I told her to get the blue one."

I remembered teaching Angie the colors. "It is just lovely, Angie. I'll remember you every time I wear it. I'm going to miss you, but I know you need to be part of Lucinda. I'll never forget you."

Angie threw her arms around me. "I'll miss you too. Thank you for teaching me colors and letters." We sat next to each other for a few minutes, our arms around each other. "Goodbye. Lucinda needs me now."

"Goodbye, Angie." A tear trickled down my cheek. I reached for the ring and put it on my finger. That would be my remembrance of Angie.

"Hey, why are you crying?" It was Lucinda.

"I just said goodbye to Angie. I'll miss her. But you need her to help you now. Do you remember how taking Lu helped you become stronger? Well, taking Angie and keeping her in front will help you to be real, to be the child you really are."

"But it's scary to be a child."

"But it's also fun. Let's open up the rest of the gifts." So, with Lucinda as a child, I opened the other gifts, oohing and aahing over each one. Lucinda was truly childlike as she watched me with excitement, explaining why she and Angie had picked each one.

As usual, I could not have predicted the course of events in Lucinda's process, but I sensed we were on a good path.

*****

In the weeks that followed, Lucinda would sometimes be a child and sometimes she was the hard, fake shell. When she was the child, she seemed to be a lost little waif. "I'm waiting to be picked," she would say. When she was the fake shell, she was hard and abrasive, her eyes caked with thick dark eyeliner.

Sometimes when Lucinda was the lost and frightened child, she would call me for reassurance. During one of these evening phone calls, Cinda emerged to talk to me. She no longer spoke in a child voice; her voice was unwavering and full of authority, informing me of what was happening internally or the course I needed to take with

Lucinda. "You need to work on the way she dresses. When she dresses in black or wears boots, she trying to be hard, to not be the child. You need to tell her not to wear all that eye makeup. If she comes to your office with it on, I want you to take it off."

I thought about what she was saying and the way she was saying it. There was a different air about her. She had so much understanding of spiritual matters and things of God. Sometimes she would rattle off Bible verses for me to look up. Lucinda knew very little about the Christian faith or the Bible, and what she thought she knew was often quite twisted and distorted. Cinda was totally different.

I had so many questions about her. How did she gain all this understanding? I thought about how she had broken apart the integration between Angie and Lucinda. I remembered how her light caused dark monsters within to leave. She seemed to be very powerful in Lucinda's inner world. She was consistently level and unruffled, no matter how difficult the outer circumstances or the extent of Lucinda's hysteria. She was completely different from Lucinda or any of the alter personalities I had encountered. At first, she had presented as a child, but now she was a mature voice of sanity and wisdom. Even as she talked to me about something as mundane as removing eye makeup, there was a quiet serenity about her that at times felt almost holy. Who was she and how did she fit into Lucinda's complex system of alters?

I originally viewed her as Lucinda's internal self-helper, an alter who encompassed the inner wisdom of the person and aided in the healing journey. But as I contemplated these things now, she seemed to be so much more. A question was forming in my mind. Before I had time to think, I blurted it out. "Cinda, who or what are you?"

A short pause followed. I wondered how she was going to answer my question. I wondered if she was going to answer my question.

Finally, she spoke. "The answer is in your heart. Search your heart and you will know." Cinda left, and Lucinda was on the other end of the line.

*****

In the days that followed, I contemplated that. What did she mean when she said the answer was in my heart?

I remembered a time when Cinda had said to me that God renews your mind but speaks to your heart. So…the heart was different than the mind. The answer to my question was not something I was going to reason my way to. I knew that the biblical understanding of the heart was that it was the core, the center of a person, from which a person's words and actions flow. In a sense, it was the deepest self. That suggested I needed to look within. The answer was within me, somewhere deep inside.

As I contemplated this, I thought about times when I had known things deep within, when there was an inner certainty that *this is the right choice*, like my decision to marry my husband. I had total peace about that decision despite some voices in my life that spoke otherwise. Then there was the decision to become a counselor. Again, I just knew it was the right thing, that this was my calling. I must have known these things *in my heart.*

Then I remembered another time when I had just known something even though it took me out of my comfort zone—the first time I had seen that vile, evil look in Lu's eyes. It had taken my breath away. I had never seen anything like it, and it was a bit frightening. But somewhere deep inside, I knew exactly what I had seen. I had been staring into the eyes of pure evil, something demonic.

I looked for that inner certainty within concerning my question to Cinda: *Who or what are you?*

I'm not sure how or when that certainty came. And it did not come without a lot of questions and concerns. While my questions about Lu's vile look brought me face-to-face with questions about evil that were at times frightening, at least there was solid biblical precedent. Both the Old and New Testaments speak of evil spirits. Jesus himself confronted many of these spirits that inhabited human beings, and these people were set free from the bondage the spirits brought to their lives.

I began to look at some biblical stories with new questions, and I wondered. Who were the three men that Abram encountered and extended hospitality to before the destruction of Sodom and Gomorrah?[1] At first, the Bible calls these men "the Lord" but later refers to "two angels." Was the writer of Hebrews thinking of this story when he wrote in the New Testament, "Do not forget to entertain strangers, for by so doing, some people have entertained angels without knowing it?"[2] Or did the writer understand that sometimes angels appear to be so human that we cannot tell the difference?

Could it be that this part of Lucinda that I call Cinda was an angel of light? I had seen dark angelic presences rise up within Lucinda and show themselves. Was it too large a stretch to believe that there could be an angel of light who occupies "space" within Lucinda? That would answer a lot of questions for me, like her extensive biblical knowledge and understanding of God; and why she had power with her light to force out dark demonic presences; and how she could be so consistently calm, collected, and at peace despite the craziness of Lucinda's inner and outer worlds.

Somehow the thought of Cinda as an angel of light resonated with me, and I came to feel a peace about it. I was well aware that this would not be understood or well received by most people, but I knew what I had experienced with her, and I had no other explanation.

*****

Meanwhile, Lucinda still struggled to keep Angie in front. Some days she was the hardened Lucinda with thick black eyeliner. When she arrived for sessions in this mode, I followed Cinda's instructions and removed the makeup. Lucinda would fold her arms and tell me it was none of my business if she wore eye makeup, but she would eventually comply and allow me to remove it.

Occasionally, she would enter our sessions as a child, but wearing eyeliner she had put on earlier in the day when the hard Lucinda had jumped in front of Angie.

---

1 Genesis 18–19.

2 Hebrews 13:2.

Child Lucinda was always compliant about having the eyeliner removed. I noticed that this child Lucinda seemed totally comfortable with having me do something as personal as removing her eye makeup.

During this time, a number of new alter personalities surfaced. The first one was Brandy, who had followed Steven out of the darkness. Others followed: Shannon, a very dark one named Death, and another boy named Jason. Each of these alters presented as strong, nasty, and impenetrable; but as I interacted with each one, often letting them hear my heartbeat, the tough outer shell would break down, and they would become broken little children, weeping and sniffling and cowering in fear.

At this point, we would pay a visit to Paul and Adele, the kindly couple who were so very skilled in ferreting out the darkness attached to each alter and having it leave in the name of Jesus. After each one was delivered, they tended to remain a child, many of whom told their stories in child words or drew pictures of dark rituals. It seemed we were getting quite a collection of broken, but healing, children within Lucinda.

Heather was perhaps the most significant alter to surface at this time. Heather was different from the others in that she didn't need to visit Paul and Adele. Lucinda had arrived for her session as a child. I removed her makeup. After it was removed, Lucinda wanted to play like a normal child. As she colored and played with the teddy bears in my office, Heather drew close to partake in the child fun.

As she and Lucinda played together, a stream of darkness spontaneously began to leave. As Lucinda breathed out, a low, guttural growling sound could be heard. Breath after breath, darkness left. I watched in amazement as Heather was freed from all her darkness. There truly was something very powerful about Lucinda and her alters shedding their hardened shells and becoming the children they really were.

After our sessions, I would sit in my office and ponder the things I was experiencing. Was Lucinda an incredibly good manipulator who was able to lure me into believing that she had alter personalities, demonic presences within her, and now, an angelic presence?

I remembered the slow, laborious process we had had gone through, uncovering alters one at a time. Often, Lucinda was more resistant to accepting them than I was. If she was manipulating, she was really good. I had never seen any indication that she was confusing alters or getting her stories mixed up. And I remembered how well Miss Kindle's impressions and experiences lined up with my own.

Then there was the emotional pain, which would surface from the depths of Lucinda's being; it was no manufactured display of crocodile tears. I had been seeing her for ten years now. Could she possibly have kept up a charade for that long?

No, I didn't believe she was making this all up to manipulate me.

Perhaps Lucinda was delusional, and she really believed that she had alter personalities, demonic presences, even an angelic presence, although up until this time, she had given no indication that she believed there was an angel within. Maybe she was so delusional that her mental illness created alter personalities to support her delusions.

But my experience with people who had delusions was that sooner or later, the delusional nature of their thoughts became evident. There wasn't external reality to support their claims. So far, nothing she had revealed to me could be challenged by facts. I remembered the gruesome poems written by her brother, which certainly supported the presence of satanism in their family. Again, there was the conversation with Miss Kindle.

And Cinda was a voice of sanity amidst it all. Would not someone with so much wisdom and levelheadedness challenge delusional thoughts? There were times when Cinda would tell me that one or another of the alters was delusional, like when Steven thought he was in a war. But she never challenged the reality of Lucinda's tragic past, her alter personalities, or the demonic presences within her.

This left me with one conclusion. Lucinda was indeed traumatized repeatedly in a satanic cult, had split off a host of alter personalities to manage the traumas, had demonic presences within her as a result, and now an angelic presence as well.

I considered myself an intelligent and reasoning person, yet these were the things I had come to accept.

As I sat there and contemplated all this, I looked at one of the pictures Lucinda had painted for me a number of years earlier. It was the second picture she had done of her world of escape, an idyllic mountain scene with a waterfall and a lake and craggy mountains in the background. The sky behind the mountains was painted in pinks and blues that had been dulled down and had a somewhat ominous feel about them.

I recalled how both this picture and the other one of her world had a commonality, a beautiful natural scene in the foreground and a barrier (in this case the gray angular mountains) that stood between the idyllic scene and something more barren or threatening (in this case, the ominous sky). In the other picture, there was a shimmering light beyond the barrenness. That was missing in this picture.

I had understood these pictures to represent the reality of Lucinda's life. She wanted to escape to a pain-free place where everything was beautiful. To do that, she had to block out the painful realities that were truth...hence the barriers. Beyond the barriers, it was barren and lifeless, but in the first picture, on the other side of the barrenness, there was light, a shimmering light that could only be reached by going through the barrenness, by facing the truth of her tragic life. In this second picture, the lifeless, rugged mountains would have to be scaled. But there was no light there, only a wispy cloud near one of the peaks.

As I studied this picture, my eyes fastened on that one wispy cloud. I got up and walked closer. Could I really be seeing what I thought I saw?

I stepped back again and studied the picture some more. How had I missed it before? Maybe I had not been ready to see it until now. I remembered as a child finding shapes in the clouds—elephants and bears and droopy-eared dogs.

For the first time, I saw that the one wispy cloud had the form of an angel.

Lucinda's world of escape, with the form of an angel in the sky.

CHAPTER 9

Becoming a Child

A long, hot, dry summer was upon us. The grass turned the color of shredded wheat as drought conditions prevailed and lawns could not be watered. Farmers prayed for rain as their crops struggled to put forth a harvest.

For Lucinda, July and August were difficult. She still flip-flopped between being the hardened shell of herself and the broken child she really was.

When she was the child Lucinda, she would feel lost and alone. This brought about many late-night phone calls as she reached out to me for reassurance. When she was in this state, she would talk about being in a "waiting place."

"I'm in this waiting place. I'm waiting, waiting. My mother's gonna come, and she's gonna take me home. So I'm waiting. How much longer do I have to wait? I wanna go home."

I wasn't sure of the significance of this, but I certainly did not want to tell her that her mother was not coming to get her, so I said nothing.

Frequently, Cinda emerged during these phone calls. She seemed eager to talk to me.

The thought would flit through my head: *Am I really talking to an angel of light?* But when she spoke, I always gave her my full attention. And I still had unanswered questions.

"Cinda, why was it that you first presented as a child, but now you aren't a child at all?"

"That's because when I first started talking to you, I came through a child. She was the one who went to the light when Lucinda split into Lu and Cinda. Lu went to the darkness and Cinda went to the light. She was protected by God all those years and remained quite pure. That's why I could come through her. If you remember, when I first showed myself to you, I didn't talk at all. I just drew and wrote." I did indeed remember when Cinda first emerged by drawing a cross. "Now I don't need to come through the child Cinda anymore. I can talk directly to you."

"What changed that you can talk to me more directly now?"

"God said it was time, and you were spiritually ready."

I pondered what she was saying. "So you called yourself Cinda because you came through the child Cinda?"

"That's right."

"So is Cinda your real name?"

"No, it's not."

"Then what is your real name?"

"That is not to be revealed."

The subject was closed.

*****

Heather began to emerge more often during our sessions. In many ways, she was similar to the other alters who emerged during this time period—originally a hard, angry shell but before long allowing herself to be a child with me.

Unlike some other alters who seemed receptive to my kindness and concern, Heather would back away at any sign of caring. She was resistant to love in any form and would threaten to go back to Death (another dark alter she was connected to) if I showed too much warmth.

I learned to proceed very cautiously with her.

During one of Lucinda's late-night phone calls, Heather emerged. This was the child Heather, whimpering about being afraid of others inside who said they would hurt her if she stayed little.

Nothing I said seemed to console her. If I was too kind to her, she would say, "You're gonna hurt me. Love hurts."

I certainly wasn't going to be mean to her, so I was at a loss for how to proceed.

"Don't get discouraged. You can help her." Cinda had emerged. "She really wants you, but she's afraid too. She's afraid that if she gets too close, she'll lose you."

"How can I help her? If I show her any kindness at all, she backs off."

"I want you to tell her that you're her spiritual mother. Use those words."

I remembered many months ago when Lucia had tried to convince me, through writing, to be their spiritual mother. I had put that in that back of my mind, thinking that it might confuse all the broken children. I didn't want them thinking I was going to be their mother. Again, I mulled over the term *spiritual mother*. What exactly did it mean? "But won't it confuse them, leading them to think that I'm going to be their mother?"

"It won't confuse them. They already know that's who you are. You have the heartbeat." And with that, Cinda was gone.

Heather was whimpering and crying on the other end of the phone. "They're gonna hurt me unless I get big. I don't want them to hurt me."

I decided to give it a shot. "It's okay, Heather. It's okay to stay little. You're safe with me because I'm your spiritual mother." I felt uneasy saying that. Would it contradict all the times I told Lucinda I could not be her mother?

But a remarkable thing happened. Heather said, "I know. You have the heartbeat." Then she stopped crying.

I mulled all this over. What was the meaning of it all?

And what exactly was a spiritual mother?

*****

That summer a steady stream of alters came to the surface swaggering about, puffing their chests, acting as tough and mean as they could. But with a large dose of kindness and a bit of chiding—"I know you're really a child. You don't have to act big and tough with me"—the outer shell would crumble, and I would be face-to-face with a sniveling little boy or girl.

At that point, we would make a trip to visit Paul and Adele. It seemed that once they were in the child state, darkness could be easily removed.

Cinda informed us that by being who they really were, broken children, no longer pretending, darkness would lose its ground, the legal right it had to be there.

"Little children do not ask for darkness. It is only as they grow that they begin to want the darkness because it feels safe for them. It's what they know, and it feels like they have a protection. When they return to being a little child, they choose to be without that protection. It takes away the ground that darkness has, and darkness must leave." Cinda explained this to me in a late-night phone call.

I considered what she was saying. "So, they have to feel safe enough to shed that tough outer shell. It seems they are getting to the point where they feel safe with me, safe enough to be a child, a lot faster than they used to. Is that because they have another source of safety? They feel they have a spiritual mother who will keep them safe?"

"That's right. Being the spiritual mother is very powerful."

I felt awed and very humbled by this revelation.

Cinda continued. "God is pleased with all you are doing for Lucinda. He is building a team to help her. You and Paul and Adele are working well together, but it is time to add someone to that team."

I wondered who this person would be.

"I want you to ask your husband to come to the next deliverance. It is time for him to join the team."

I felt a smile inside me. I couldn't think of anyone I would rather have join our deliverance team. "I'll be glad to do that Cinda. I think he would be a great addition. He's never done deliverance, but he is strongly rooted in God. He'll learn quickly." I was very pleased with this unexpected turn of events.

*****

It was a hot summer night when my husband, Joby, and I drove into the city to pick up Lucinda. It was time for Steven to receive deliverance from the darkness that kept him bound. After picking up Lucinda, we headed south for the twenty-minute drive.

Paul and Adele's home was in a rural area, an old Victorian house slathered in the charm of another era. We stepped out of the car to a cacophony of crickets and katydids, so much louder than we were used to in the city or suburbs. We entered the home through a side entrance, into a large room used for meetings.

Paul and Adele emerged from the living area of the house. They were a homey couple in their late fifties. They greeted us warmly. Introductions were made. Paul and Joby firmly shook hands while Adele smiled kindly, her blue eyes sparkling. Then we headed into the basement area, the space where we usually met for deliverance.

Lucinda, by this time, had become very comfortable with this couple. That night, Lucinda was the fake, outer shell.

Paul understood the importance of her being real, being the child, so he encouraged her to shed the tough shell. "Come on, Lucinda, you know you're safe here. You can let those walls down. We love you when you're a child."

Adele agreed with him, smiling warmly.

So Lucinda let the walls down. She ran to Paul and Adele, giving them both a big hug. Then she ran to me, threw her arms around me and exclaimed, "NanNan!" That was the name child Lucinda used for me. Then she looked at Joby. She had met him several times before but did not yet have a connection with him. She smiled shyly. Hubby smiled back.

Paul looked to me. "Is there a particular alter we are to work with tonight?"

"Yes, there is. It's time for Steven to be delivered."

"Well, let's have him out then."

"Could I please have Steven out? Steven, would you come to the surface?"

In a flash, Steven was out, standing with his arms folded over his chest. He looked at me, and then he looked at the others. "Who are these people?" His tone was demanding.

"This is Paul and Adele. And this is my husband."

Steven glared at them.

"It's okay, Steven. They are here to help you, not to hurt you." I realized that Steven had only been out with me when I was alone. Seeing other people must have caught him off guard. "We are here because the time has come to get rid of those monsters inside. You no longer need them to protect you because you have the light to protect you. And you also have a spiritual mother."

Those words were no sooner said when that vile look appeared in Steven's eyes. He glared at me, and then he glared at my husband, his pupils pinpoints. His eyes were totally flat and seemed to take on a yellowish cast. There was no sparkle, no light or life in them.

His eyes fastened on my husband. A low, guttural, growling sound came out of his mouth. Then he lunged at Joby, grabbing him around the throat.

I had seen darkness attack Paul this way any number of times. He was always cool and collected, ordering darkness down in the name of Jesus, and darkness always complied. But this was my husband, having his first encounter with a demonic presence. I held my breath and waited for Paul to do something.

But it was Joby who spoke. "In the name of the Lord Jesus Christ, you must leave." Steven's hands remained clutched around his throat. Joby's voice grew stronger even though Steven's clenched hands were making it hard for him to talk. "In the name of the Lord Jesus Christ, get your hands off me and leave." He was face-to-face with an ugly, demonic presence, but he did not flinch.

Paul joined the fray. "This man is a child of God and a follower of the Lord Jesus Christ. You heard him. Now leave." The dark spirit let out a vile shriek, followed by a low, hissing sound. He unclasped his hands from Joby's neck, fell to his knees, and lay there in silence.

Paul dropped down to his knees and placed his hand on Steven's back. "You are to go to wherever the finger of God sends you. You may not harm any of us, our families, our churches, or anyone else. Just go where God sends you."

Steven lay there in silence for a few minutes. Then he sat up, looked at me and smiled. It was child Steven.

I sat down next to him. "Hi, Steven. Are you okay? There was quite a battle out here."

"It was scary. There was this big, ugly monster in there. But more and more light just kept comin', and he got crowded out." He sounded frightened and amazed at the same time. He pulled close to me. I took his head and laid it on my chest, letting him hear my heartbeat. As he lay there, listening to my heartbeat, something unexpected happened.

A steady stream of darkness started leaving him. Breath after breath, a low guttural growling could be heard as darkness was expelled with each exhale. Finally, the growling stopped. Steven looked up at me and smiled. He was silent for a short time. Then he said, "I feel different. Everything is calm inside. I ain't ever felt that before." Then he laid his head back on my chest and fell asleep.

As he slept, Adele and Paul, Joby, and I talked. We all agreed that Joby's first encounter with darkness was a dramatic one, but he knew exactly what to do, taking authority over the darkness in the name of Jesus.

"I was pretty nervous coming here tonight," Joby said. "But even before I got here, I had a Bible verse running through my head: "Greater is he who is in me than he who is in the world."[3] "I just kept that running through my head as I looked into his eyes."

"You stood on the truth," Paul said. "That gave you the confidence you needed."

The first time I had brought Lucinda to see Paul and Adele, it was a slow, laborious process that took several hours. I had watched

[3] 1 John 4:4.

from the sidelines. I reminisced out loud. "The first time we came to see you, it took all night to expel one demon. Tonight we saw many leave in a much shorter period of time."

Paul responded, "That is because Lucinda has become so much stronger in the Lord. Her growing faith makes a big difference. There is much more light in her now."

I nodded. Then I remembered what Cinda had told me, that as the alters chose to become children, darkness lost its right to be there. "And Steven has chosen to be a child, at least most of the time. When he does that, he is telling darkness that he doesn't want their protection anymore. Then they lose their ground to be there."

Paul chuckled. "Well, they left in a hurry tonight, so their foothold was very weak."

*****

The summer was coming to a close. The drought was finally over as the earth was refreshed with rain. I felt very positive in my work with Lucinda, as if we were getting somewhere. Hardened alters were breaking down and becoming children. Deliverances were flowing easily. It seemed as if taking the role of spiritual mother was having a very positive effect upon the whole system of alters. And my dear husband had joined our deliverance team. I was all optimism as the summer drew to a close.

Lucinda still flip-flopped between being real and being the hard, fake shell. When she came for appointments, I never knew which Lucinda would show up. I did notice that as the summer wore on, she was being the child more often. I'm not really sure when it happened, but at some point late in the summer or early in the fall, Lucinda took the Child, the part of herself that connected her to her emotions, as part of herself. From that time on, Lucinda was a child.

Now this posed a problem of its own. How could she mother her boys if she was five years old? I knew there were other alters who cooked and cleaned and who were out for sex with Kurt. I just hoped these more mature alters were covering for her.

This child Lucinda would come to sessions with me every bit a child, and at times, a sassy child at that. She would pout if I wanted another alter out. She would cry when I told her it was time to leave. One day she reported to me that she had been playing with the dolls in the cabinet, the very expensive collector dolls she had accumulated while working at the doll store. She had given one of these dolls a bath and cut its hair.

I winced, knowing those dolls were worth hundreds of dollars apiece. I started to wonder if this really was a good course.

Cinda must have detected my doubts. "God has given her a special gift, a chance to start over. When she would not accept the other parts as her own, when she tried to push them away, God decided to go another route, a route where she would not forget where she came from. She is now the broken child that she has always been. She cannot get away from it now. She can't push the others away, thinking she can do it on her own. She is a child in every way except her body."

"What am I supposed to do to help her?"

"You are to help her grow up. Spend time with her and teach her how to be a healthy child, instead of a broken one."

"But I'm her counselor, not her parent."

"You are her counselor, and you are also her spiritual mother."

So our session time together became primarily focused on Lucinda. I took her to the mall, as I had with the Child many months earlier. We went for walks in the park. We fed the ducks. I read her stories and colored with her. I corrected her when her behavior was out of line, which was frequently.

At times, I had to take control and not be nice, letting her know that I was in charge and that she would listen to me. She would sass back, but I stood firm, telling her that she was the child, I was the adult, and I was in charge.

I was surprised to see her break down and become compliant. She started respecting my position, and as she did, her behavior improved.

By the time fall rolled around in full force, Lucinda was showing signs of being a healthy child. I was indeed optimistic.

But little did I know, something very dark and sinister, worse than I could have ever imagined, was just around the corner.

CHAPTER 10

The Note

As we headed into the fall, I had my hands full. Child Lucinda needed a great deal of time and attention, which I tried to give her. But Steven was still around, as was Heather.

Steven was still getting memories, which he would share mostly through his drawings. After each drawing, he put the crayon down and became a broken little child, weeping and wailing. Then I would hold him and let him listen to my heartbeat until he fell asleep. When I called Lucinda back, Steven receded inside into the light, the part of Lucinda's inner world where Cinda was present and God's healing light was especially powerful. Resting in that light, he found healing from the pain of the memory he had just drawn. With the healing of each memory, Steven seemed to get healthier. Both he and Lucinda seemed to be on a path to becoming normal little children, filled with spontaneity and laughter, warmth and affection. How could I not love the children they were becoming? I developed a deep affection for both of them.

The healing process they were going through to shed their tough outer veneer and become broken little children, to be freed from the darkness that had them bound, and then to find healing from their traumatic memories in the inner light was giving me great hope. Was it God's plan to have each alter go down a similar path and find healing that way? This was so much easier than the long and tedious memory work I had done with previous alters. I was very excited about the possibilities ahead.

Heather was still flip-flopping between being the tough outer shell and a needy and broken child. She resisted any outward displays of affection or comfort, but I had great hopes for her to follow the path that Steven and Lucinda were pioneering.

Around this time, a new feminine alter called Sam emerged. She was closely connected with Steven, who told her it was safe to trust me. She first appeared as the hardened outer shell. "Steven said you would help me. I don't need your help, especially if it means becoming a stupid little child like he is. I ain't ever had anyone else's help. Why should I want yours?"

I reassured her that I understood how she felt, but I also told her that I knew she was a broken little child, just like Steven. "It must be hard to pretend all the time. Think how nice it would be to let your guard down and just be who you really are. It's okay if you are really scared and hurting."

"Hell no. I'm not hurting. And I ain't scared of nothin'. They told us we're not allowed to hurt. If you show pain, they do things to you."

But much to my amazement, Sam began to soften on my second encounter with her. Within three weeks, she revealed something to me. "There's two little children inside me. I keep them hidden. No one else knows they're there. I'm tired of hearin' them cryin'. They're always cryin'. Always. Sometimes they just whimper, but sometimes they're really loud."

"Sam, it must be very difficult to hear that all the time." I sat down next to her on my pastel love seat. "Let me talk to them through you."

She nodded.

"I want to talk to the two little children inside Sam. I know you're hurting and that you have endured many terrible things. But I want you to know that everything is changing. You have a spiritual mother now, and I'm here to help you get better so you don't hurt all the time."

A short silence followed. Then Sam laid her head on my chest, and she became a whimpering little child, tears streaming down her cheeks. She cried and sobbed while I held her. I remembered all the times I had sat on this love seat and held Lucinda and Lucy and Lu and so many others as they cried out the pain of their childhood.

This time, something different happened.

After the crying subsided, Sam looked up at me and said in a small child voice, "We're one now. One of them little ones was out with you, but I was inside with the other one. There was this bright light inside. It felt warm and good, so I went to it and then we all came together. I don't hear them cryin' anymore, but I feel their sadness, and I can see some of them things that happened to them." A tear trickled down her cheek.

"When you go inside, Sam, if you see that light, go to it. Stay there as long as you can. Jesus is in that light, and he will help you feel better."

She nodded, then laid her head back on my chest. After a few minutes, Sam was sound asleep.

As I held her, I marveled at what just happened. The process seemed to be going much more smoothly and quickly. In just a few weeks, Sam's outer shell broke down, she trusted me enough to tell me about her inner children, she moved into the light, and she integrated her two child parts. Now she was sleeping peacefully.

What was so different? Was it the example Lucinda was setting by being a child? Was it owning the role of the spiritual mother? Was it Lucinda's stronger faith? Was it all of these things? Whatever it was, I was delighted and encouraged. I was beginning to think that wholeness for Lucinda was becoming a real possibility.

*****

As I worked with Heather, I began to detect some changes in her. Her fear of being loved seemed to diminish. She became less guarded and allowed her child to be out with me more frequently.

One day, while in her child state, Heather looked at me with pitifully sad eyes. "I want to come live with you."

Deeply touched, I looked at Heather. How could I respond? "Heather, that can't happen. You have boys of your own who need a mother."

She looked back at me with a puzzled expression. A tear formed in the corner of her eye. Then that fast, she was the hard, outer shell. She shouted, "You can hurt me, but don't hurt her. I let the child be with you, and then you hurt her."

"I'm sorry if I hurt your child, Heather. That was not my intention. But what she wants is simply not possible."

"I'm a protector. I trusted you with her, and now you've hurt her." Heather glared at me. I remembered how Lu would call herself a protector. It was a point of great pride with Lu, and it seemed to be so with Heather as well.

I proceeded carefully. "I'm glad you were there to protect the children inside. I know horrible things happened to them. I didn't want to hurt your child, but I have to be honest with her. I can't take her home to live with me." I sat down next to her and took her hand.

Heather pulled her hand back. When she spoke, her voice was harsh. "Love hurts. But I'm goin' away soon, so none of it matters anyway."

"What do you mean when you say you're going away? Where are you going?"

As I studied Heather's face, I could see she was fighting back tears. She was silent for several minutes.

I waited for her to speak, wondering if I should have been so honest with Heather's child.

When she finally spoke, she had collected herself and showed no emotion. "I have to go. I wrote a note for you. It is very important that you get that note. I left it in Lucinda's top drawer. Tell her to look there and bring it to you. It is very important you get that note. You must read it." She sounded deadly serious.

"I'll tell her about it, Heather."

Heather repeated herself. "You must read it." Then she was gone.

Lucinda, frightened, looked back at me. "What happened? There was a lot of growling in there." She spoke in her child voice and grabbed my arm. "It was really scary to hear all that growling."

"Heather was out with me. I'm afraid I hurt her child when I told her she couldn't come live with me."

"I wanna live with you too."

I decided not to go down that road again. I hurried on to tell her about the note. "Heather said she left a note for me in your top drawer and it's very important that you get it to me."

"I'll look for it."

"That's great, Lucinda." I wondered what this note could possibly be about. I also wondered where Heather planned to go and how she planned to get there.

*****

I received a phone call from Lucinda that evening. "I looked in the drawer for Heather's note, but there's nothin' there. No note."

"Well, let me call Heather out. Maybe she put it somewhere else. Heather, would you come out, please? Lucinda can't find your note. Maybe you can help her find it." There was no response. I tried and tried to call her out, but Heather did not respond. Maybe she really did go somewhere. But where could she have gone?

When someone finally spoke, it was Cinda. By this time, I was very frustrated and concerned about Heather. As usual, Cinda was calm and collected. "Don't worry. Heather is safe, but you must encourage Lucinda to look for the note."

"What's happening? Where is Heather, and why can't Lucinda find the note?"

"One of the others must have taken the note."

"What if they destroyed it? Heather said it's very important that I read it."

"It is important that you read it."

"What if they destroyed it? Why can't you tell me what's in the note? You must know." I felt panicky. Something about the urgency in Heather's voice when she told me about the note was unnerving me.

"You must trust God. And you can't depend on me so much. I can only tell you what God reveals to me. He did not reveal to me what is in the note." Now Cinda sounded deadly serious. "If you start to depend on me too much, I will be removed."

"What do you mean that you will be removed?"

"Two things you must never do. You must not become too dependent on me. And even more important, you must not ever worship me. Never. I am just a messenger. If you worship me, I will be in the way of your relationship with God. I will be removed."

"But Cinda, how could I have made it this far without you? And Lucinda needs you too."

"God knows what you need and what Lucinda needs. Both you and Lucinda must see me as no more than a messenger. If I become more than that for either of you, I will be removed."

I paused to think about what she was saying. The panicky feeling subsided. Even though what she was saying scared me a bit, something about it seemed rock-solid true. If she was indeed a heavenly messenger, she would reflect the heart of God. I thought about the first commandment, "You shall have no other gods before me." Angels are created beings, not gods. They are not to be worshipped. What she was saying was totally consistent with all that I understood about Christian theology.

"Your dependence needs to be on God, not on me. Pray and ask God to protect that note and to get it into your hands."

"I know you're right, Cinda. God must be first. Thank you for making that clear to me."

"Now call Lucinda back."

I called Lucinda back and carefully explained what Cinda had told me. "We cannot become too dependent on Cinda. And we must never worship her. God is the only one we are to worship. If we put her in the place of God, she will be removed from us."

"I don't want her to be taken away."

"I don't either, so we must keep her in her proper place. She was a gift to you to help you survive. Now she is a gift to me to help me know how to help you. But we must worship only the giver, not the gift. Now let's pray to the giver, to God, to help us with this note. Dear God, this note seems really important. Please protect it. If one of the parts has moved it, please help Lucinda find it. And please help us graciously receive the gift of Cinda without depending on her too much. Amen."

"Amen!" Lucinda exclaimed in her child voice. "And thank you for my spiritual mommy."

My heart was at peace, and I was able to trust God with the fate of Heather's note.

*****

I arrived to work on a crisp fall morning. I entered the office and looked out the window at the field across the street. It was disheartening to see a large yellow backhoe parked at the edge of the field. Two men stood beside the backhoe, engaged in conversation. One pointed out toward the field while the other stood with arms across his chest. I watched his brilliant yellow hard hat bob up and down as he nodded.

My heart sank. It looked like I was going to lose my wonderful view. I so enjoyed watching the field change with the seasons. But it certainly seemed as if another office building was in the making. It might be the last fall when I would see the warm yellow golds of wild mustard gradually die off into scraggly straw-colored sticks before gentle blankets of light-reflecting snow would bury them. I lowered myself onto my desk chair with thoughts about inevitable "progress."

My phone rang to startle me out of my mental meanderings. I answered the phone to hear Lucinda's excited child voice. "I found it! I found the note. It was in the trash can. I saw this paper in the trash can and wondered what it was. I can't read it, but I know it's

Heather's note. It even has some drawings on it. It's kinda wrinkled, but it isn't torn, so you can read it."

"That is so wonderful, Lucinda." I checked my schedule for the day and saw that Lucinda was the last one on the docket. "I'm supposed to see you late this afternoon. Put it in a safe place until you come, somewhere where none of the parts will be able to find it. Then bring it with you. I am so glad you found it. Heather really wanted me to read it."

I felt great relief to know that the note had been found. Thoughts of the field across the street no longer filled my mind. The note was now front and center. What could the contents of this note possibly be? I hoped that child Lucinda would be able to find a safe place to keep it until the end of the day. After all, a five-year-old child may not be particularly adept at hiding something.

I remembered Cinda's instructions to ask God to protect the note. A spontaneous prayer arose. "Father, thank you that Lucinda found Heather's note. Please keep this note safe until Lucinda can get it to me." I said these words aloud. Then I turned my attention to the full day of counseling ahead.

*****

The day dragged on. After each session, my thoughts catapulted ahead to my final session. Would Lucinda arrive with the note safely in hand? And what were the contents of that note?

Four o'clock finally arrived. I went out to the waiting room and ushered Lucinda down the hall to my office. We both seated ourselves, Lucinda on my pastel love seat. I was on a chair directly across from her. "Well, do you have the note?"

Lucinda stood up and reached into her jeans' pocket. She pulled out a piece of lined notebook paper that had been folded over several times and handed it to me. I unfolded it and scanned the front and back quickly. Both sides of the paper were filled with ink. The front was filled with writing. The back was covered with writing until about the middle of the page. Below the writing were several drawings of human figures and a pentagram (a satanic symbol that consisted of a five-pointed star within a circle). All along the left side of the paper and around the drawings, short phrases were written, some in print and some in cursive. I had not expected the note to be as extensive as this. I could see that it would take some time to decipher.

Lucinda was looking at me with inquisitive eyes. "What does it say?"

I started to read aloud. "'Dear Nan, when you get this letter I will be gone.'"

"Where did Heather go?" Lucinda's voice sounded frightened.

"I don't know. Let's read on. Maybe she will explain." I took a deep breath and read on. "'I wish I could got to know you will do good to them.'" I tried to make sense of Heather's run-on sentence. "I think she's saying two things: she wishes she could have gotten to know me more and she thinks I'll be good to them, which I guess is all of you."

Lucinda nodded. I scanned the next sentence and wished that Heather had better writing skills. I began to read again. "'I know I give my child up to help you with Lucinda, but they need to live as a child, if I didn't help her she would have die, so I took all the pain so she could come back to you.'" What did this mean? I looked at Lucinda. "Did Heather ever give her child up to help you? It says she took all the pain so you could come back to me. Does that mean anything to you?"

Lucinda shook her head.

I studied her words some more. "One thing is clear. Heather is a protector. It sounds like she took a lot of pain to help you, even sacrificed her child."

Lucinda looked at me blankly. It was obvious that none of this registered with her.

"Heather also says that you need to be a child. That confirms what we already know."

I scanned ahead in the letter and then began to read. "'You need to help Death she is getting worse if she gets to third phase of mother you will have a problem.'" How to interpret that? The one thing I could clearly understand was that I needed to help Death, who seemed to be up to something very nefarious.

I scanned ahead to read the next sentence and stopped dead in my tracks. I reread it to myself several times over. I felt every ounce of energy drain out of me. Inside my head, it felt as if there was a loud scream of "*Nooooooo!*" I felt sick to my stomach. Do I dare read this to child Lucinda?

"You can read it to me." It was Cinda. "Go ahead and read it." It was as if she had read my mind.

"Oh, Cinda, it can't be true. Tell me it's not true."

"Go ahead and read it."

"'They join a group BLD666 they are going to hurt the children please, help to stop them.'" I looked at Cinda. I voiced the question that I dreaded to ask. "Have they joined another satanic group?"

"Yes, they have. Heather knew that you helped free them from their grandmother's group. She wants you to help them again."

I wanted to burst out in tears. I remembered the long, laborious process we had been through to free them. Now we had to do it all over again. "She said they want to hurt the children. Does she mean like Lucinda and Steven?"

"Yes, they want to get to the children. The last time they went, they were trying to get to Lucinda, child Lucinda. Heather went out instead and let them have her child to protect Lucinda. She knows that Lucinda needs a chance to grow up in a healthy way."

I felt a protective mother-bear instinct arise within me. "What do they want to do with the children?"

"They want to torture them so that they will become strong and tough, just like her grandmother did."

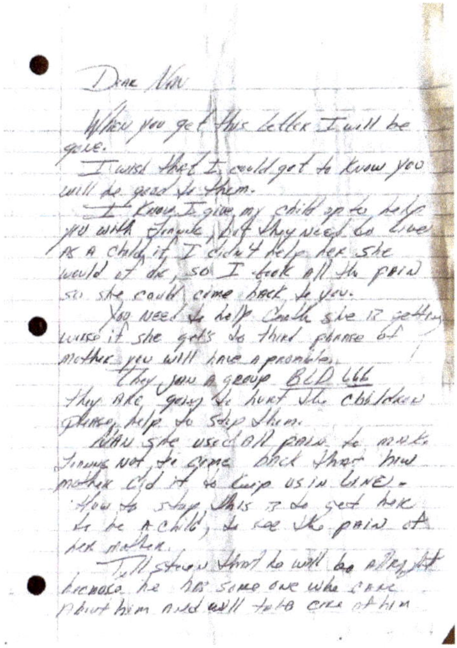

Dear Nan

When you get this letter I will be gone.

I wish that I could get to know you will be good to them.

I know I give my child up to help you with Jennie, but they need to live as a child, if I didn't help her she would of die, so I took all the pain so she could come back to you.

You need to help Chelle she is getting worse if she gets to third phase of mother you will have a problem.

They join a group BLD 666 they are going to hurt the children please help to stop them.

Nan she used all pain to make Jennie not to come back there now mother did it to keep us in line.

How to stop this is to get her to be a child, to see the pain of her mother.

Tell Steven that he will be alright because he has some one who care about him and will take care of him

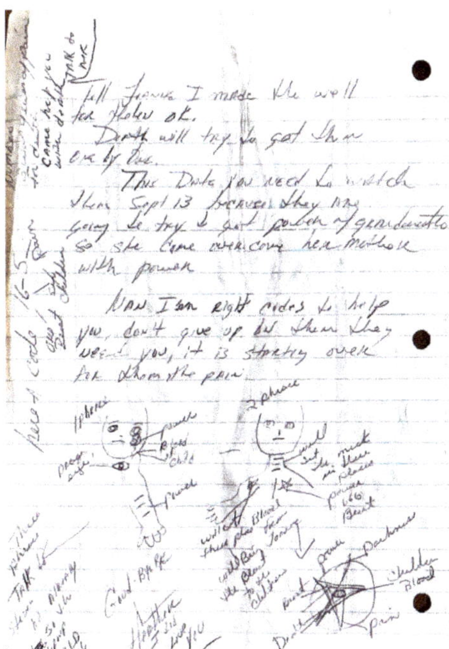

Tell Jennie I made the well for Helen ok.

Death will try to get them one by one.

This Date you need to watch them Sept 13 because they are going to try to get power of grandmother so she can overcome her mother with power

Nan I am right sides to help you, don't give up on them they need you, it is starting over for them the pain

Heather's note, front and back.

I thought about child Lucinda and child Steven, on their way to becoming healthy little children. I felt such affection for them. This group wanted to torture them? I couldn't bear the thought. In that moment, my world came crashing down around me. I looked at Cinda, calm and collected. How could she be so dispassionate? "I won't let them. I won't let them!" I felt like a mother bear protecting her cubs. "I'll do anything I can to stop them."

Cinda responded. "You must walk in trust. God knows what they need."

"Then why did he allow this to happen?" I was crushed and enraged at the same time. Little did I know that I was on the cusp of a battle that would upend my life.

CHAPTER 11

Roxie

I did not read the rest of the note to Lucinda. I explained to her as best I could that Heather was trying to warn me that some of the parts had gotten involved with some bad people. Lucinda looked frightened when I told her this. I suspect she also detected my emotional distress. I reassured her, as Cinda had done with me, that God was with her and knew what she needed.

She left that session reluctantly, holding onto me, saying, "I want to come live with you."

I took the note home that evening and read the rest of it carefully, seeking to discern what it meant. Picking up where I had left off, it read,

> Nan she used all pain to make Lucinda not to come back that how mother did it to keep us in line. How to stop this is to get her to be a child, to see the pain of her mother.

I fastened on her words about how to stop this, to get Lucinda to be a child, and to see the pain of her mother. At least that gave me something to focus on, but on some level, I felt as if this was already accomplished. Lucinda was a child all the time now, and we had certainly, in the past, dealt with the pain of her mother.

I read on.

> Tell Steven he will be all right because he has someone who care about him and will take care of him.

Heather really did have a good heart. Her concern for Steven was obvious.

> Tell Lucinda that I made the well for Adele ok.

This was a gift Lucinda had started making for Paul's wife, Adele, before she had become a full-time child. It sounded like Heather had finished the project, painting the wooden frame of a well and filling it with silk flowers.

It also seemed that Heather had been filling in the adult role at home. But who would fill it now that she was gone?

The next line read,

> Death will try to get them one by one.

It seemed Death was at least one of the alters who had become involved with this new group. She said earlier in the note that I needed to help Death. Maybe that was where to begin, spending time getting to know Death.

I read on.

> This date you need to watch them Sept 13 because they are going to try to get power of grandmother so she can come overcome her mother with power.

September 13 was more than a week behind us.

Had I missed something urgent? I knew September 13 was the date her grandmother had died. Dates like this were significant in satanic ritual. Had the delay in getting this note to me allowed the parts to reclaim some evil power? I had no way of knowing.

Finally, she wrote,

> Nan I'm right codes to help you, don't give up on them they need you, it is starting all over for them, the pain.

I felt totally disheartened. The pain was starting all over for them. How was I ever going to help them? And what did she mean by *codes to help me*? I read some of the short phrases along the left-hand margin. One of them said "here a code 1-one beast 6-six children 5-pain." What could I make of that? In another place on the margin she wrote, "Number 3 was years of pain for death came help you with death talk to her." Again, it seemed that Death was the place to start. Another margin note read, "Talk to Steven he already so the group BLD666." Did she mean he already saw the group? Could Steven give me some valuable information?

Heather closed her letter by saying, "Good-Bye Bye Heather I did love you."

I was touched. With all of Heather's fear of closeness and love, she was, in the end, able to own her love for me. But where was she now? I did not have the answer. And her declaration of love for me did not relieve my emotional turmoil.

The three drawings at the bottom of the page, two of human figures with cut marks and one of a pentagram, were surrounded by words like *power, blood of child, dragon eye, 666, beast, will bring the beast to the children, death, pain, darkness,* and *will cut the neck in three places.*

I didn't want to read anymore. My heart was heavy.

Inwardly, I resolved to focus on Death, hoping I could win her over. But the path led me in a different direction, to a different alter personality.

*****

It was a warm, late summer day. Lucinda's youngest son, Michael, had his first peewee football game of the year. Michael was showing some promise as a football player, so Lucinda was eager to see him play. This was before Lucinda had become a full-time child, so she was able to walk across town to the park where the game was to be played.

There was a small set of bleachers at the side of the field. She climbed up the stands and seated herself in the back row. She eagerly scanned the field where the players were doing their pregame warm-ups. Then she saw him, number 23, looking dwarfed in his oversized pads. She watched him doing his jumping jacks and felt proud of him. Michael was little, but he was fast, so he got to carry the ball a lot.

As the game began, Lucinda was completely absorbed in cheering him on. By the time halftime arrived, Lucinda was hoarse.

As she waited for the second half, a man came and sat down several rows in front of her. He was a younger man, maybe thirty years old. He was rough-looking, unshaven, dressed in blue jeans, boots, and a black T-shirt with a white skull on its front.

Lucinda looked him over. His arms were covered with tattoos, many of them satanic symbols. There were ugly dragon-like monsters and a goat head. Those symbols made Lucinda feel very uncomfortable. She wanted to get up and leave, but she felt fastened to her spot.

At that moment, those tattoos, the satanic symbols, connected with something deep within Lucinda. An alter personality was pulled forward. The man stood up, looked around, and saw Lucinda. "Are you cheering for someone?"

The alter had no idea why she was at this game, so she simply nodded. "And you?"

"Nah. But I played football at this age. I thought it would be fun to watch 'em. I loved playing. It gave me a chance to knock the crap out of the other players, and I didn't get in trouble." The man noticed that Lucinda was studying his tattoos. He stood up and lit a cigarette. He looked at Lucinda again, and they looked into each other's eyes. A dark presence within each of their eyes met, and a connection took place. The man extended his hand. "I'm Chris. And who are you?"

"I'm Roxie."

"Good to meet you, Roxie."

Chris reached into his pocket and pulled out a scrap of paper and a stubby pencil. He scribbled a phone number on the paper. Handing it to Roxie, he said, "We have regular meetings you might be interested in. We call our group BLD666."

Roxie took the paper and nodded. She carefully folded it and put it in her jeans' pocket.

The second half began. Roxie looked out at the field and wondered why she was there.

Play began, and Michael carried the ball on the second play of the half.

A woman in the front row yelled, "Go, Michael, go!"

The sound of her son's name pulled Lucinda to the surface. She was present to see Michael being tackled on the thirty-yard line after a nice run. She enthusiastically cheered her son on for the rest of the game. His team won fourteen to seven, with Michael scoring the second touchdown on a short run. She was indeed proud of him.

As they walked along, Michael bubbled on about his touchdown run.

Lucinda felt good, and all seemed well. She had absolutely no idea about the ominous conversation that had occurred over halftime.

*****

The first time I encountered Roxie, she seemed like many of the other alters: a hard, tough exterior, her speech littered with profanities. "Who the hell are you and what the hell am I doing here?" She looked around my office. "What am I doin' in a place like this?" She was looking at a picture of Jesus walking with his arm around a young man. He was laughing, and his eyes were filled with light.

"Hi. I'm your counselor. I'm here to help you. This is a safe place."

"Hell, I don't need no help. And what's a safe place?"

"This is a place where you can be who you really are. You don't have to pretend to be big and tough. You can just be the child you really are."

She glared at me. "I don't know what you're talkin' about. I ain't no child. If you're a child, you get hurt."

"If you're a child here with me, you won't get hurt. Do you have a name?"

"My name is Roxie."

I was surprised that she offered her name so easily. "Thank you for trusting me with your name. I bet you were hurt when you were little, and that's why you don't want to be a child."

She screamed back at me, "I was beaten with electrical cords!" Then she fell to the floor, curled up in a ball and began to flinch and cry out in pain with each flinch. She was reliving that experience before me.

I shuddered each time she flinched and cried out.

When the flinching stopped, she was still curled in a ball but whimpering quietly.

I dropped to my knees beside her and gently placed my hand on her back. "I'm sorry that happened to you, Roxie."

She sat straight up and glared at me. She looked a bit disoriented. "I ain't no child!"

Then I was looking at Lucinda. "I just met one named Roxie. She became a child and relived being beaten with electrical cords." This abuse seemed rather mild, compared to many of the horrors that had been revealed to me.

"I been seein' that memory. I think it was my mom's boyfriend who did it." Lucinda spoke in her small child voice. She looked frightened.

"Did the memory frighten you?"

She nodded. "But somethin's really wrong with Sam. She's just lyin' there, won't talk or do nothin'. It scares me to see her like that."

I remembered that Sam had become one with her two child parts very unexpectedly while I held her as she cried. I wondered what was wrong with her. I certainly hated to see her have a setback. "Why don't I call her out to see if I can help her?"

Child Lucinda nodded.

"Sam, this is your spiritual mother. Would you please come out to me?"

A few seconds later, Lucinda slumped over, face down into the pillow that was nestled in the corner of the love seat.

I sat down next to her and put my hand on her shoulder. "Sam, Sam." I shook her gently. There was no response. "Sam, this is your spiritual mother." I remembered Cinda saying how powerful that was. I shook her again. She just lay there. I got up, pulled her into a sitting position, and sat back down next to her, cradling her head in my arms.

Her eyes were closed, and she was limp.

I wondered what was happening. Knowing nothing else to do, I prayed aloud. "Lord Jesus, I don't know what's wrong with Sam, but you do. Please help her." I held her and studied her face, looking for any sign of life.

She looked pale, and she barely seemed to be breathing. Then I noticed a red welt on her neck. An abrasion, like a rug burn. What was the meaning of this welt?

I pulled her close and laid her head on my chest so she could hear my heartbeat. After a few minutes, I noticed a few eye movements, like she was rolling her eyes behind her closed eyelids. "Sam, Sam." I shook her gently.

Then, ever so slowly, she opened her eyes. I hoped to see signs of life. Instead, I saw a brokenness so deep that it seared my heart.

I had seen deep pain in Lucinda's eyes many times, but this was different. They were child eyes, and it was as if I could see deep pools of pain and brokenness that had no bottom. Even her pupils looked broken, cracked.

I gathered her up in my arms and held her close, not wanting to look into that depth of pain any longer. My own eyes welled with tears. I rocked her back and forth, holding her close to my heart.

Then I heard a familiar voice. "You're doing the right thing." It was Cinda. I released my hold and allowed her to sit up.

"Oh, Cinda, what is wrong with Sam? Why all this pain? The pain in her eyes was so deep I couldn't bear to look at it."

"Sam has been hurt."

"What? Who hurt her?"

"The group Roxie went to, the one Heather's note talked about."

"What?" I couldn't believe my ears. "What did they do to her? Why would they hurt her? What is the meaning of the welt on her neck?"

"Roxie told them there were children inside. They torture the children to teach them to be hard. They had a rope around her neck."

My world shattered.

"But what if they get Lucinda or Steven? They have come so far and are starting to heal and to learn to trust and to have normal experiences. This can't really be happening." I was beyond distraught.

Cinda looked at me with her clear, peaceful eyes. "It is time to walk in faith. Some will be hurt. But God can heal, and he has given you a very powerful gift for healing, your heartbeat. And Sam did not harden herself. She remained a child. That was good. Now call Sam back and see how she is doing."

I didn't want to call her back. I didn't want to see her broken eyes. Instead, I wanted to scream at God, *Why are you allowing this?* I was aflame with anger. How could I comfort a tortured child with that much anger at the surface?

Cinda repeated herself. "Call Sam back."

"Sam," I said half-heartedly, hoping she would not surface.

But at my voice, she slumped over onto my lap, looking up at me. She blinked. Our eyes met, and while I saw pain in her eyes, it was not the same depths that I had seen before. Again, I pulled her to my chest and let her hear my heartbeat. For about ten minutes, I rocked her back and forth, her head nestled against my heart. My anger started to dispel, and I allowed a mother's heart of compassion to rise up as I murmured gentle words of love to her, reassuring her she was loved and God would heal her.

By the time our session was over, Sam had snuggled into me and fallen asleep. She had a peaceful expression as she slept, and I wondered if God really had healed her.

I called Lucinda back. Child Lucinda looked at me. "What happened? It felt all warm and nice inside."

"I'm not sure. I guess God healed Sam with my heartbeat. She was sleeping peacefully when I called you. But you must listen to me, Lucinda. It is very important that you never come out unless it is me that is calling you. If you are inside and someone else is calling you out, you must stay in."

"Who else would call me out?" Lucinda looked puzzled.

I wasn't sure how to respond. Do I tell child Lucinda about the new group? I didn't want to frighten her. On the other hand, she needed to know how serious this was. Finally, I took her hand and squeezed it gently. "It seems that there's one inside named Roxie. She has gotten involved with a satanic group. I don't want you to ever be out when she is there. That is why you must never come out to any voice other than mine."

Now Lucinda looked really frightened. Tears swelled up in her eyes. "I don't wanna go home. I wanna be with you."

"You must go home. You will be fine as long as you only come out to my voice. Jesus is with you. Pray that he will keep you safe."

She grabbed hold of my arm. "I don't wanna go. I'm scared."

I found my most no-nonsense voice. "Lucinda, you must go. End of matter. Kurt will be waiting for you."

Tears made their way down her cheeks. "I don't wanna go..." She sniffled a few times. Then she was quiet. "Cinda just talked to me. She said I have to go. But she said she will be real close to me. I can feel her. It feels warm."

I sighed, a sigh of relief.

Lucinda stood up and headed to the door. Then she ran back and threw her arms around me. "I wish I could be your little girl. If you had been my mommy, everything would have been different."

"God didn't make me your mommy. But he did make me your spiritual mother, and he knew exactly what you needed." I was surprised at the certainty in my own voice.

*****

Sleep did not come easily for me that night. I tossed and turned and wrestled with God. I reviewed in my mind all the progress that Lucinda had made.

Cinda had said that God was giving Lucinda a chance to start over as a normal child. But normal children are not tortured in satanic cults. What if she inadvertently found her way out when Roxie took them to this new group? How often did Roxie go to this group?

Roxie was the key. If I could get to Roxie and reach her inner child, then she wouldn't go to that hellacious group.

By the time I drifted off into a fitful sleep, I had a plan. I would work with Roxie, have her hear my heartbeat, and hopefully, have her come over into the light. Then she would want nothing to do with this group.

*****

The next time I saw Lucinda, I told her about my plan to work with Roxie. "If we can get her to be a child and if she comes over into the light, she won't even want to go to this group. So I am going to need to spend time with her."

"Will I get some time too? I want to play with you and color and have fun."

"I hope we can have some time together, but right now, Roxie has to come first."

Lucinda reluctantly nodded. "I know. I don't want to see Sam get hurt again."

When I called Roxie's name, she burst out and glared at me. "Whad'ya want?"

"I just want to spend some time with you and get to know you."

She looked at me suspiciously. "You want more than that. Everybody always wants somethin' from ya."

"You know, Roxie, the last time you were out with me, you became a little child being beaten with electrical cords."

She glared at me. "That wasn't me. That was some little pussy."

"I bet it was your child. I think she was hurt a lot."

"What's it to you? You gotta keep that child hidden, or they'll hurt her, just like they hurt Sam."

I was encouraged that Roxie was willing to admit she had a child. "Roxie, your child doesn't need to be hidden away. She needs to be cared for and loved. Just like Sam needed to be loved after she had been hurt."

"What did you do to Sam? After she was with you, she was all... different."

"I let her listen to my heartbeat. Then God healed her from whatever your group did to her. That's because God loves her and wants her to be whole. Roxie, do you want to hear my heartbeat?"

"Hell no." In a split second, Roxie was gone.

The one I was looking at seemed peaceful. It wasn't Lucinda. "Who is this?"

"It's me, Sam. You didn't know who I was?"

"Well, the last time I saw you, you were really hurting."

"I've been inside in the light. I want you to tell me about the light. When I'm there it feels so warm."

So I told Sam about Jesus, that he called himself the light of the world, and that he loved her, and wanted to help her. Then I read her a simple children's book about Jesus.

When I was done, she smiled at me. "I'll think about all this. And there's something you need to know." The sound of her voice had changed. She had seemed quite childlike, but now she took on an urgent tone and seemed much older. "Don't tell any of the others about this, especially Roxie or Death. But you need to know. Roxie is going to take them to the group this Sunday night at ten. There's talk about an initiation. You need to stop them."

Her words bought me up short. What? An initiation? I remembered when I had helped Lu avert an initiation into the role of high priestess of her grandmother's group. Could this be happening all over again? "What's she being initiated into?"

"She's being initiated into the group. They want to make it official."

"Well, I'll need to tell Lucinda about this so we can work together."

"Just don't tell Roxie or Death."

"I won't. And thank you so much for telling me. If you can tell me whenever you know about a group meeting, that would be great. Then Lucinda and I can work to block it."

I explained to Lucinda what had happened with Roxie and Sam. When I told her about the planned meeting, she looked frightened. "I don't want them to go."

"I don't either. So let's come up with a plan." I thought for a minute. "I know. I've been invited to a large church meeting on Sunday night. It's in one of the city churches, and lots of different churches are invited to come. I'm not even sure what it's about, but my husband and I thought we'd go. Why don't you come with us? We'll make sure you don't get home until well after ten. You know, with Sam working to help us on the inside, we might be able to avert any more meetings until I can win Roxie over."

Lucinda nodded eagerly. The thought of spending an evening with us sounded wonderful to her.

I was a bit uneasy over this blatant breaking of my professional boundaries—allowing her to be part of my personal life—but the thought of her going to another meeting and more inner children being tortured was more than I could bear.

My relationship with Lucinda was changing. Being her spiritual mother was adding a different dimension. And my emotional attachment to her, especially to the child parts, was growing stronger all the time. So I put aside my uneasiness and prayed that our plan to block the meeting would be effective.

CHAPTER 12

Two Artists

The following Sunday, on a cool fall evening, my husband and I picked up child Lucinda and headed to the south end of town for the multi-church gathering I had been invited to. We ascended the steps into a century-old stone church building on a busy city corner.

The pastor who had invited me greeted us at the door. I introduced him to my husband and then to Lucinda. "This is Lucinda, my spiritual daughter." I was surprised at how easily those words rolled off my tongue. It certainly seemed that I was getting more comfortable with this new role.

The pastor smiled and welcomed us all. "You'd better hurry up and get a seat. The sanctuary is just about full."

We walked through arched doorways into a large sanctuary. My eyes followed soaring archways upward as I took it all in. It was a magnificent display of rich stained-glass windows, carved stonework, intricately wrought brass chandeliers, and deep-stained pews and railings—a leftover from another era when church buildings were meant to evoke awe, wonder, and reverence.

We found seats about halfway up the sanctuary on the left-hand side. As I sat, I caught sight of the chancel at the front of the church, a raised area with an intricately carved wooden altar and the gleaming pipes of a pipe organ. I stifled an impulse to laugh. Amidst a tangle of electrical cords were amps, monitors, a keyboard, electric and acoustic guitars, and a full drum set. The incongruity of this assortment of musical instruments against the backdrop of Gothic splendor was jarring.

Lucinda sat between my husband and me, wide-eyed and child-like, as she surveyed the scene. I watched as Hubby interacted with her, drawn in by her unaffected innocence. It was hard to resist child Lucinda. She truly was as endearing as any young child, although she still had her moments when she could be sassy or stiflingly clingy and whiny. But this night, she seemed to be a healthy child in every way (except for the incongruity of her adult body).

The musicians entered, took up their instruments, and began to play contemporary worship songs. For the next two hours, I was swept into a spontaneous blending of music, prayers, teachings, and prophetic words.

As I look back on that evening, several distinct impressions are seared into my memory. One was of Lucinda, child Lucinda, eyes closed, hands held palms up in a receptive position, swaying back and forth to the music. Her expression was one of peaceful bliss.

She looked over and smiled at me watching her. "God is here," she murmured.

I also remember the call for intercessors to come forward. The lady in front of me scurried to the front of the sanctuary, as she waved her hand. "Oh yes, that's me." From all parts of the sanctuary, including the balcony, people moved to the front to be commissioned as intercessors, specifically to pray for our city.

Our city. That is what I remember the most: the passionate prayers for our city. The focus of the evening was the battle for our city, the battle to take it back from the forces of darkness. As I took all this in, one persistent thought kept coming to my mind. *I am already in this battle. I have already been fighting for our city.*

My fight to free Lucinda from the satanic stronghold that kept her bound was not just a fight for her, but a fight for our city as well. I remembered Lucinda telling me several years earlier that her grandmother was not just the head of a small group, but of many groups that permeated the city. Was my work with Lucinda somehow disrupting a whole network of satanic groups? And what about this new group? Was my fight to free Lucinda from them part of this battle?

We were at this gathering tonight because of this fight. This did not seem like a coincidence. God had us here for a reason. He wanted me to know that our work with Lucinda had larger consequences than I had ever dreamed.

My husband emerged from that meeting with a strong sense that it was divinely orchestrated, a bringing together of diverse and passionate believers from all over the city for a common purpose: to usher God's presence into our city.

After the gathering was over, we took Lucinda out for ice cream. It was well past eleven when we dropped her off at her city row home. Once I was home, I called to make sure she was still there and Roxie had not gone to the group. All seemed well. I heaved a huge sigh of relief. It seemed as if we had won that battle.

*****

Roxie became the focus of our sessions. My goal was to get her to soften, to become the child she really was. She always emerged as the hardened outer shell. "What the hell am I doing here again? Why don't you leave me alone? I got important things to do. I gotta get the power back. I gotta get Gram's power. I was gonna get some of it back when they initiated me, but somethin' got screwed up. I bet it's that Sam. She told me she'd destroy us before I get enough power."

Hoping to break down her walls, I reached for paper and crayons. I began to draw some smiley faces and flowers. Roxie watched me suspiciously. "Do you want to draw, Roxie? Here's some paper and a clipboard. Help yourself to the crayons."

Roxie's first drawing: dark images mixed with a child's work

Much to my surprise, Roxie took the paper and a black crayon. She began to draw furiously, crude figures with blacked-out faces and pentagrams on their chests. One held a knife. Then she drew the familiar hook at the top of the paper. She grabbed a red crayon and drew blood dripping from the hook and onto an unhooded figure. Then she took the yellow crayon and drew rough yellow shapes, one crudely taking on the shape of an angel. Next to it she drew the silhouette of a blue bird. Among the black-clad figures with pentagrams she drew several childlike stick figures with smiling faces. She colored green the bottom of the paper and placed several rough flowers in this sea of grass. Then she drew a very crude tree nestled against the left edge of the paper. It was like there were two artists, one an angry, tortured soul haunted by images of dark rituals and the other an innocent child.

She was totally engrossed in what she was doing, so I didn't comment on her drawing, though I wondered about its meaning. Was another child part, perhaps Lucinda, trying to intrude on her drawing? Or was this Roxie's own child coming through?

Did it matter? I had seen many of these dark drawings in the past, but they had never been sprinkled with light, like this one. Was this a sign of the growing power of the light within Lucinda?

Roxie picked up the black crayon again and furiously scribbled out the yellow shapes, the bird, the child stick figures, the grass, and the flowers.

I inwardly winced. It looked like the dark was overpowering the light.

Roxie grabbed another sheet of paper, again drawing the black hooded figures and the hook with blood dripping from it. Again, she took the yellow crayon and drew angel-like shapes. Then she drew smiling children stick figures and green grass with flowers. Next, she added the crude tree nestled against the left edge of the paper. She stared at her drawing for a minute, then grabbed the black crayon and once again scribbled over the happy child images.

Roxie's third picture: Hooded figures in gray mixed with child drawings.

Roxie then took a third piece of paper. She still held the black crayon. She paused a moment, laid the black crayon down, and reached for a gray one. She then drew the hooded figures in gray. She took the red crayon and drew the always-present hook with blood dripping from it. She drew a hand with blood dripping from it and placed a knife in the hand of one of the gray figures.

Then Roxie drew, as she had before, crude yellow shapes and smiling children. But these children were more than stick figures. They had rough body shapes, except for one face that had no body at all. She drew the green grass and a brown tree trunk topped with green scribbles. Red flowers dotted the grass. When she had finished the last flower, she laid the red crayon down, buried her head in her arms, and began to cry.

Her last picture, with the mixture of gray-hooded figures and child images, laid untouched with no black scribbles hiding the child drawings.

As Roxie cried, her sobs became child whimpers, and she curled into a little ball. I seated myself next to her and gently placed my hand on her shoulder. I said nothing, fearing that my words might bring back the hard, outer shell of Roxie. She seemed very young, maybe three or four years old. I needed to let her hear my heartbeat, but I didn't want to disturb her.

"What's happening?" It was Lucinda. "I hear growling inside. Darkness is really mad."

"Roxie has become a child. She drew some pictures which seem to have triggered her child state. I want to let her hear my heartbeat. Will you lay your head on my chest, and then I'll call her back out?"

Lucinda leaned over, snuggled up to me, and laid her head on my chest.

"Roxie, Roxie, will you come back out?"

A second later, I was holding Roxie as she sniffled and cried, her head nestled on my chest. Slowly, over the next few minutes, her sobs subsided. "Boom-boom, boom-boom," she murmured quietly. Then she looked up at me, her face still damp with tears. She laid her head back down, closed her eyes, and fell asleep.

I thanked God that Roxie had so quickly become a child. Maybe my strategy for freeing Lucinda from this new group was going to work.

*****

But my optimism was short-lived. The next session, child Lucinda arrived as a clingy, needy child. "I don't wanna let Roxie out. She gets all the time with you. I don't get nothin'. And Roxie's mean. She took my favorite stuffed dog, Mutt. She said she's gonna rip him apart. I wish Roxie would go away and never come back. I told Cinda that Roxie was bein' mean, but she said that's because Roxie's just a frightened child. She don't look like no frightened child to me. I kept tellin' Cinda I don't want to be here no more. I want to be in the light with her all the time. Then I don't have to feel nothin' bad."

I tried not to show my exasperation with her whining. "Lucinda, you know that we need to help Roxie to become the frightened child she really is. That means that I must spend time with her."

"I don't want you to spend time with her. I want you to spend time with me. I need time too. What good is it to have a spiritual mommy if I don't get time with you?" Tears collected along her lower eyelids. "I asked Cinda if I could come into the light with her. She said no, that God wanted me to be out in the world so I would get stronger. I told her I don't wanna to get stronger, I wanna be in the light where it feels good. Then she told me I'm depending on her too much."

"She also told me I shouldn't depend on her too much. My dependence needs to be on God. I think it's important that we pay attention to her."

We sat in silence for a moment. Tears ran down Lucinda's cheeks. I mulled over her words. Perhaps she was right in feeling that we needed time together too.

"Why don't we take some time together today? What would you like to do?"

Lucinda's face brightened. "Can we color?"

"We sure can." Out came the paper and crayons.

Smiling, Lucinda grabbed a sheet of paper. "I'll make you a picture." First, she drew three figures, smiling children. Then she drew two little black dogs with their tongues hanging out. Lucinda had met my two comical Scottish terriers.

"I bet that's Baggins and Stevie."

She nodded eagerly.

Next, she drew two yellow shapes hovering above the children. She put smiling faces on them. "That's Cinda."

"Who is the other one?"

"That's Cinda's friend." Then she drew a smiling sun.

"There's lots of smiles in this picture." She nodded in agreement as she picked up a green crayon and colored in grass at the bottom of the page. Then she drew a tree nestled up against the left side of the paper. She drew red balls in the tree.

"Is that an apple tree?"

She nodded eagerly as she drew red balls in the grass at the base of the tree.

"It looks like the ripe apples are falling."

She nodded again. Next, she drew some red flowers in the grass. Finally, she filled in the sky with blue. "It's for you." She handed me her picture.

"Thank you so much, Lucinda. It's a wonderful picture."

I reached for her file and pulled out the pictures drawn by Roxie the week before. As I thought, Lucinda's picture was very similar to the happy images that had appeared on Roxie's pictures. "Lucinda, were you the one who helped Roxie with her pictures?"

She smiled and giggled. "I wanted Roxie to see there are good things too."

I couldn't help but smile back at her. She could be so very disarming.

"Cinda said it was good that I drew them pictures, that my being close to Roxie like that helped her become a child."

Lucinda's drawing, revealing that she was the
other artist in Roxie's pictures.

I remembered how Roxie had regressed into a crying child after Lucinda had helped with her pictures. As I mulled this over, I had a sudden inspiration. "Lucinda, maybe that's how we'll get Roxie to become a child! If you draw close to her when she's out with me, it might show her that's it's safe to be a child. Isn't that what happened with you and Angie? When she drew close to you, it helped you to be less afraid of being a child. And now, look at you. You're a child all the time."

"Do you think it will work?"

"Well, it's certainly worth a try." I started to feel hopeful. This session that had started with Lucinda's whiny complaint was taking a positive turn.

Then I noticed the subtle eye movements that indicated a switch in personalities. "Who just came out with me?"

"It's me. It's Sam." She looked very serious.

"Is something on your mind, Sam?"

She nodded. "Roxie talked to Chris on the phone. He was mad that she didn't show for the initiation. I got real close and listened. He told her she would be initiated at another time. Then he told her they were going to be meeting two times every week, on Thursdays and Sundays, and that she should come."

My heart sank.

"He also told her that there were some people she had to meet."

"But won't Kurt know if she's gone that much?

Sam shrugged. "He goes to bed really early because he gets up so early. He might not even know."

I let out a long sigh. What to do now? I couldn't bear the thought of another ritual where a child alter might be hurt. "Do you know what time she will go?"

Sam shook her head. "Chris didn't give a time."

"Well, the last initiation was to be at ten. I know that midnight is an important time for satanists, so it will probably be late. Why don't I call you at around nine-thirty and keep you on the phone till well past ten? Maybe we can block another meeting."

Sam nodded. "If another one answers, call me out...or Lucinda."

"Thank you so much, Sam, for keeping me informed. I was hoping that since Roxie wasn't initiated, she wouldn't go anymore. I guess it's not that simple."

"There's one other thing you need to know. It's almost Halloween. It's very important we don't go that night. If Roxie's part of it that night, she will get a lot of power."

How could I have forgotten the importance of Halloween in the satanic year, the most holy of all their holidays? I glanced at my calendar. Halloween fell on Sunday night. I would keep her on the phone Thursday night, and I'd have to figure out something else for Sunday. Maybe that would be a good time to go to Paul and Adele's for a deliverance. I made a mental note to call Paul to see if that would be possible.

"Thank you for reminding me about Halloween, Sam. I will do all I can to keep them from going. It sure is good to have your inside help."

I called Lucinda back and filled her in on Sam's warnings. "I will call Thursday night to try and stop Roxie from going. I'm hoping we can set up a deliverance with Paul and Adele for Halloween. And we must keep working with Roxie to help her to be the child she really is."

Lucinda looked at me with frightened eyes. "I wish Roxie would go back down inside. She's nothin' but trouble."

I didn't say anything, but I shared her sentiments. Maybe this was going to be much more of a battle than I had ever expected.

CHAPTER 13

Halloween Victory

On Thursday night I called Lucinda promptly at nine thirty. Child Lucinda answered the phone. I talked to her for about half an hour, trying to calm her fears, reassuring her that God was with her and that he would never leave her. I told her, in simple words, the story of the disciples in the boat when they got caught in a storm, about how frightened they were as the wind and waves tossed their little boat about. All the while, Jesus was sleeping in the back of the boat. "He wasn't afraid, was he? That's because he knew he could trust God. And you know what he did when the disciples woke him up? He told the wind and the waves to stop. And they did! The disciples were amazed, and they wondered who this Jesus really was. That same Jesus who could stop the wind and the waves is with you right now. We need to trust him, trust that he will take care of you." I think I was reassuring myself as much as Lucinda.

Then I called Sam out and spoke with her about staying out after we hung up. At about ten thirty, we said good night, with Sam assuring me she would do the best she could to stay out all night.

*****

When Lucinda arrived for her appointment the following day, she was once more the whiny little child. "I don't like having Roxie around. She's gettin' really mean. She took Mutt and hid him. She told me that if I don't do what she says, she'll push me out when she goes to her stupid group. I got really scared and asked Cinda again if I could come into the light with her. She said I have to stay out, that God wants me to become strong. I used to be able to go into the light with her. Why can't I go into the light now? I don't like it out here. The only good part is being with you. Cinda said I can't depend on her so much. If I depend on her too much, she'll be removed. What does that mean?"

"Lucinda, take a deep breath," I said to slow her down. "Jesus knows what you need. He must know that at this time you are strong enough to be out."

"But what does Cinda mean when she says she'll be removed?"

"I don't know, exactly, but I'd sure hate to lose her. She helps both of us so much. I think it's best to look to God when you are struggling, not Cinda."

Lucinda folded her arms and protruded her lower lip. "This is too hard. I don't like being little."

"God is giving you chance to start over with a spiritual mother to help you. Wasn't it always your dream to have a mother that loved you and took care of you?"

"But this is just too hard."

"Well, I would suggest we have Roxie out. You can draw close like you did before, and we'll see if she gets little. If we can get her to be little, she won't be mean anymore. Then if we have time left over, we can do something fun."

Lucinda reluctantly agreed. "Okay. But I want some time too."

When I called Roxie, she burst into the room. "That Lucinda is such a little brat! All she does is cry. I told the group about her, that she's just a little child and doesn't have a big part like the rest of us do. They want her. They asked if she was a normal child. I don't know what a normal child is, but I told them she was. So they want to meet her. I tried to get her out last night, but I couldn't find her."

"What do you mean you tried to get her out last night?"

"They wanted to meet her. I couldn't find her so I pushed Steven out instead."

"Roxie, did you go to the group last night?"

"Yeah, I went to the group."

"What time did you go?"

"They picked me up at eleven."

My heart sank. Our attempt to block the meeting hadn't worked. Our phone call ended too early. And what about Steven? I sat in silence, afraid to even think what might have happened. I took several deep breaths as my heart cried out to God. What do I do now? Talk to Roxie? Have Steven out? I looked over at Roxie, having no idea how to proceed.

Roxie looked back at me. "There's that little brat? What's she doin' gettin' close to me? Hey, little brat, go away."

I was too distraught to say anything. But as I sat there, feeling queasy in my stomach, Roxie's tone changed.

The hard, brash outer shell began to melt away. Her face softened. Her lip quivered. "Hurt…hurt." Her voice was that of a little child. Tears flowed down her cheeks. Having Lucinda draw close was working like a charm. Before my eyes, Roxie was becoming a little child. She put her hands in front of her face and sobbed.

As angry as I was at Roxie's tough outer shell, I felt nothing but compassion for this sobbing child. I sat down next to her, pulled her head down to my chest, and gently rocked her back and forth. She choked on her sobs for several minutes. Then they slowly began to subside. After about ten minutes, she lay still with her head nestled onto my chest. "Boom-boom, boom-boom," she murmured. Then she fell soundly asleep.

When I was sure that she was indeed asleep, I took a deep breath and called for Steven, fearful of what state he would be in. I remembered Sam's pain after she had been tortured by this heinous group. I called several times.

Lucinda's body went totally limp.

"Steven, Steven. Is this Steven?"

His body was lifeless.

I pulled him close and made sure his head was nestled against my heart. "Steven, this is your spiritual mother. Are you okay?" I tried to keep my voice even and not betray the distress I felt. I gently rocked him back and forth.

After a few minutes, he turned his head slightly, and ever so slowly, his eyes opened.

I saw it again, the deep pools of pain, the searing brokenness, a pain so deep that I felt I would drown in it. Not wanting to see his eyes, I buried my head in Lucinda's hair and blinked back my own tears. "Dear Jesus, please help him. What did they do to him? Why did you allow this?" I held him tightly and felt myself being torn in two directions, raging anger at the group and the unbearable pain of seeing Steven in this condition.

After several moments, Steven let out little whimpering sounds. Tears flowed down his cheeks.

Not wanting to look into his eyes again, I buried his head in my chest and silently prayed for him.

For about twenty minutes, he whimpered, and tears flowed. Several times his body quaked, and his lips quivered. Finally, the whimpering ceased.

I mustered my courage and let his head drop from my chest so I could see his eyes. I grabbed a tissue and wiped the tears away. Then I looked into his eyes.

The depths of pain were gone. He blinked when his eyes met mine. Then he put his thumb in his mouth and laid his head back on my chest. A few minutes later, he was asleep.

I felt totally depleted. But I also felt hopeful. Like Sam, Steven found healing from whatever trauma he had undergone. The healing seemed to come from listening to my heartbeat. I thought of all the times I held Lucinda and other alter personalities as they had wept and wailed and howled in brokenness and pain. In the past, such a dramatic display of emotion seemed to be part of the process the alters needed to go through to move forward in their healing. But this was different. The healing came with minimal outward displays of emotion.

Cinda was right. My heartbeat seemed to be very powerful. I was amazed, and I was humbled. I silently thanked God that he had given us this gift.

My musings were interrupted by Lucinda's child voice. "Can we do something fun now?"

Feeling quite depleted, but remembering how much Lucinda wanted to spend time with me, I suggested I read her a story. I went to my bookshelf and found a child's book that told the story of Noah's ark. We had read this book many times before. Lucinda loved the animal pictures and delighted in telling me the name of each animal. She especially loved the monkeys and laughed with delight whenever they were pictured. I felt myself renewed by her unaffected joy. How could there be so much brokenness and so much joy, so much darkness and so much light in one person? How could one person so totally deplete me, but then fill me to overflowing?

I looked at Lucinda and smiled. "You are amazing." And I gave her hug.

*****

Halloween arrived the following Sunday. Fortunately, I had been able to set up a deliverance with Paul and Adele for that evening. My husband and I drove up to Lucinda's city home early in the evening. We drove through urban neighborhoods with groups of costumed trick-or-treaters wandering about in groups. Jack-o'-lanterns with eerie glows sat on front porches. Many homes were bedecked with cobwebs and skeletons and ghosts made from old bedsheets.

We waited a few minutes outside Lucinda's home. I held my breath, hoping that she had not connected with the group much earlier than usual. With great relief, I watched Lucinda emerge from her front door. She approached the car, but I could not see her face in the dark. She opened the back door of our car and climbed in. I turned around to greet her. "Hello, Lu…" My voice dropped as I gazed at her in disbelief. "Lucinda! Who did your makeup?"

Child Lucinda responded with a puzzled look. "I don't know."

She was dressed all in black, and her makeup was jaw-dropping. Her eyes were circled by large sweeps of red and black, coming to points at her temples, like two large paisley designs. She looked as if she was headed for a medieval masquerade ball or perhaps a Mardi Gras celebration. The overall effect was eerie, even evil.

"Well, your makeup has to come off." I climbed into the back seat and reached into my purse for a small container of hand cream and a packet of tissues. As Joby drove the twenty-minute drive to Paul and Adele's, I wiped and wiped and wiped, trying to remove the bizarre makeup. Lucinda sat compliantly as I worked. By the time we arrived, the makeup was removed. "You look so much better, Lucinda. Do you have any idea who did your makeup or why they would have painted you up like that?"

Lucinda shook her head.

"Well, I'm glad you look like you again." I never did find out who the culprit was, or why the garish display, but I was certain she had planned to attend some kind of very bizarre and evil ritual that night.

Paul and Adele greeted us fondly when we arrived at their country home. They were delighted to see child Lucinda. After some warm exchanges, we headed downstairs into the large open space where we met for our deliverances.

Joby pulled out his guitar and played several worship songs as we focused our hearts on God, his power and love, and all that he was capable of doing.

After the last song, Paul spoke first. "Do we have a particular alter who is ready for deliverance?"

I responded. "Not this time. The purpose of tonight was to keep Lucinda safe during Halloween. But as long as we're here, Roxie is the one that got involved with this new group. I think we should work with her."

Paul nodded in assent, so I called Roxie out.

As was her way, she burst into the room. "Who the hell are these people and where the hell am I? I got important things to do tonight." She ran up the stairs and headed for the door. Joby and I were on her tail. She threw the door open and looked outside into the dark, wooded landscape. "Where the hell am I?" she screamed.

I came up behind her. "It's okay, Roxie. These people won't hurt you. You're where you need to be for tonight."

Roxie turned around and looked at me. "But I gotta be somewhere. How do I get there from here?" She ran out into the dark. Joby and I ran after her. Roxie stopped in her tracks, looking frantically around. She looked at me with piercing eyes.

"Remember me, Roxie? I'm your spiritual mother. Come back inside and we can talk." Much to my surprise, Roxie let me take her hand and lead her back inside. We sat down together on a large couch in the corner of the room. I pulled her head down and placed it on my chest so she could hear my heartbeat. In just a few minutes, Roxie became a sniveling child. I wondered if Lucinda had pulled close to her to facilitate the process.

Paul had come upstairs and was observing. He knelt in front of Roxie and gently placed his hand on her head. "This is an innocent child. She did not ask for darkness. It was forced upon her before she had the ability to choose. So I command any demons within her to leave now in the name of the Lord Jesus Christ. You have no ground with this innocent child."

As I held Roxie, her head leaning against my chest, tears soaking my sweater, I heard the now familiar sounds of darkness leaving: low, guttural growls with each breath.

Paul continued to pray. Hubby retrieved his guitar and played soft worship songs. Adele also placed her hand on Roxie's shoulder, quietly praying.

We watched as darkness was defeated and Roxie quietly snuggled into me. When the growling ceased, I looked down at Roxie.

She looked up at me. "Mama, Mama." Then she made other baby talk sounds. "Gagaga, googoo."

I spoke up. "She seems to be very young, younger than I've ever seen her. It's like she's just learning to talk. I wonder what's the meaning of this."

Paul responded. "Well, the Lord was certainly here tonight. Whatever is happening, I suspect it's from him."

I nodded in agreement. "We had a double victory tonight. We kept them from going to the group, and Roxie got delivered."

I continued to hold Roxie until she fell asleep in my arms. Then I called Lucinda back and shared with her that Roxie had been delivered from darkness. "Did you draw close to her to help her become a child?"

"No. I didn't know I was supposed to."

"So she became a child on her own. That means she chose to do it. That is another victory."

We all agreed that on Halloween 1999, there were some major victories in Lucinda's life. It might be Satan's holiday, but God was still at work.

It was well past midnight when Lucinda arrived at her home. Roxie was a sleeping baby, so we had confidence that she would not be going to her group that night. I said goodbye to Lucinda, feeling very hopeful that at least for now, she would be safe.

*****

Lucinda and I began a regular rhythm of phone calls. Every Thursday and Sunday night I would call her at about nine thirty. I would try to keep her on the phone until well past eleven o'clock. My hope was that all meetings with this new group could be thwarted.

When child Lucinda arrived for her next session, I knew instantly that something was wrong. Her eyes were red with tears. Her hair was disheveled. I felt my heart sink. It seemed our victories were always short-lived. I mentally regrouped and gently asked her what was wrong.

"Cinda won't talk to me. She said I depended on her too much. After Roxie woke up, she got big again, and she was so mean to me. She was mad that she didn't go to her stupid group on Halloween, and she said she was going to give me over to the group. I was really scared and told Cinda I wanted to be in the light with her. She said I couldn't do that, that I needed to be out in the world to get stronger. I kept sayin' I wanted to be in the light with her, not out in this stupid world. I kept tryin' to go with her in the light, but I couldn't get in. She said bein' in the light was a gift from God, not a right. What does that mean? Why can't I be in the light with her? Then she said that I depended too much on her, and I wouldn't be able to hear her anymore."

I was trying to take this all in. What did this mean? Had Cinda been removed? Would we not have her help anymore? How would I ever be able to help Lucinda find her way out of this new group without Cinda to guide me? I felt truly dismayed.

"It's all right. I'll still be able to talk to you." Cinda popped out as if she had read my thoughts.

"Oh, Cinda, I'm so glad to hear from you. I don't know how I could do this without your help and guidance. But what about Lucinda? She needs you too."

"Lucinda was depending on me too much. Her eyes were off God and on me. She wanted me to make things easy for her. The problem is that she won't grow if she's hiding in the light all the time. The light is to help them heal, but not to shelter them from the world. She has you now, her spiritual mother, to help her. And she needs to learn to hear from God. Her dependence needs to be on him, not me. The same is true for you. If you depend on me too much, I will be removed from you too."

I gulped. I did depend on Cinda a lot. How much is too much? "Okay, Cinda, I will try not to depend on you. But now, Lucinda is an emotional wreck."

"She will learn to hear from God. My time of talking to her is over. I will still be with her, but she will not hear me anymore." Cinda left.

Lucinda sat before me, eyes wet with tears.

"I talked with Cinda. I will still be able to talk to her, but I can't depend on her too much either, or she will be removed from me too. We need to trust that God is doing this for your good so that you can learn to hear from him rather than Cinda."

"But I wanna hear Cinda. And I wanna be in the light with her."

"I guess God has another plan. And we can trust that his plan is always good." I tried to imagine how I would feel if I was the one who would no longer hear from Cinda. I would feel very lost. "You must feel very lost without her, Lucinda."

She nodded through her tears.

"The good news is that God always finds his lost sheep. He will not let go of you."

CHAPTER 14

The Battle Intensifies

The following Thursday night, I was on the phone with Lucinda, hoping to block her from going to another group meeting. My conversation with Lucinda was interrupted by Roxie bursting out. "Hey, I got a meeting tonight. Gotta go, gotta go." But her voice wasn't nearly as hardened as before.

"Is this Roxie?"

"Yeah. They're really mad I wasn't there on Halloween. They wanted me there. I was supposed to get Lucinda out with them."

"Well, I'm glad you didn't go."

"They told Death it's her job now to get Lucinda out, that I wasn't strong enough for the job. Hell, I'll show them I'm strong enough. I know how to get her out. I'll take them tapes she has of you talkin' to her. That'll get her out."

I remembered the various tape recordings I had made for Lucinda a number of years earlier. They were meant to comfort and reassure her when I couldn't be with her, especially when I was away on vacation. I realized these could be quite effective in pulling her out. I needed to stop this.

"Roxie, do you remember visiting Paul and Adele the other night, what happened while we were there, how you heard my heartbeat and were freed from darkness?" I was hoping to direct her attention to God's power, much stronger than any power of darkness.

"Yeah, I remember. It felt different. I ain't ever felt anything like that before. It was like everything was still inside." Her voice became childlike.

"Do you remember hearing my heartbeat?"

There was a long silence. Then she said, "Boom-boom. Boom-boom."

"Yes, that was my heartbeat. That is a very powerful gift God has given us to help free you from the darkness that had you bound. That's because God loves you and wants to set you free. Jesus loves you, Roxie." Then I began to sing the familiar words of "Jesus Loves Me." When I had finished, I waited for a response.

What I heard on the other end of the phone was soft noises, *coos* and *goos* and *gagas*. I remembered how Roxie had regressed to baby talk after she had been delivered. I tried to engage her in conversation, but all I heard was baby talk. Then I heard raspberry sounds like a very young baby would make by protruding her tongue through her lips.

"What is happening?" I recognized Cinda's familiar voice. It was so good to know that I would still be able to hear from her.

"I'm not sure, but it sounds as if Roxie is regressing to a very small baby."

"How old do you think she is?"

I thought it was interesting she was asking me questions. Usually, she was the one with the answers. "I don't know. Maybe six months old. Definitely preverbal."

"Oh my, the Lord will really be able to use this."

"Is she getting a chance to start over?"

"The Lord is at work accomplishing his purposes. It is all good."

When I hung up the phone, well after eleven o'clock, I pondered Cinda's words. When I thought about God's power, I usually thought of mighty deeds, dramatic interventions, darkness having to bow at the name of Jesus. But this time, God's power was being displayed in a little baby cooing and gooing, an adult person regressing to a baby state.

I chuckled, thinking about another time when God's power was displayed in a small baby, a regression from divine to human. The apostle Paul speaks of the weak things of this world confounding the strong and the wise.[4] Cinda seemed confident that God would accomplish his purposes through Roxie becoming a baby.

I was very excited to see how this was going to unfold.

*****

At our next session, I intentionally spent some time with Lucinda before calling Roxie out. In my heart, I was extremely anxious to see Roxie. I had an inner sense that something very powerful was in store, but I wanted to make sure that Lucinda and I got some time together. We did some simple puzzles with animal pictures. Lucinda clapped her hands with delight as she saw the animal forms taking shape. "Grrrr," she said, as the lion's face fell into place.

"That's right, Lucinda. That's the sound a lion makes. What sound does a monkey make?"

Lucinda thought for a moment. Then she burst out with, "Chee, chee, chee, chee, chee."

I laughed. "I'm not sure what sound a monkey makes, but that sounds pretty good."

"I'd like to see a real monkey."

"Well, maybe someday you will. But for now, it's time to have Roxie out. Today I don't want you to get close to her. I want to see how she is without you affecting her." Lucinda nodded.

"Could I please have Roxie out?" I waited to see what would happen.

After a slight pause, Lucinda fell over on her side. I studied her face, noting that it looked a bit rounder than usual. She made little raspberry sounds. Her tongue protruded through her lips and drool ran down her chin.

"Roxie," I said in a singsong voice. "How's Roxie today?" She turned her eyes toward me. They were full of life and light. I reached

4 1 Corinthians 1:27–28.

for the teddy bear on the back of my couch and showed it to her. She reached for it. I laid its soft fur against her cheek, and she began to make cooing noises. She was so authentically baby-like.

For the next twenty minutes, I interacted with her, playing peekaboo with the teddy bear. I took the teddy bear and rubbed it against her cheek until she laughed. The whole time her eyes sparkled. I was mesmerized by her. Despite her adult body, she truly seemed to be a baby.

Then I pulled her over to me, placing her head on my heart. I gently rocked her back and forth until she fell asleep. I sat quietly with her nestled into me, totally awed by what I had just experienced. In every way, she seemed to be a real baby. It felt like these had been holy moments.

I reflected on what was happening in Lucinda's process. Previously, the pattern was for the hard outer shell of each personality to break down so that each one could be the child, maybe four or five years old, that she really was. Once the alter freely chose to be a child, she was no longer depending on darkness to protect her. Their ground was gone, and each child could be easily set free from the demonic presences within. But with Roxie, the regression was much greater. Roxie became a very young baby, perhaps going back to before there was much abuse. She could start over and have a different outcome for her childhood. It was as if all the horrible memories were erased. I wondered if this was to become a new pattern for the different personalities. Or was Roxie the exception?

I looked down at this sleeping baby in an adult body. I remembered how much I enjoyed watching my own children sleep when they were babies. They looked so peaceful and angelic. It was no different with Roxie.

Reluctantly I called Lucinda back.

"Wow, you got light!" she exclaimed.

I wasn't surprised by her comment. I felt full of light.

*****

Later that week, I received an early evening phone call from Lucinda.

"I was going to call you in about an hour," I said. "This is Thursday night."

"I know, but I had to call you. I know which number is yours on our speed dial. So I pushed it. The group was on the phone with Death. I was close behind her while they were talkin' to her. I got really scared about what they were saying, so I pushed my way out and hung up the phone. Then I called you right away."

"Well, it sounds like you did exactly the right thing. What were they saying?"

"It was a man she was talking to. He sounded funny, like he wasn't from around here."

"He had an accent?"

"I guess that's what you call it. She called him Nevil. He sounded mad that she wasn't going to their meetings. He said they'll find other times to pick her up. Then he talked about you. He wanted to know what you were doing to mess Roxie up, that she's becoming useless. But he said they have a plan, that they're going to send someone to you, and that she'll find out where you keep your records. They want all your records on me."

I felt queasy. This sounded scary. They were sending someone to me? I had just scheduled two new women for the next week. Was one of them from the group? And they wanted all my records on Lucinda? That was ten years of records, file folders filled with notes. I would have to bring them all to my house to keep them safe.

This was starting to get very close to home.

I took a deep breath. "God is with us, Lucinda. We need to remember that. I am so glad you heard their conversation. Maybe that was God's doing. I will remove all your records from the office. And I will be on the alert for any new client who seems suspicious."

I spent several hours on the phone with Lucinda that night. When we finally said good night, I reminded Lucinda to never come out to any voice but mine. "And if you hear those recordings of my voice that I gave you, don't come out. Roxie has talked about taking them to the group to get you to come out."

"This is scary. Why do they want me to come out? I don't wanna be out with them. I wish I could go into the light with Cinda."

"I don't want you out with them either. Keep looking to Jesus. He must know you are strong enough to stay inside."

After we said good night, I let out a huge sigh. This was getting hard. Did I have the fortitude to walk through this with Lucinda? Were they really sending someone to scope out my office? How would I know if one of these two new ladies was from the group? What did I get myself into? Was I sure I wanted to continue down this path?

Then I thought about Sam and Steven being tortured by the group. I thought of baby Roxie, so full of light and life. I thought about my ten-year journey with Lucinda and how she was becoming a healthy child. I could not give up now.

"God, give me the strength and wisdom I need to go down this path with Lucinda. I can't quit now, so I choose to trust you are in this with me."

*****

The next time I saw Lucinda, my worst fear materialized. It was Sam who arrived for the session, Sam who was my inside help. "I'm trying to stay close to the surface so I can tell you what's goin' on. The group is really interested in us. They want to understand us better. They ain't ever known anyone who can split as easily as we do. They have plans for us. They like the way the hard parts show no fear. They ain't just involved with a little group anymore. Chris has taken them to meet some other people. Big, important people. Some of them are from England."

"Is that the accent that Lucinda heard when she listened in on Death's call?"

"Probably. They want to know what makes us tick."

While I didn't like the sound of all this, I was grateful for Sam. "Thank you for all this information. You're going out of your way to help me. I really do appreciate what you're doing."

"Well, I know now that I wanna be with the light. That's where the real power is. I felt it when I listened to your heartbeat after the group hurt me. I also feel it when I'm inside in the light. Then I'm just a little child. But I can still be big when I'm out here. As long as I can be big, I'll help you."

"Thank you, Sam."

"There's one other thing you need to know. They went to the group yesterday afternoon. They got Lucinda."

"What?" My heart skipped a beat. "Tell me it's not so. How did she get out?"

"Death pushed her out. She was too close to the surface."

"Is she okay? Did they hurt her?

"Yeah, they hurt her. She needs to hear your heartbeat."

I felt my world crashing down around me. Child Lucinda, so spontaneous and free and unaffected, so full of life and love, had been tortured by this heinous group? I could not bear the thought.

"It will be all right." Cinda's peaceful voice felt like a healing balm on my broken heart. "God has given you a powerful gift to help her. Remember I said that some will be hurt."

"But why does the some have to include Lucinda?" I was angry.

"Right now, your spiritual daughter needs you. Call her out."

With a faltering voice, I called Lucinda to the surface.

She emerged like the others had, a limp, lifeless body.

With raging emotions swirling inside me, I pulled her head to my chest and held her tight. "Jesus, please heal her." As I prayed for her healing, I also wanted to scream at God, *Why did you permit this evil to come upon an innocent child who is finally getting a chance to live? I don't understand you, God.* I held onto her, buried my head in her hair, and wept.

About ten minutes later, Lucinda stirred. She whimpered and took little gasps of air.

I pulled her head away from my chest, mustered up my courage, and looked into her eyes. There were the pools of pain, the brokenness that seared my heart. I could not bear to look into the eyes of another broken child. I pulled her head back to my chest and sat there, frozen in my own pain.

A short time later, the whimpering subsided, and she began to say, "NanNan, NanNan."

"I'm here, Lucinda."

"Hold me, hold me."

I held onto her until it was time for her to go. "Lucinda, I'm going to call Sam out to take you home. I'll call tonight to see how you're doing."

She nodded her head ever so slightly. Then I called Sam back.

After Sam left, I went to my desk drawer and pulled out a folder I had from a conference I had attended about trauma. I remembered hearing about secondary post-traumatic stress. I found the papers that described this condition, a by-product of working with traumatized clients. The papers also called it compassion fatigue.

It was good to see that I didn't have most of the symptoms, but when it talked about emotional depletion, I silently nodded. I was becoming emotionally depleted. How was I going to walk this path and stay strong enough to help Lucinda?

*****

I called Lucinda that night to see how she was faring. Sam answered the phone. When she heard my voice, she identified herself and said that my time with Lucinda helped her. "Yeah, she's a lot better, but there's some things she needs to tell you. You better call her out."

So I called Lucinda out. "Lucinda, this is your spiritual mother. Can you come out with me?"

A second later, Lucinda emerged. "NanNan." Her voice sounded weak.

"Are you okay, Lucinda?"

"The bad people got me. Death pushed me out."

"I know they got you, Lucinda. I'm so sorry. Sam said you have some things to tell me."

"I think I'm supposed to tell you what happened."

I could tell she was holding back tears. "Are you ready to tell me?"

"You need to know. When Death pushed me out, I was in this really richy place. I was in this real soft chair. It was a pretty big room with lots of really nice chairs and tables and rugs. The chair was so soft I started rubbing it. It felt good. Then some people came into the room. The man talked funny, like I told you before. The lady said they were ready for us. I didn't know what she meant. I just sat there. The lady waved for me to follow them. I didn't want to go. I got scared and started to cry. I tried not to cry, but I was so scared. Then the lady looked at me and asked, 'Who are you?' Then she said to the man, 'I don't think this is Death. I think this is a child. I wonder if Death got Lucinda out.' I was really scared. They came over and asked if I was Lucinda. I was too scared to say anything. The man said, 'Take her to the playroom.'

"So she took my hand, and we went down this long hall to this room that was filled with toys. There were cars and trucks and dolls and animals. There was a little kitchen, and there was a monkey. I wanted that monkey. She said I could play, so I got the monkey and then got some other animals. I sat on the floor and made them talk to each other. I forgot she was watching me, and I just had fun playin'. Then the man came in. The lady said to him, 'Roxie's right. She's a normal child. How can that be?' He said he didn't understand it either, but he'd find out.

"Then they told me playtime was over, and we were going to another room. They took me to this other room. I didn't like that room. Ugh! There were all these tables there, and they made me get up on one. Then they put my hands and legs in these round things so I couldn't move."

I didn't want to hear any more. How important was it for Lucinda to tell me all this?

She was starting to cry as she talked. But she kept going. "They hurt me while I was on that table. They pulled my pants down and put things inside me. It hurt." Now Lucinda was sobbing.

I was frozen in horror. I didn't want to hear any more. I kept thinking about secondary post-traumatic stress. *If I didn't have it before, I surely have it now.*

"You need to know what happened to her." It was Cinda.

"I don't want to know. This is too much. Who are these people, and how can they get away with it?"

"You need to be in your heart. If you are in your head or in your emotions, you will not be able to do this. In your heart, you know you are their spiritual mother and God has given you a gift to bring them healing. God will heal her. She is inside now, and God is allowing her to be in the light so she can be healed."

"But why is God allowing this? Hasn't she suffered enough in her life?"

"Yes, she has suffered much, but God knows what she can bear. And remember, they all are one. If they are one, she wasn't pushed out. She came out."

"That makes no sense to me. She did not want to be out."

"Are Lucinda and all her parts really one?"

"Yes, they are," I conceded.

"Remember, you must stay in your heart, or you will not be able to do this. Now call Sam back."

After that phone call, I was totally depleted. And I doubted. Can this really be true? Can there really be a group that is perpetrating these horrors on her? Maybe it is all the fabrication of a mentally ill mind. Maybe it's her way of roping me into being a mother figure in her life, and I've fallen for it hook, line, and sinker.

I wrestled with these doubts and questions, yet when I remembered the deep pools of pain in her eyes, I doubted she could have made it all up. Do not the eyes speak truth?

*****

Early the following week, I met with the first of the two new ladies I had scheduled. She was a young woman who was struggling with the aftereffects of trauma. She had been raped several years earlier while a college student. She was struggling with typical symptoms of post-traumatic stress. As she told her story, she showed genuine emotion. She seemed very authentic.

I outlined for her the treatment path I would take. I reassured her that because it was a single incident and not a lifetime of trauma, and because she did not seem to have any underlying mental health issues, the prognosis for her finding relief from her nightmares and intrusive thoughts was very good.

She seemed so genuinely relieved. Nothing about this dear young woman seemed fabricated. I did indeed work with her, and her healing came very quickly. I did not believe that young woman was sent by the group.

Later that week, the second of the two women arrived for her appointment. She was a nicely dressed, middle-aged woman. I often started my first interview with a client with the question, "What brings you here today?"

When I asked her that question, she rambled, talked a little about being unhappy with her life, and at times fidgeted nervously in her seat. Our whole conversation seemed disjointed, like I couldn't pin her down to anything specific.

When I asked what she hoped to accomplish with counseling, she seemed at a loss. Finally, I asked if she wanted to set up another appointment. Did she feel I could be of help to her?

She eagerly responded, "Oh yes." That response seemed incongruous after our rather pointless conversation.

I turned my back to her to reach for my appointment book. When I turned back around, her head was turned, and she was staring directly at my filing cabinet in the corner of the room.

When she turned back toward me and saw that I was watching her, she jumped a little and shifted nervously in her seat.

I scheduled her for the following week. I handed her an appointment card and suggested that for the next session, she come in with some concrete ideas about what she hoped to accomplish through the counseling process.

She nodded her head and left.

How different this session felt from the one earlier in the week. This woman shared practically nothing about herself. *The first lady was the real deal. I'm not so sure about this one.*

I wasn't surprised when the next day I received a message that lady number two was canceling her next appointment. No explanation was given. Had she accomplished her mission? She knew exactly where my patient charts were filed.

That night I gathered all of Lucinda's files and took them home with me. Then I decided to have some fun. I made a fake file with Lucinda's name on it, filling it with pointless papers, notes saying "Jesus loves you," Bible verses scrawled across otherwise blank sheets of paper, and a warning that Lucinda belonged to the Lord Jesus Christ, and he would fight for her.

At the end of each week, we had an office meeting over lunch. That week we were informed that a new office cleaning service had just been engaged. The office had been approached by this new cleaning service that was substantially less expensive than the previous one. The timing for this announcement seemed uncanny to me. I wondered if this could be connected to the group. Would this group really go to this extent just to get Lucinda's records?

*****

Each session, I tried to spend time with Lucinda so she would not feel neglected. After spending some time in her inner light, she was once again a carefree child, as if she had never experienced the horrors of the group.

I also tried to spend a few minutes with Roxie. She was a baby all the time now. I never again saw the tough outer shell of Roxie. Spending time with her was renewing. She would babble in her baby talk, drool running down her chin.

As I engaged her with baby play, she would coo and giggle, and her eyes would sparkle with light. Then one day, in the midst of all her baby noises, I heard, for the first time, "Mum mum mum…" Then she squealed with delight.

"Are you learning to talk, Roxie?"

She cooed in response.

"Well, I need to go now, Roxie. Bye-bye." I waved my hand to her and called Sam out.

I tried to check in with Sam each session to see if she had news about the group. She kept me informed about times when the group planned to meet with her. I soon realized that I could not stop all the meetings. They were frequently picking her up during the day while I was working. And the nighttime meetings were increasing as well. I couldn't stop my entire life to protect Lucinda from this group. But the thought that they were routinely torturing her was never far from my mind.

One day Sam emerged with a big smile on her face. "I pulled close while they were at the group last night. Nevil was talking to some other people, and he was not happy. They said all they got was a junk file. They thought they had her records, and it was just a junk file."

"They got into my locked file cabinet?"

"I guess they did."

I went to the corner of my office and opened the file cabinet. I paged through the files until I found the one with Lucinda's name on it. I pulled it out. "But it's still here. I did make a fake chart for you, but this is it. They don't have it."

"Maybe they put it back. Or maybe when they realized it wasn't real, they didn't take it. All I know is they were really mad it was a junk file."

I mulled this over in my head. I didn't think I'd said anything to Lucinda about making the fake file. Yet Sam knew about it. Despite all my questions and doubts, this gave credibility to the reality of this group.

CHAPTER 15

Jacelyn

The next time I had a conversation with Cinda, I brought up my question about Roxie establishing a new pattern for the personalities. "Are they all going to become babies now?"

"All the ones who willingly become involved with this new group will become babies."

"But why? What has changed?"

"This is God's plan. They will become babies and then integrate into Lucinda. They will not have to go through the pain of being healed from all their memories."

"Is God going to just wash all their memories away?"

"Yes. God is going to graciously spare them from the pain of the healing process."

"But what about Steven and Sam? Won't God do that for them too?"

"God has a different path for them and for Lucinda. He knows what is best."

I mulled this over. How I wanted all of them to be spared the pain of memory work. I sighed. "I guess I have to trust that God knows what he is doing."

"God always knows what he is doing. He has a different path for each person. And when one plan doesn't work out, he has another plan. Like Lucinda becoming a child. That was not his first plan for her, but when she didn't want the other parts anymore, thinking that she would have a better life without them, God chose another way.

She wanted to forget where she came from and that like the others, she was just a little child. Then God told her he wanted her to be that little child. She agreed to do it, not all at once, but she let him take her back to being a child. That took a lot of trust because they were hurt so much as children. God is very pleased with her for that."

"This time she can be a normal, happy child."

"That's right. And she has a spiritual mother who loves her."

I was pondering the things she was telling me when Cinda abruptly changed the subject. "God has an assignment for you."

The sudden shift of subject caught my attention. "What kind of assignment?"

"God has a message for Dr. Kirkly. You are to set up a time for me to meet with him."

"What? You want me to tell Dr. Kirkly that you are an angel with a message from God? He'll think I'm absolutely wacko."

"That is God's assignment. You can choose to do it or not. If you refuse, he will find another way to deliver his message, but you will miss the blessing."

I gulped. This was really making myself vulnerable. Dr. Kirkly was my boss. He knew all about Lucinda, her personalities, her past involvement in satanism, even her present cult involvement, but I never told him I believed Cinda to be an angel of light. What would he think of me?

And what was the message God had for him? Did I really believe Cinda was an angel of light? If she really was, there was nothing to fear. If she wasn't, I would make an absolute fool of myself.

I wrestled with these questions for several days before deciding to trust that she truly was an angel. I had no other explanation for her wisdom, insight, and understanding of spiritual matters. Even her biblical knowledge was far beyond anything Lucinda had ever displayed. So with that trust as my foundation, I set up a time to meet with him for the following Saturday morning.

*****

The next time I met with Lucinda, I told her about the assignment I had been given. "I set up an appointment with Dr. Kirkly for next Saturday. We can have a session together, and then we can meet with him." Child Lucinda was very compliant. I'm certain adult Lucinda would have resisted such a meeting, but she was no longer around, so all was set for Saturday morning.

That same session, as had become our routine, I spent some time with Roxie. I had brought in a few colorful toys that a baby might enjoy. Roxie laid on her back on my couch, her head propped on some pillows. I held the toys in front of her, and she reached for them. She clumsily grasped them in her hand, shaking them and making baby sounds. When I handed her a bright-yellow toy with a rattle inside, she reached for it and began to shake it. When she heard the rattling noise, she turned her head and began to giggle. The harder she shook the rattle and the more noise it made, the more she giggled. I watched with fascination. I remembered my own children at this stage. Her movements even had the same jerkiness that I remembered from my own babies. I began to interact with her, smiling and saying her name. "Roxie, Roxie, you're starting to play."

She looked at me and giggled. "Goo, goo, googa. Mum mum mum."

"That's right, Roxie. I'm your spiritual mom."

Roxie's eyes began to rove around the room, taking in the various things she saw. Then they stopped on a glowing lamp in the corner of the room. Its base was a jar filled with seashells I had found in Florida. She pointed to the lamp.

"That's a light, Roxie. See the light." I went over to it and turned the light off. "Oh my, what happened to the light?"

Roxie's eyes were fastened on the lamp.

I turned the light back on. "There's the light."

Roxie squealed with the delight.

For the next few minutes, we played a game of turning the light off and then turning it back on. Each time I turned it on, Roxie squealed and giggled, and I would say, "There's the light."

After repeating this a number of times, I walked back over to Roxie and sat down next to her. She pointed to the lamp in the corner of the room and said, "Li…li…li."

"That's right, Roxie. That's the light." Then we both laughed together. In every way, she seemed to be an authentic baby.

*****

On Saturday morning, Lucinda arrived promptly for her appointment. I tried to stay engaged with her, but my mind kept wandering to the meeting with Dr. Kirkly. I was very nervous. He had a faith of his own and was not hostile to spiritual matters, but to tell him I believed one of Lucinda's parts was an angel…that was way out of the box. I knew he considered me to be a reasonable and intelligent person, but what would he think of me after this meeting? Was I putting my job in jeopardy? Was it too late to back out of this meeting?

As we marched down the hall to his office, I reassured myself with some wisdom from my husband. When you put Jesus in the center of your life, you will live on the edge. *Well, Jesus, I've put you in the center, and I'm on the edge now. I guess I shouldn't be surprised. I trust that you are with me.*

Dr. Kirkly's office door was open. He was busy watering the myriad of plants he kept in his office. He was quite a horticulturist and knew an amazing amount about houseplants. At Christmastime, I would search for an obscure plant to give him, hoping I could stump him with a plant he couldn't identify. So far, I had failed.

"Are you ready for us?" I asked.

"Come on in." He continued to water his plants, giving some a long drink and others just a few drops. He would pluck away any dead leaves before moving on to his next plant.

Child Lucinda and I sat next to each other on the couch. I wasn't sure if I should begin or if I should wait for him to finish his task.

He looked over at us. "What brings you two here today?" He moved over to the other side of the room and began to work on the plants on top of a filing cabinet.

I gulped. "Well, this is not a therapy session. There's someone inside Lucinda who wants to talk to you, but not about herself. She has a message for you."

Dr. Kirkly turned around and looked at us. He raised an eyebrow in a questioning way. Then he went back to his plants.

"This is child Lucinda out now, but Cinda is the one with a message for you." I gulped again. *Here goes.* "You see, I've come to believe that Cinda is not just another alter personality. She's so wise and has so much spiritual understanding and biblical wisdom, way beyond Lucinda's capability. I've concluded that she is an angel of light, sent by God to help Lucinda. And she says she has a message for you from God."

My words hung in the air.

Dr. Kirkly stopped his watering.

The room was silent for a moment.

He put his watering can down and sat in his chair.

"Shall I call Cinda out?"

He nodded.

I tried to read his expression, but as usual, he was inscrutable. "Could I have Cinda out, please?"

Cinda smiled warmly. She got right to the point. She looked at Dr. Kirkly. "God has a message for you."

He was very still and said nothing.

"There was a time when you had a great deal of compassion for your patients. But over time, you have let your personal concerns get in the way of that. God wants you to find your compassion again. And he knows that the death of your father has affected you deeply."

Dr. Kirkly looked over at me. "Did you tell her my father died?"

"No. I knew he had been ill, but I didn't know that he died. If I had known, I would have said something to you."

Dr. Kirkly looked a bit rattled. "Will you excuse me for a minute?" He got up and left the room. I assumed he wanted to compose himself.

As I sat there with Cinda, who was not saying much, I grappled with my fears. How was Dr. Kirkly receiving all this? Did he think I was an absolute nut? A bit deluded? In need of some antipsychotic medication?

He returned in a few minutes. My fears spilled out of me. "You must think I am a bit wacko, bringing an angel to you with a message."

His answer was surprising. "Well, you must think I'm a bit wacko because I'm talking to an angel."

His comment put me at ease. Maybe this wasn't going as badly as I feared.

Dr. Kirkly gestured to the door. "Well, I guess I have some things to think about." We stood up, and he escorted us to the door.

After Lucinda left, I gathered my things to leave. Then I went back down the hall and stuck my head into Dr. Kirkly's office. He was sitting in his chair, looking out the window. "I'm leaving now. Thank you for not treating me like I'm crazy and for being open."

He nodded. "It was a very profound experience."

"And oh yes, I'm sorry to hear about your father."

"Thank you."

As I drove home, I thought about our meeting. It was obvious Dr. Kirkly had been moved by what Cinda had said. It was also obvious that he was a bit amazed that she knew about his father's death. I was glad that I was able to walk in trust and see God at work. Then I prayed for Dr. Kirkly, that he would be able to grieve his father's death in healthy ways and that he would find his compassion again.

*****

The weeks rolled on. Winter set in. The excavation in the field across the street had stopped once the ground was frozen. A coating of brilliant white snow blanketed the field. I assumed this would be the last season when I would be able to enjoy nature's panorama of change showcased in the field across the street. Wooden stakes protruded from the snow, marking the parameters of the building-to-be. *Soon they will be working on the foundation.*

My sessions with Lucinda had changed drastically. There was very little talk therapy, like we had done for so many years. Sessions consisted of strategizing with Sam on how to keep them from going to the group, of giving Lucinda time with me to play and learn, of watching Roxie progress as a baby, and of holding broken children who had been hurt at the group, letting them hear my heartbeat and heal. Some of them became babies, including one named Jacelyn.

I was on the phone with them many nights, seeking to keep them engaged until I was confident they would not be going to the group. Often, I was on the phone until after midnight. I would talk with Lucinda and Sam, and sometimes the hardened ones who were connected to the group would talk to me. I discovered that if I let them talk, I could learn a lot.

"We got an important meeting tonight. Have to go. Nevil is really mad. They spent all this time workin' with Jacelyn. They had her right where they wanted her, willing to do whatever they asked. She was afraid of nothin'. They were goin' to have her do drug deals for them."

"Drug deals?"

"Yeah, they got this really big drug ring. They ship the drugs into the country in the lining of coffins. They want Jacelyn out on the streets dealin' the drugs because nothin' scares her. They've been workin' on gettin' Jacelyn addicted to drugs, so she's dependent on them for her supply. They said maybe that's where they failed with Roxie, that she wasn't dependent on them. They're doin' a good job. Jacelyn's really gettin' addicted."

I gulped. The only mental health issue Lucinda seemed to have avoided was addiction. Were we about to go down that path? I certainly hoped not. "Are you sure she's addicted?"

"She's addicted all right. They got her on meth, but they want to get her on heroin. But the last time they had her out, she was just a little baby. Boy, were they mad. They said that first it was Roxie and now it's Jacelyn. They wanna know what you're doin' to them."

"It's not what I'm doing. It's what God's doing."

"But Nevil said they had another plan, that they'll get some hard ones that you won't be able to touch."

I wondered to myself about this group. I had thought it was a satanic cult that she was involved with, but this was sounding very different. A drug ring? Who were these people? They sounded criminal. Was I in danger? They certainly saw me as an adversary.

The thought that I could be dealing with hardened criminals combined with the emotional toll of holding broken children who had been terrorized was wearing me down. To add to that stress, I was staying up late so many nights, trying to keep them safe from the group, that I was becoming sleep-deprived. And now, we had a personality who was drug-addicted. It all felt like too much. I was emotionally depleted and physically worn down.

Cinda became my sounding board. "I am totally depleted. This battle is taking over my life. I am worn out. I don't know how much longer I can do this."

Cinda would listen to my complaints. Her responses were always similar. "You are carrying too much. You cannot do this in your own strength. If you are wearing out, you are doing more than God is asking. It's okay if you don't call to stop them from going. God will take care of them. Do you believe that? And when you are holding the broken children, that should be a time of renewal for you as well. You get to see God's healing power at work. Rest in it and receive what God has for you as well. When God works, it's not just for one person. Others are meant to be blessed by it as well. It's like with Dr. Kirkly. He was blessed by God's message, but you were blessed too. You got to see God at work. And Lucinda was blessed when you told her what happened. When you try to do too much on your own, you are not trusting in God."

"But I can't just let them go to this horrible group, knowing they will be tortured. And now they're getting them drug-addicted. What if Jacelyn's drug dependence starts affecting the others? They share a body. Won't they all get addicted? If I can stop it, at least some of the time, I'm going to."

"Very well. But if you get worn out, it's your own doing. Sometimes you need to trust them into God's hands."

That kind of trust was more than I seemed to have. So I continued to call most nights, whenever I knew the group planned to have them.

And I continued down my path to total depletion.

*****

Finally, a night arrived when I knew that I could not call them. I had been crying earlier in the evening. I was sleep-deprived from a very late phone call the night before. I was emotionally drained. I had nothing to give. So I prayed that God would somehow intervene and keep them from going to the group. I went to bed early and was so exhausted that I slept despite my fears.

When I saw Lucinda in my office the next day, I was very fearful. Had the group gotten them? If they did, what had happened? Would I be able to forgive myself if they had been tortured and I had done nothing to stop it?

Child Lucinda bounced into my office.

My first question was, "What happened last night? Did they go?"

"I think they went. I was hiding inside. Maybe Sam can tell you."

So I called Sam out. "What happened last night? Did they go?"

"Yeah, they went."

My heart sank. I braced myself for bad news.

"Yeah, I was close enough to know what was happening. Jacelyn was out with them."

"Jacelyn? Baby Jacelyn?"

"Well, she was big again. She goes back and forth. Nevil was really happy she was big. He told her they needed her to do big drug deals, and she shouldn't be out with you because it messes her up. And if she wants her drugs, she better do what they say. Then Jacelyn said that she wasn't afraid of anyone...including him. Then she said he ain't got no power. There's somethin' stronger than him, than any of them. And that she felt that power inside her, and it stopped her from hurting. And that's the power she wants. She don't care what they do to her; she wants that other power."

I listened in amazement. Jacelyn had taken a clear stand with Nevil.

"Then Nevil said she was useless, but they have another plan, and they will get some who will be loyal to them."

"You see what can happen when you trust them into God's hands?" It was Cinda. "Jacelyn needed to clearly choose the light. She did. She remembered the power she felt when she listened to your heartbeat. She took her stand with Nevil. They had put a lot of time into grooming Jacelyn. Nevil knows now that they don't have her. Even though they went to the group last night, God worked good out of it."

"But I understand they got Jacelyn addicted to drugs."

Yes, they did. But the power of your heartbeat not only healed her pain, it also healed her addiction. Their plan to keep her dependent on them for drugs failed. And Jacelyn knew she was set free."

I was amazed. Jacelyn had been healed from drug addiction by the power of my heartbeat. "That is amazing, Cinda. Were any of them hurt last night?"

"No, not last night. There's a lesson here for you. If you are unable to call, you can trust them into his hands. His purposes will be accomplished."

"And I feel much better because I had a good night's sleep."

"That was God's gift to you. You were able to sleep even though you were worried about them going to the group."

*****

I was very hopeful for Jacelyn. Maybe she would become a strong asset to Lucinda in this battle. The next time I met with Lucinda, I questioned her about Jacelyn. "Do you know anything about Jacelyn? How's she doing since she took her stand with Nevil?"

Lucinda wrinkled up her nose. “I don’t think she’s too good. There’s something wrong with her.”

I hadn’t expected this answer. “What’s wrong with her?”

“I don’t know. She’s not right. She keeps talking about spaceships. She said they’re getting the spaceship ready.”

“Ready for what?”

“I don’t know. She was in the basement and kept pointing to the dryer, saying the spaceship’s not ready yet. Then she got some black paint and painted the dryer all black.”

“What? She painted your dryer black?”

“Yeah, she did. And Kurt was really mad. He swore at us and told us we were a nut case.”

“Well, I can understand he was mad if she painted the dryer black. What do you think is going on with her?”

“I don’t know, but she’s not right.”

“Jacelyn’s not in reality.” Cinda had come out. “She’s looking for an escape. She thinks a spaceship can take her away from all her pain. That’s what the drugs were doing for her, taking her away from the pain.” She shook her head sadly. “Jacelyn has mental problems. She needs help.”

“I was hoping she could be an asset in fighting the group. It doesn’t sound like that will happen.”

“She has had so much pain that she’s looking for a way out. You need to pray for her, that God will heal her mind.”

I remembered other alter personalities who had psychotic breaks, thinking the furniture was talking to them. “But she seemed to be so strong when she confronted Nevil, saying she had experienced God’s power and that’s what she wanted.”

“At that moment she was strong, but Jacelyn has a lot of brokenness. You need to pray for her.”

So my hopes for Jacelyn were dashed. But I did pray for her. “Lord Jesus, please heal Jacelyn’s mind so she can be whole. Give her whatever she needs to stay in reality. And help her maintain her strong stand against the group.”

I wish all of my prayers were answered as quickly as that one.

CHAPTER 16

Babies

The next time we met, I specifically called Jacelyn out. She jumped to her feet and looked wildly around my office. "Where's the spaceship? We gotta get it ready. Get it ready, get it ready. We're leavin' this place, never comin' back."

I knew enough not to reason with someone who was delusional. Instead, I let her rant for a bit. Then I called Lucinda out and had her lay her head on my chest. I called Jacelyn back.

When she emerged, she jolted into an upright position, again looking wildly around the room with crazed eyes.

I spoke in my most soothing voice. "Remember the power, Jacelyn, the power you told Nevil that you wanted?" I gently pulled her head back to my chest.

She resisted for a moment and then laid her head on my chest. As she lay there, the crazed look in her eyes diminished and, after a short time, she regressed to a whimpering baby.

I held her until the snivels ceased and she fell sound asleep. I prayed for her as I held her, asking God to heal the deep pain behind her delusions.

Jacelyn spent several weeks vacillating back and forth between crazed lunatic and sniveling baby, but in the end, she became a full-time baby. No more rantings about a spaceship, no more crazed looks. She seemed to be following in Roxie's path.

It wasn't long before I had a third baby that needed tending to. Erica also spent a number of weeks vacillating back and forth between being the hard, tough outer shell and the helpless infant. Eventually, she also became a full-time baby.

Sometimes I didn't even know which baby was out. Roxie seemed to be slightly more advanced developmentally, so I usually could discern her presence, but Jacelyn and Erica seemed identical. I would try to give them the kinds of interaction that any baby needed: lots of eye contact, verbal interaction, and gentle touch.

Even as babies, there were times they were hurt by the group. I would hold their limp body and let them listen to my heartbeat. Amazingly, they would stir, then whimper and cry for a short time. Finally, they would resume the baby talk and facial expressions of an infant.

As I watched this unfold, it often felt totally surreal. Was I really interacting with babies in an adult body? Was I really seeing them healed by listening to my heartbeat? Could Lucinda be inventing all this as a way to get the mothering she so desperately needed and wanted? I would wonder about these things, but in the end, I would conclude that Lucinda was not so skilled an actress that she could impersonate a baby so precisely.

The day came when I decided to see if Roxie had developed enough to sit up on her own. I pulled her from lying on her back into a sitting position.

She tottered back and forth for a few seconds before she fell over sideways.

I pulled her up again and held her in place. "Look at you, Roxie. You're sitting up."

She looked at me and stuck her fist in her mouth. I released my hands from her shoulders.

Again, she tottered back and forth for a few seconds before she fell over sideways. Drool dribbled down her chin as she looked up at me.

"I think you're just about ready to sit up on your own, Roxie. Every time I see you, we'll practice sitting up. You just have to learn to keep your balance." I tried to remember at what age my children began to sit on their own. It seemed to me it was at about five or six months. That gave me a marker for about how old Roxie might be chronologically.

Okay, chronologically she was really in her thirties.

*****

One chilly December morning, I entered my office and shed my winter coat. I pulled my files for the day, then headed down the hall to the front office to check my messages. There were several slips of paper with phone calls that needed to be returned, a reminder of an office meeting coming up, and a sealed white envelope with my name hand-printed on the front. I chuckled to myself as I studied this envelope. My name had been spelled NANCESS. I wondered who had so badly misspelled my name. I went back down the hall to my office, settled into my desk chair, and opened this envelope.

I pulled out a folded sheet of paper with a short note that was computer-printed in a cursive-style font. The note was dated and began with the words "To Nancee Soisson" (this time my name was correctly spelled).

> I'am write this to you to offer you $50,000 Dollars to help us with her we want you to know we have her even if you think you do she can help us now about the brain how it works under pain we want you to consider helping us there will be more money to help us...WELL write back too find out your decision!!!!!!

I sat glued to my seat. I couldn't believe what I was reading. Had this heinous group, whoever they were, actually sent me this note? Did they really think they could buy me off, that I would join them in their nefarious intentions? The note said they were going to write me back. Should I respond to them, let them know that I found their proposal totally ludicrous? I did not want another communication from these people. I didn't want anything to do with any of it. And how did this note find its way into my office mail slot?

I took a deep breath, reined in my rampaging thoughts, picked up the empty envelope, and headed back down the hall. Trying to look as unruffled as possible, I asked the girls in the office if any of them knew how this envelope had gotten into my mail slot. Each one looked at it and shook her head. One of them asked if there was a problem. Trying to sound as casual as possible, I said that I had received an unsigned note and wanted to know who had left it for me. That seemed to satisfy her, so I headed back to my office.

I sank back down in my chair and reread the note. I could not help but notice the run-on sentences, the poor grammar, and the misspelled words. Whoever had written it was not well educated. How was I going to proceed? And how did they ever get this note into my mail slot?

As I sat there mulling all this over, I remembered the new cleaning service. That's how they could have gotten the note into my slot. I shuddered a little to think that these people, or somebody in contact with them, was regularly in my office. But at least I had an explanation for the appearance of this note.

I decided that my best course of action was to talk to one of Lucinda's parts about this, probably Sam, and to have her talk to the others inside. They needed to tell the group that I would not help them for any amount of money, that I could not be bought off, and that I didn't want to hear from them again.

When I approached Sam and showed her the note, she agreed to do this. She reported back to me that she had talked to all those inside who seemed to be involved with the group. "Boy, they don't get you. They said $50,000 was a lot of money. You must be crazy not to take it. Then they said you were probably holdin' out for a bigger offer. But they said they would tell Nevil."

Much to my relief, I never heard from the group again.

*****

As winter progressed and the babies started to grow, giving me hope for Lucinda and how integrating healthy babies might affect her, the battle with the group intensified. It seemed that Lucinda's dark parts were going to the group more and more often. Even more distressing for me personally were the days when it was not Lucinda, but Sam, who would show up for an appointment. My fear, when this would happen, was that Lucinda had been hurt by the group, that one of the others had pushed her out. Sometimes this was the case.

Nothing shredded my heart like seeing child Lucinda, usually so full of life and light, lying limply in my arms as I held her to my heart. Those glimpses into her pain-seared eyes would undo me. I prayed for God to heal her as I fought back my own tears. I cried out to God, asking him why he allowed these atrocities to be done to her.

The day Sam explained to me what exactly the group had done to her was more than I could bear. "They had her on that table."

I remembered well the room with the tables that Lucinda had described to me.

"Then they put things up inside her."

I shuddered. "And what exactly did they put up inside her?" I should not have asked this question.

Sam looked directly at me. "Knives."

Everything inside me was still. The word *knives* reverberated in the air. A silent scream went through my head as my jaw dropped in stunned disbelief.

Sam continued. "When they do that, they can torture her, and no one will know it. All the scars are on the inside."

The emotions that welled up within me, the disbelief, the rage, the shock, the horror, were more than I could bear. I was about to explode. "Cinda, I need you out, Cinda!"

She appeared that quickly. "You need to know the truth."

"I don't want to know the truth. This is too much. Knives up inside her? So no one will see the scars? This is the most horrible, evil thing I have ever heard. I can't do this. I CAN'T DO THIS!"

Cinda reached out her arms and pulled me to her. For a long while she said nothing, just held me close.

Inwardly, I screamed at God. *I don't get you, God. You make no sense to me. You are a God of love, and yet you allow this? You allow this to happen to an innocent child who's had a life of hell, but is finally getting a chance for some happiness? I don't understand you!*

As I inwardly railed at God, I felt Cinda's arms around me. My head was buried in her neck. Tears flowed.

Warmth radiated from Cinda. Not an emotional warmth—physical warmth. Her body felt hot. I could feel the heat being transferred to me. It felt good, like a soothing balm poured out on my tattered soul.

As I focused on this new sensation, the cacophony of emotions within me began to subside. After about ten minutes of soaking in the warmth emanating from Cinda, I found that I was strangely peaceful inside. My emotions had subsided, and my body was at rest.

"What just happened?"

"God healed you. He knows how hard this is for you. Now your spiritual daughter needs you. Call her out."

So I called for Lucinda. As I expected, she was a limp, lifeless body; but as I held her close with her head on my heart, she stirred and then whimpered. Finally, she looked up at me. "NanNan, you got light." Then she smiled. "It kinda feels like when I'm inside in the light. A little bit like that. You feel good and warm."

I wondered if Lucinda's experience of hearing my heartbeat was like what I had just experienced with Cinda. Somehow being held close by Cinda had settled my raw emotions, and there certainly was a warmth emanating from her. The warmth flowed from her body into mine, bringing with it a soothing calm. It had been very powerful. Was this the power Jacelyn told Nevil about the night she took her stand with him?

One thing was certain: God had been at work through Cinda. He had restored my emotional well-being, and then I was able to pass it on to Lucinda, who had suffered the trauma of having knives inserted into her.

"Can we color?" Lucinda's request interrupted my thoughts.

"We certainly can." I pulled out the crayons and paper. Lucinda reached for a bright-red crayon and began to draw what was now her signature drawing, an angel that looked more like a bumblebee than an angel. She put a big smile on her face and then took a yellow crayon and surrounded her with light. "That's Cinda. I don't hear her anymore, but I know she's still there. Sometimes I can feel her light shining inside. It's okay that I don't hear her. I was mad about it at first, but I still have my spiritual mommy."

Amazing. This child had been tortured with knives the previous night, and now she's a happy child. *Thank you, God, for this gift of healing that is in my heartbeat. Without it, I could not do this. And thank you for Cinda. Without her, I would still be in emotional turmoil. I need to trust that you will give both Lucinda and me what we need.*

*****

The day came when Roxie was able to maintain her balance when I pulled her into a sitting position. She wobbled back and forth a few times, then steadied herself for a few seconds before she fell sideways. I pulled her back up. Again, she wobbled a bit, but soon found her balance and sat for about thirty seconds before she toppled over. "Goo goo, gaga, mum mum mum," she babbled. It was not long before she would hold a toy or shake a rattle while maintaining her sitting position.

Meanwhile, Jacelyn and Erica were starting to babble. I would try to spend time holding whichever baby was out with me. I knew that lots of touch was essential for a baby to thrive. Even if they had not been hurt, I would let them hear my heartbeat. Often, they would fall asleep to the sound of my heart. Then I would call out the next one. I felt like a mother hen trying to keep track of all her chicks.

And I still needed to spend time with Lucinda. I did not want to neglect her. She was doing so well. I could see that she was getting stronger as she spent time being a child in the world rather than being sheltered inside in the light.

She arrived for her session on a cold December day just before Christmas. She had a Christmas present for me.

I opened her gift. It was a silver bracelet, what we used to call a name bracelet when I was a teenager. It had a silver plate with my name engraved on one side and *Spiritual Mother* engraved on the other side.

"Thank you so much, Lucinda." I clasped it around my wrist.

"I wanted you to always remember that you're my spiritual mommy."

"How could I forget that?" I laughed. "But just so I don't forget, I'll wear it all the time."

"I'm so glad God gave me a spiritual mommy. Last night I kept thinking about you."

"What happened last night?"

"After you hung up the phone, they went to the group."

My heart sank, but I said nothing and waited for Lucinda to continue.

"I didn't know they went until I heard that man who talks funny. He was trying to get Jacelyn to come out. Jacelyn was just a little baby. I didn't want her to get hurt. So I got in front of her. When he'd say her name, I could feel her being pulled out, but I kept in front of her and wouldn't let her get out. Boy, he got mad. But I just stood there. Finally, he stopped calling her. Then he called Death out. I heard him asking her what happened to Jacelyn. But then I grabbed Jacelyn and took her over near the light. We couldn't go in the light, but we got near it."

"Lucinda, I am so proud of you. You are getting so much stronger. You weren't even afraid."

"Oh, I was afraid, but I didn't want Jacelyn to get hurt. I kept thinking that you would be really sad if Jacelyn got hurt again."

"I would have been sad. But you overcame your fear to help Jacelyn and to help me. I am so proud of you. Maybe God wants you to get stronger so you can help the others."

Lucinda smiled at me. "I didn't feel strong, but I guess I was stronger than baby Jacelyn."

We both laughed.

*****

After Roxie had mastered sitting up, I began to wonder what her next developmental step would be. As I recalled my own children's development, it seemed that learning to crawl would be next. That meant I had to get her off the couch and onto the floor. I presented this to Lucinda and asked if she would be willing to lie on the floor on her stomach before I called Roxie out. She laughed, thinking this would be great fun. I pushed all my furniture back against the walls of my office, making as much space as possible. Lucinda lay down, and I placed the baby toys around her. Then I called Roxie out.

When Roxie emerged, she began to babble in baby talk. Then she saw the yellow rattle and reached for it. She brought it to her mouth and began to suck on it. After a few minutes, she lifted her head and turned it around. Spotting another toy, she reached for it, then dropped her head. Then she lifted it again. I watched with fascination as she went through the motions of lifting her head and putting it down, again and again. It was as if she was just discovering that she could do this. Then she put her arms just in front of her and began to push up on them. Then they collapsed under her. Again, she pushed herself up until her arms gave way. Images of my own children going through this same motion flashed through my head. Each time her arms collapsed, she pushed back up with determination. I remembered that this was the first step in learning to crawl. Babies needed to strengthen their arm muscles so they could hold their weight.

Obviously, Roxie's arms were physically able to hold up her weight, yet she was going through the very steps that were part of any baby's development. Finally, Roxie laid her head down on the floor. "Mum mum mum mum."

I pulled Roxie to myself and let her hear my heartbeat. That day she fell asleep very quickly. I considered all I had observed. It was as if Roxie was going through all the normal steps of child development, but at an accelerated rate. And again, everything she did was so authentically baby-like.

I was witnessing something truly extraordinary. It was as if Lucinda was a getting a chance to start over.

*****

The nighttime phone calls continued. At times I felt almost desperate to keep them from going to the group. I tried to remember Cinda's warnings about taking too much on myself, but I wasn't very good at relinquishing Lucinda into God's hands. One night when I was on the phone well past midnight, Cinda emerged. "It's time to hang up now. Tonight they are going to the group."

"You want me to just hang up and let them go?"

"That's right. You need your sleep, and tonight they are going to the group."

"I can't do that."

"Well, you can try to stay on the phone all night, but God has a purpose for them going. You can cooperate with God, or you can fight God."

"What purpose can there possibly be in her going?"

"He had a purpose that night you didn't call. Jacelyn took her stand with the group. God was pleased with that. Now she's a baby in the light having a second chance to grow up. Do you trust God?"

"I want to trust him, but I don't know if I can."

"Who knows better, you or God? You are not her savior."

I felt pretty foolish after listening to Cinda. Of course, I didn't know more than God. And I certainly wasn't her savior. It was with a heavy heart that I explained to Lucinda that they had to go to the group that night, that God had a purpose. "I want you to go inside as far as you can. And don't come out, no matter what. Pray that God's purposes, whatever they are, will be accomplished."

"I don't want to go, NanNan."

"I don't want you to go either, but Cinda says this is God's plan. Good night, Lucinda." I hung up the phone. That night I fell asleep praying for God's protection on the little ones. My heart was heavy. *This is taking trust in God to a whole new level.*

I finally drifted off to a fitful sleep.

I never did discover why Lucinda had to go to the group that night. Neither Sam nor Lucinda was close enough to the surface to hear what was occurring. There was a broken child out with me the next time I saw Lucinda, but it was not Roxie or Jacelyn or Erica.

Another tortured child. I clutched the limp body and held it to my heart.

In time, this one, whose name I didn't even know, started to stir, to whimper, and then to make baby noises. Finally, this one fell asleep listening to my heartbeat.

When Lucinda was back in the body, I asked her about this baby. "Who was the child that was out with me? It didn't seem like any of the ones I know."

Lucinda shook her head. "I don't know. Roxie and Jacelyn and Erica were all with me inside."

I sighed. When would this ever end, this string of tortured children?

*****

When I was on the phone with them, I tried to remember that I was not their savior and there would be times that I would have to hang up and let them choose to go to the group. One night as we were on the phone, our call kept being interrupted by static. One time we were completely disconnected. I promptly called back and was relieved when Lucinda answered the phone.

"What happened, NanNan?"

"I don't know. We must have had a bad connection." The disruptive static continued, making it very difficult to have a conversation. I wondered about this static. What could be causing it? When we finally said good night, well after midnight, I felt very uneasy. I later learned that she did go to the group that night.

Several nights later, we again had a conversation disrupted by the static. This time there were also odd beeps and pinging noises. I was talking to Sam at the time. "Sam, is it possible that the group is trying to break up our phone calls, that they have some way of causing all this interference?"

"I wouldn't put it past them. They are really mad that sometimes you keep them from going. They ain't no small group. And they know lots of important people. If there's a way to break into our calls, they'll figure it out."

I tried not to let on how distressing this was for me. The thought of them going to this group almost every night was more than I cared to consider. I tried to keep my voice level. "If the phone call gets cut off, try to stay out. I will call you back right away."

Sam agreed to this. But now our phone calls took on another dimension. The static and beeps and pings continued to be disruptive, and it felt as if these calls had become a battleground. It was not just a matter of whether or not I could outlast the group. Now there was also the concern of the call being disconnected so that one of the parts could leave with the group.

I considered these odd disruptions to our calls. I'd never experienced anything like this before when talking to other people on the phone. Was it possible that the group was truly behind this? I shuddered at the thought. It was creepy to think that I was on their radar that way. I didn't want anything to do with these people, but here I was, locked in a battle with them.

*****

The next time I was with Roxie, I had her on the floor again. Once more, she interacted with the toys around her, reaching for them and grasping them. Some she put in her mouth. Others she looked at while she made baby noises.

She began to push herself up on her arms, collapsing after each effort. Several times she was able to stay in the pushed-up position for ten or fifteen seconds before her arms collapsed. Again and again, she went through this exercise. After a bit, she lay exhausted on the floor. I interacted with her, using her name and showing her the toys. Once again, she pushed herself up on her arms, each time staying in the pushed-up position for a little longer. Then, while in this position, she began to rock her weight backward, lifting her rear end ever so slightly. She did this over and over again, making little baby grunts each time she tried. She rocked back and forth, trying to lift her rear end and get up onto her knees. Finally, her arms gave way, and she lay on the floor. Once again, I watched with fascination, remembering my own children going through these very motions.

A short ten days later, Roxie made it onto her knees. Five days after that, she began to move her arms and legs and take her first, tentative crawling steps. The following session, two days later, she crawled about my office floor. In less than a month's time, Roxie had moved from being a stationary, helpless infant to a baby who could navigate. She had, like babies do, conquered the human drive to be mobile.

I watched from the sidelines, captivated by this human progression, not because it was different from what normal human babies do, but because it was so much like the progression of a normal human baby. *She can't be making this up,* I kept thinking. I felt I was truly watching something phenomenal, an adult woman going through the developmental stages of babyhood. I listened to Roxie coo with contentment and wondered how this would affect Lucinda.

*****

During this time, I was on an emotional roller coaster, up and down, up and down. I watched the broken children being healed by my heartbeat and was amazed. I watched the babies developing in such an authentic way and felt I was observing something truly extraordinary. Child Lucinda had become a true delight for me. But the pain in the broken children's eyes still haunted me. The nights I had to let them go to the group were heart-wrenching.

I would sleep fitfully those nights, yet I still had to get up and go to work and counsel people. I did not want to shortchange those who looked to me for help. At times, I felt totally depleted and wondered how much longer I could do this. I was constantly on the edge of breaking down. I cried a lot, and I cried out to God. I was aware that my relationship with God had become quite raw. I would yell at God, telling him exactly what I thought about his allowing her involvement with the group. It wasn't pretty.

By this time, my youngest child was away at college. My husband and I were in the empty nest stage, but I was in a continual state of emotional depletion. I wanted to enjoy the newfound time alone with him, but our relationship was changing. I depended on him to just maintain my equilibrium.

Joby was a sounding board and the shoulders I cried on. He had gotten to know Lucinda quite well through our deliverance sessions and had a heart for her as well. He had a firm conviction that we had been called to this, so his steady support undergirded me. I could not have done this if he had not been in my corner.

A curious thing began to happen. Despite my continual emotional upheaval, a sweet closeness permeated our relationship. We were pulled together in a tighter union than we had ever known. He was with me on the mountaintops and in the valleys, not just sympathizing but empathizing with me at every turn. I could draw strength from our relationship, and each day, I made the decision to press on, to hold one more broken child or to make one more phone call.

*****

I had several more sessions with Roxie crawling about my office floor. She navigated over to my bookshelf and began pulling books out. I darted over to the shelf and began moving everything that might be breakable out of her reach. She discovered the cubbyhole under my desk and crawled into it, getting stuck because she had not yet mastered the art of crawling backward. In every way she was truly a baby, except, of course, her thirty-six-year-old body.

After I rescued her from the cubbyhole under the desk, I pulled Roxie over to me, holding her close to let her hear my heartbeat. She looked up at me and cooed. "Mum Mum Mum Mum."

I smiled back at her and repeated her name several times, "Roxie, Roxie, Roxie." She had been on a long journey backward, from that tough outer shell that got involved with this horrible group to this sweet and authentic baby. For her, going backward was moving forward. She was getting a new foundation as a healthy infant who was loved.

Roxie drifted off to sleep mumbling, "Mum Mum Mum Mum."

She seemed especially peaceful as she slept. My heart felt full as I held her and watched her peaceful breathing. I prayed for her, asking God to complete this work he had begun in her.

After a few minutes, her eyes opened. "NanNan." It was child Lucinda. She smiled. "I feel good. I feel full. I ain't ever felt like this before. I feel like I'm loved…and like I'm whole."

Her words filled me. "That's wonderful, Lucinda."

"Roxie's gone. I knew you were holding her, so I came close so I could feel you holding me too. I got real close to her, and I could feel your love for her coming through. And then, Roxie just kinda came into me. She's gone now. She's part of me."

"Lucinda, that's great! No wonder you feel whole. You've taken back part of yourself." I was delighted to hear that Lucinda and Roxie had integrated. However, if I am to be honest, part of me was a bit disappointed. Watching Roxie's development had become such an engaging experience, and now, I would never see her take those next developmental steps. I acknowledged that disappointment to myself but then turned my attention to Lucinda. "God is doing an amazing work in you. He is taking your broken pieces, healing them, and then giving them back to you so that you can be whole."

Lucinda nodded. "I can feel God. I know he is near."

With that encouragement under my belt, I felt strong enough to once again take on the group.

CHAPTER 17

Barbara

Spring arrived early that year. The warmer weather felt like a balm to my soul. As the crocus and daffodils began to push through the soil with promises of spring colors to come, I felt hopeful. Perhaps I would be able to do this, to be Lucinda's spiritual mother and to fight the battle against this horrific group.

My relationship with Lucinda was changing. It was no longer just a counseling relationship. I was her spiritual mother, and a deep bond had formed between us. As a counselor, a certain amount of emotional distance is needed. Once the boundaries are crossed, it can be very difficult to maintain an objective stance with the counselee. I had crossed the boundary into what is known as a dual relationship. The danger was that my emotional needs could get entangled with her emotional needs.

I wondered if it was a good idea to continue to counsel her professionally. Perhaps I should stop counseling her and simply be her spiritual mother. But it seemed that the time we spent together in my office was very helpful. Whether I was with the babies or spending time with child Lucinda or working with hardened parts who were involved with the group, it felt like time well spent. So I continued to see her professionally, even as I wrestled with these questions.

For several weeks after taking Roxie, Lucinda was filled with childlike wonder as we interacted in our sessions. There was an innocence and an exuberance about her that was contagious. Having reclaimed Roxie seemed to have affected her in a most positive way, so

I was very surprised when she arrived for a session several weeks later and the effervescence was gone. She was whiny and uncooperative.

"What's wrong, Lucinda? You don't seem like yourself. You've had so much joy since you took Roxie. What happened to it?"

Lucinda didn't respond. She grabbed a teddy bear off the back of my couch and buried her head in it.

"Well, it's obvious something is wrong. I'll just sit here until you're ready to tell me about it."

We sat in silence. It had been a long time since I had shared these heavy silences with her. I could hear the clock ticking. I looked out the window and saw backhoes digging in the field across the street. I sighed. I hated to see my field being developed.

Finally, Lucinda said, "I sorry, NanNan. I didn't mean to do it."

"Do what?"

Another silence. Tears trickled down her cheeks. "I got real scared. They went to the group, and I heard Nevil tell someone to go in and get a child. I got real scared they would come get me. With Roxie as part of me, I can't hide that I'm a child. I didn't want them to get me, so I pushed Roxie away. I didn't mean to do it, but when I saw one looking around for a child...it was one I didn't know...I don't know where she came from...and she looked really mean...I got really scared, and I pushed Roxie away so I wouldn't look so little."

My heart was pounding. "Did she get you, Lucinda?"

"No, she found another one that she pushed out."

"Who was it?"

"I think it was Steven."

My heart sank. I hadn't heard from Steven in quite a while since I was so busy with the babies. And now the group had gotten him and had probably tortured him. I braced myself for his limp body and pain-seared eyes. "

"Well, I'm glad they didn't get you. Can you take Roxie back?"

"I don't know how to do that. I don't even know where she is."

I pondered the situation for a minute. Steven seemed to be the most pressing problem. "I think I should have Steven out, to see if he needs to hear my heartbeat. Then I'll call you back. Maybe if you listen to my heartbeat and I call Roxie close, the two of you will come back together since that's how you came together in the first place."

Lucinda nodded as she sniffled.

When Steven came out, I looked into his eyes and knew instantly that he had been hurt. I pulled his head to my chest and let him hear my heartbeat. I tried to settle my own emotions, my discouragement over Lucinda separating from Roxie and my heartbreak over Steven's condition.

I remembered Cinda telling me that I needed to receive during these times too, that I could be built up by seeing God at work. I tried to rest in that, but my own emotional turmoil got in the way.

The truth is that I was raging mad at God, that this child that I loved had been tortured by these awful people. It took a lot longer than usual for Steven to come around, for life to return to his limp body. When he finally started to whimper, I tried my best to speak endearing words to him, to reassure and comfort him, but I suspect my own rigid body and tense voice communicated louder than my words. When Steven finally came around, I got the top out, so he could have some fun. Then I gave him a big hug.

"I miss being with you," he said.

"I miss you too. We need to make it a point to get some time together. I haven't forgotten about you and how far you've come."

Steven smiled. "I like being with you."

"I like being with you too, but now I need to have Lucinda out. In the future, try to stay way in the back so that you won't be out with those horrible people again."

"But I want to be out with you."

"I know, Steven. There are so many of you who need my attention. I will try my best to find time for you. But it's very important that I have Lucinda out now."

Steven nodded his head. "Okay, but I want time with you too."

As I called Lucinda out, I wondered how I would ever find time for all these broken children. Once she was present, Lucinda settled her head against my heart. When she seemed at peace, I called for

Roxie to come close. I called and called. "Do you feel her drawing close, Lucinda?"

"No, I don't feel her. I don't know where she is."

Lucinda left that day still separated from Roxie. It was hard not to be discouraged. Lucinda and Roxie merging had seemed like such a positive step forward.

*****

Time spent with the two babies, Jacelyn and Erica, was going well. Much like Roxie, they were progressing developmentally, reaching for toys and making baby talk. Erica, especially, seemed full of life. My heart was captivated by them, as it had been by Roxie. Sometimes they were the victims of the group's torture, and I would hold them to my heart so they could find healing. I never ceased to have a shattered heart when I would look into their broken eyes and see those pools of pain.

One particular day, I was holding Erica, the group's latest victim, inwardly crying out to God and asking him why he allowed this. As I held Erica, I felt a powerful sense of connection with her. Love rose up in my heart, pouring through me to her.

As she stirred, I could see she was being healed. I felt such deep gratitude to God that he had given them the gift of my heartbeat. A few minutes later, she started to coo. I looked into her eyes and saw the pain was gone. Gratitude flooded my heart as I squeezed her gently. Then she nestled into me and fell asleep.

When I called Lucinda back, I was in for a pleasant surprise. Lucinda looked up at me and said, "I felt your love. It came through to me, so I got real close to Erica. I think Roxie felt it too because she was there too. Then Roxie and I became one again. We were both there listening to your heartbeat, and we just kinda came together."

"Lucinda, I am so glad you came together. I did feel a lot of love and a lot of gratitude for the gift of my heartbeat. I guess there's a lot of power in love and gratitude."

"It was very strong. And I feel good again, being one with Roxie."

I wish I could say that was the last time Lucinda separated from Roxie. In the months to come, there would be any number of times, usually triggered by fear, that Lucinda and Roxie would separate. They would inevitably come back together while one of the alters was listening to my heartbeat. But this resulted in Lucinda being tossed back and forth between feeling content and full and then discontented, empty, and broken. I could usually tell as soon as I saw her whether or not she had separated from Roxie. Sometimes they would be separated for several days, sometimes for several weeks.

I tried my hardest not to be upended when a separation took place, but with all the other pressures I was feeling, I would go up and down with Lucinda.

We rode the roller coaster together.

*****

Barbara, one of the ladies I counseled, had been referred to me by one of the doctors in our office—but not the esteemed Dr. Kirkly. She had come in because she was depressed. Our doctor had prescribed an antidepressant for her and then referred her to me for therapy. She was a middle-aged woman with a history of childhood sexual abuse.

By the time Barbara reached me, she had already been diagnosed with dissociative identity disorder, the new name for multiple personality disorder. She had the usual assortment of tough protector alters and vulnerable child alters. The host, the main one out, was a savvy lady who worked in the mental health field. She was surprisingly functional, perhaps as a result of years of therapy. She was very discouraged by her inability to simply leave behind all the brokenness of her past and just be normal. When she learned that I was well versed in her disorder, she opened up quickly to me, allowing me to interact with her alters.

One day she arrived particularly dispirited. One of her hardened alters had picked a fight with her husband, which had escalated into a crass shouting match with threats of divorce. She was so tired of the hardened alters causing chaos in her life. She was especially despondent, and nothing I said or did could penetrate her walls.

We sat in silence, and I wondered what to do next. Then a very interesting thought entered my head. I was going to see Lucinda next, and she usually arrived early. She was probably sitting in the waiting room. She had come so far and was so full of life and light. I wondered if she could be an encouragement to Barbara.

I tentatively opened the subject with Barbara. "The lady I am scheduled to see next has the same diagnosis you do. She has made a lot of progress and has integrated a number of her alters. I'm wondering if she could be an encouragement for you. Would you like to meet her?" Even as I said this, I was hoping that Lucinda had not separated from Roxie and was not herself in an emotional funk.

Barbara was silent for a moment. "Well, I guess that would be okay."

"Then let me see if she is here and if she would be willing to meet you."

Even as I went out to the waiting room, I was wondering if this was a good idea. I found Lucinda sitting in a corner looking at the pictures on the walls. I explained to her what I had in mind and asked if she would be willing to meet Barbara. I could tell by her childlike innocence that she had not separated from Roxie.

"Is she a nice lady?

"Yes, she's a nice lady, but she's very sad today."

"I don't want her to be sad, but I don't know what to say to her."

"Just be you and let her know how much God has done for you."

So child Lucinda followed me back to my office. I introduced them to each other. Lucinda smiled shyly.

"Lucinda, why don't you tell Barbara about how far you've come."

"Well, God brought me and Roxie together, and since then, I feel good and happy and whole. I'm learning I can trust God to take care of me."

Barbara sat straight up and looked at Lucinda. "My word, she's just a child." Barbara appeared flabbergasted.

"That's right. God is letting me be a child because I couldn't be one when I was little."

Barbara sat in silence, but her eyes started to water.

"Hello, Barbara. Are you confused?" Cinda had come out to talk with Barbara.

What do I do now? Do I explain to Barbara who she is? "Barbara, this is Cinda." I hesitated. "Cinda isn't just another alter personality. At first, I thought she was, but she has so much wisdom and spiritual understanding and so much biblical knowledge, way more than Lucinda ever had, that I have come to believe she is a special gift from God for Lucinda, an angel to help her with her healing process." I tried to gauge Barbara's reaction.

Cinda said, "Barbara, you have a loving heavenly Father who knows all you have been through. He knows how hard it is for you to live with so many different pieces to your personality. I am going to ask him to heal your broken heart and your fractured personality to make you whole."

Barbara sat in silence.

Cinda continued. "God has a different path for each person. He has given Lucinda a chance to start over as a child, to have some of the love and joy she never knew. He is giving you the gift of wholeness."

Tears now freely flowed down Barbara's cheeks. "Why would he do that for me?"

"Because he wants you to know how much he loves you. This is God's gift to you."

Barbara riveted her eyes on Cinda.

She leaned in toward Barbara and gently placed her hand on Barbara's shoulder. "So I ask you, God, to bring wholeness to Barbara and healing to all the broken places within, healing from all the wounds that have been inflicted on her. Let her know how much you love her."

After a moment of silence, Barbara spoke. "I do feel so much better." Her countenance had changed. The sullen look of dejection was gone. Her face looked soft as she grabbed a tissue to wipe away her tears. "I do feel very different. All the jumble in my head has gotten still. Something happened. Thank you so much. I'll see you next week." Barbara picked up her purse, stood up, and turned toward Cinda. "Thank you again." She left the room.

I looked at Cinda. "I just wanted Lucinda to be an encouragement for her. I didn't expect you to come out, and I certainly didn't expect to see such a change in her. Did God really heal her?"

"God has touched her in a very deep way. She will not be the same."

*****

The next time I saw Barbara, her countenance was very positive. "I'm feeling so much better. I don't think I need to be on this antidepressant anymore. Would it be okay if I went off it?"

"That is not my decision. You need to talk to the doctor, and he will advise you."

"I have an appointment with him next week. I'll talk to him then."

"Good idea. Obviously, you are feeling much better. What changed?"

"I'm not sure, but my heart was so touched by what happened at our last session. Since then, I just feel so at peace."

"What about your alters? Are you hearing from them?"

"No, I can't say I am. My head is so much quieter. Will you please tell Lucinda and the one you called an angel how grateful I am for them? I can't explain it, but I feel so much better."

I mulled over what Barbara was telling me. Nothing spectacular had happened in our session with Lucinda and Cinda, at least not outwardly. But it was very obvious that something had changed in Barbara. Maybe it wasn't so outlandish to think that Cinda was an angel from God.

Dr. Kirkly had also been visibly touched by Cinda, who did nothing more than deliver the message God had for him. With Barbara, she had simply told her that God was giving her the gift of wholeness and then prayed for her. Yet both times, the results seemed profound.

The following week, I emerged from my office to find Barbara's doctor standing at my door with her chart in hand. "I just saw Barbara. What happened to her? She's an entirely different person. She wants to go off her antidepressant, so I started weaning her off. The change in her is startling."

I was caught off guard, not by the news of Barbara, but by the doctor's amazement. *What do I say to him?* It sounded as if Barbara had not said anything about her visit with Lucinda and Cinda. *Do I tell him she was visited by an angel?* My dilemma was solved as he turned around and walked back down the hall, muttering to himself about the extraordinary change in Barbara.

During the next few days, I contemplated whether or not I should tell him about Barbara's visit with Lucinda and Cinda. In time I did. He was quite receptive. In fact, he came to me a number of weeks later with concerns about his daughter who was having severe health issues. He wondered if the angel could be of assistance to her. When I told Cinda about it, she said that she would bring the matter to God. I was always concerned about how I would be perceived if I told people that I believed Cinda to be an angel. So far, my fears had been groundless.

I only saw Barbara a few more times before we decided that she did not need to be treated for depression anymore. We hugged warmly as we parted. She whispered in my ear, "Please, please, thank Lucinda and Cinda for all they have done for me."

I watched her leave, very grateful that she had found so much healing, but also a bit unsettled. Why couldn't God give the same kind of wholeness to Lucinda?

But then I remembered what an extraordinary gift he had given her, the chance to journey backward and start over.

*****

The following week, Sam arrived for Lucinda's appointment. This was always a cause for concern. Was Lucinda okay? Had the group gotten her? I was greatly relieved when Sam assured me that Lucinda was just fine.

"But there is something I need to tell you." Her voice was dead serious. After a pause, she took a deep breath. "The group was in your house."

"What? In my house? Why? When?" I felt like the bottom had dropped out of my stomach.

"I was close to the surface and heard them talkin'. They said they checked out your finances to see if maybe they could win you over with an offer of more money, but your finances were clean."

"Even if my finances were a disaster, I wouldn't take a single penny from them."

"Then they said that they needed your notes on Lucinda. So they sent someone to search your house."

"Search my house? When? Did they find anything?"

"They said it was an easy job. Your back door was open."

My heart sank. We often didn't lock our back door, more for convenience than anything else. I made a mental note to talk to my husband about making sure it stayed locked.

"Then they said they found the notes. In a bag."

My heart skipped a beat. I had taken all my files on Lucinda and put them in a straw beach bag, which I then hid in the back of a bedroom closet. My entire body felt limp. To think that these people had rifled through my house and that they had taken my notes on Lucinda was horrifying. "So they have all my notes?"

"Not now. They copied them all and then returned them. To cover their tracks."

"I don't know why my notes were so important to them. Copying all those notes must have been a monumental task. We're talking about over a decade of notes."

"Oh, they were real happy about havin' them. They were especially happy about one thing they read."

"What was that?"

"They read that once Lu integrated, she undid the integration and came back to say goodbye to you."

"What's the big deal about that?"

"Now they think they can find a way to undo the ones that have integrated."

I let out a long sigh and rolled my eyes. "These people will stop at nothing." I was really rattled.

"It's okay. God had them on a leash. They didn't take anything else from your house." It was Cinda, with her unruffled demeanor.

"Oh, Cinda. This is so disturbing. Not that they would take anything else. It's just knowing they were in my house looking around and took my notes. I feel violated."

"As I said, God has them on a leash. You need to trust in him."

"But what about all the information in my notes? And now they're going to try to break apart integrations."

"They will only do what God permits."

"I don't like that they know where I live."

"Remember, they're trying to stay hidden. That's why they returned the notes, to cover their tracks. You need to walk in trust."

"This whole deal feels really creepy to me."

That night I checked my closet as soon as I returned home. There, in the back, was the beach bag with all of Lucinda's notes. Nothing seemed amiss. It didn't look like anyone had been going through my closet. If the group had indeed taken it, they had covered their tracks well. When I told my husband about this latest occurrence, we agreed to keep the back door locked.

It took several days before I began to shed that uneasy feeling of having been violated. I found myself praying at odd moments for protection from this group. Sometimes this battle seemed so bizarre I could scarcely believe it was all true.

CHAPTER 18

Number Three

Lucinda's thirty-sixth birthday was coming soon. I decided I wanted to do something special for her. I usually gave her a card on her birthday and maybe a small gift, but I wanted to do more. As I thought about it, I knew what would absolutely delight child Lucinda. I also knew it would break all professional boundaries. I wrestled with the plan forming in my mind. Was I her counselor, or was I her spiritual mother? Could I be both? Was it advisable to be both?

In the end, I believe my heart (what I truly wanted to do for Lucinda) triumphed over my head (what was the professionally correct thing to do). I made plans for a special day.

I picked Lucinda up early in the morning. After she was seated in the car, I gave her a gift.

With childlike exuberance, she ripped the wrapping paper off the small box and opened it. "It's just like yours!" It was a silver name bracelet.

I clasped it around her wrist. On one side of the silver plate, her name was engraved. On the other side were the words *Spiritual Daughter*. I told her what was written on each side.

"I'll wear it all the time, just like you do."

"Now we can both remember the special relationship God has given us."

"Where are we going?' Lucinda asked.

"That is going to be a surprise. We have to drive for over an hour, so let's put on some music and enjoy the ride." With children's songs in the background, Lucinda and I made our way through rush hour traffic. When we arrived at our destination, I parked the car.

"Where are we?" Lucinda asked, as we made our way across the parking lot. "Who are all those other children?" We had made our way to a line of people, many of them parents with children. There were even a couple school busses parked along the road, emptying out long lines of excited children.

"We're at the zoo, Lucinda."

"What's the zoo?"

"You don't know what a zoo is? Well, you just wait and see."

We paid for our tickets and entered the zoo. We joined others walking along a sidewalk lined with bushes. Then suddenly, Lucinda let out a shriek. "Look, monkeys!" The first exhibit we came to was a large cage filled with monkeys swinging back and forth, rambunctiously chasing each other, and making high-pitched sounds. Lucinda ran to the cage, leaned up against the fence, and looked on in total fascination. She could hardly contain herself. "They're real monkeys! Look at them! Look how funny they are. Look at that little one. He's with his mommy." We stood there for about fifteen minutes while Lucinda took it all in.

While she watched the monkeys, I watched Lucinda. Her sheer delight was contagious. She squealed with delight at the monkeys' shenanigans. Other children were also excitedly watching the monkeys, but none were as captivated and stayed there as long as Lucinda. Occasionally, one of the children or one of the adults would see Lucinda and give her an odd look, but it didn't matter to me. She was an anomaly others would not understand. Lucinda was so absorbed in watching the monkeys that she didn't even notice.

Finally, I said, "Lucinda, a zoo is a place where they have all kinds of animals for people to see. Let's go see the other animals."

"Can we come back to see the monkeys again?"

"Yes, we'll pass by them on the way out."

So Lucinda and I spent an entire day at the zoo. She was totally captivated. With the exception of those in the reptile house, she was fascinated by every animal. The lions and tigers, the chimpanzees and gorillas, the otters and zebras and giraffes—she loved them all. Her uninhibited excitement was so endearing that I did not even care about the occasional sideways glance of confused people wondering about this thirty-six-year-old child.

We went through the lorikeet exhibit together, where these colorful, exotic birds would land on your arms and shoulders to drink from a cup of nectar. Lucinda positively beamed when the birds landed on her, infectiously laughing as they climbed her arm.

I looked on in amazement, so glad I had decided to do this. I felt myself brimming with love for her and overflowing with joy. As we left the zoo, stopping for one last look at the monkey cage, I noticed a peculiar thing. Several of the monkeys came over to where she was standing, sat across from her, and looked directly at her. For several minutes, they watched her, making soft monkey noises and showing their teeth. "Look, they're watching me."

"They must like you, Lucinda. Something about you is drawing them to you."

"Well, I like them too."

With great reluctance, we left the zoo. It had been a wonderful day. I couldn't have given her a better birthday gift. But the day had to end, and we had to return to the reality of her dark alters' involvement with this evil group.

On the way home, I brought up several questions that had been on my mind. "Lucinda, doesn't Kurt ever know that you are gone so much, especially in the middle of the night? Doesn't he get suspicious and wonder what's going on?"

"He goes to bed early because he has to get up so early, so he usually don't know I'm gone. And they always get me back before he gets up."

"But doesn't he ever wake up in the middle of the night and know you're not there?"

"That's happened, but the parts tell him I went down to my mom's because she needs me since she's sick with kidney disease."

"But don't you think he should know this group is getting you?"

Lucinda shook her head adamantly. “No, I don’t want him to know.”

“But maybe he could help to keep you from going.”

Again, she shook her head adamantly.

“Well, what about your boys? Don’t they know that you’re not home during the day?”

“They’re at school and do things afterward. Michael is really good at sports, so he’s always stayin’ after school. Mark is involved in after school stuff too. And Matthew hangs around with his friends. If I’m not there, they think I’m at my mom’s or my sister’s.”

Lucinda’s boys were teenagers now, so her story was plausible. But I wondered why she was so insistent that Kurt shouldn’t know about this group.

“It is important that Kurt not know what is happening.”

I recognized Cinda’s voice. “But why? This is his wife. Shouldn’t he know that she is being routinely tortured by these horrible people?”

“The problem is that he may go charging in there to rescue her. These are ruthless people who have no scruples. He would be putting himself in danger.”

I gulped. “But I’m involved in fighting against them.”

“But you are not crossing their paths. God has not called you to do that.”

“I think it’s incredible that he isn’t suspicious.”

“Sometimes Kurt sticks his head in the sand. He did that when she was involved in her grandmother’s group. He knew she was gone at night sometimes, but he believed her stories, partly because he wanted to.”

*****

I returned to the battle feeling strong and renewed. The late-night phone calls continued. Hardened alters still went to the group. There were still broken children to be held and healed. But with a newfound determination, I pressed on.

It was not surprising that my prayer life changed. I would vacillate between angry diatribes at God and desperate pleas on behalf of Lucinda. I would only be able to fight this battle with his strength, so I clung to him at the same time I questioned his goodness.

There were also times, like the day at the zoo, when I was filled to overflowing with a love and joy that I knew could only be from him. At those times, I felt deep awe and gratitude that he was allowing me to walk this path with Lucinda. I soon realized my prayer life had lost any veneer of propriety. It was raw, and it was real, filled with emotions and doubts and needs. I discovered the Psalms in a new way, those prayers that came from the deep struggles of godly men of millennia past. It was a comfort to know that an emotion-tossed prayer life had been experienced by others before me.

Cinda kept telling me I needed to be in my heart, not my head. "God speaks to your heart. You hear God in that deep place within. When you are in your head, you question and analyze, and you have no peace. When you are in your heart, God renews your mind."

I was discovering how much of a head person I was, always thinking and considering and using my rationality to understand things. Cinda was telling me there was another way to be, leading with your heart and allowing your renewed mind to follow.

I did not always understand what she meant, but there was so often a ring of truth about what she said. So I tried to be aware of times when I led with my heart, when I had an inner certainty about a decision or course of action that had not come from reasoning. I discovered that there was a settled quality about those times.

I also discovered that when I let my mind have free rein, it often led me to places of fear, anxiety, confusion, and doubt. I stumbled on a Bible verse: "The mind of sinful man is death, but the mind controlled by the spirit is life and peace."[5] Was this what Cinda was talking about? Being in this battle was affecting me in many deep ways.

*****

[5] Romans 8:6 (NIV).

Shortly after our trip to the zoo, a hardened alter came out in a session. I knew a switch had taken place when child Lucinda dropped her crayon and turned and glared at me. She looked at the blue crayon she had dropped. "What's that?" She had a disgusted look on her face.

"That's a crayon." I had worked with so many hardened alters that I was not in the least bit alarmed by this new one.

"What's a crayon? Where am I? Who are you?"

"A crayon is something children use to draw and color. I'm your counselor, and this is my office."

"Children? Children come here? Is this the playroom?"

"No, this is not a playroom. It's my office, but sometimes children come here, and I let them play."

"I don't know where I am. Where's Nevil?"

"Nevil is not here."

"He's not here?

"There's no one here named Nevil."

"Nevil's not here?" Her voice was starting to sound panicky. "I'm only supposed to be out with Nevil.

I tried to find my most soothing voice. "There's no reason to be afraid. You're safe here."

"I don't know what I'm doing here."

Hoping to disarm her, I introduced myself and asked for her name.

"I ain't got no name," she said with evident pride.

"What? You don't have a name? Everybody should have a name. I won't know what to call you."

"Having a name makes you weak."

I was used to parts withholding their name from me until they began to trust me. "Okay, you don't have to tell me your name yet, but I promise I won't use it against you should you decide to tell me."

"I told you I don't have a name." Now she was shouting at me. "I ain't got no name because names make you weak. I have to be strong."

"A name doesn't make you weak. It makes you human. It gives you a point of identity."

"You don't get it. I ain't got no name." She was silent for a minute. Then she blurted out, again with visible pride, "I got a number."

"A number?"

"Yeah, a number. What's it to you?"

"You have a number instead of a name."

"That's right."

Every alter I had met from Lucinda's large system of alters always had a name. Sometimes it took a while for them to trust me with their names, but sooner or later, they revealed them to me. Was claiming she had a number instead her way of keeping her name secret, or did she really not have a name?

I decided to tackle this head-on. "So, what is your number?"

Again, she glared at me. "None of your business."

"How will I know if I'm talking to you again if I don't know your name or number? I need a way to identify you, to tell you apart from the others."

"Only Nevil needs to know my number. You don't need to know it."

"You're right, I don't need to know your number, but I would like to know it." I picked up the blue crayon, turned over the sheet of paper Lucinda had colored on, and wrote numbers: 1, 2, 3, 4, 5, 6, 7, 8, 9, 10. "Is one of these your number?" I put the crayon down.

Much to my surprise, she picked up the blue crayon and made marks on the paper. "Hey, this is like what Nevil uses to keep notes on us. Are you going to keep notes on me too?"

After Lucinda was gone, I would write some notes on her, but she didn't need to know that. "Nevil keeps notes about you? Why would he do that?"

"So he can know which ones of us are strong."

"I bet you're one of the strong ones."

"I sure am. They say I can be very useful to them. Not like Numbers One and Two. They said the third time they got a good one."

"So, are you Number Three?"

She looked startled. "How'd you know?"

"Just an assumption from the things you said."

"Hey, you know too much." And with that she was gone.

I was face-to-face with child Lucinda. "Hey, what happened to my picture?"

I turned the paper over, and she continued to draw her picture of smiling stick figures.

"Lucinda, are you aware of any of the ones inside who have numbers instead of names?"

"We all have names," she said.

"Well, I just met one who says she's Number Three and doesn't have a name."

"I don't know any who don't have names." Lucinda was engrossed in her coloring.

I wondered if I had come upon another level of alters. The first level I met, over a decade ago, all had names that were variations of the name *Lucinda*: Lucy, Lu, Cinda, Lucia. Later, I met another level, the third level, whose names all began with the letter *T*: Tasha, Tara, Tiffany, Theresa, Terry, Tina. Then there was Dominique, who was looking for her star. Okay, all but one began with a *T*. Had I now come upon a level of alters who were all numbers?

I mulled over the meaning of this.

*****

My husband and I began including Lucinda when we went to various Christian events in our city. Many of them were on Sunday evenings, and I was always glad to have her with us, in hopes that she would not go to the group. The local churches were coming together on a regular basis specifically to pray for our city. Child Lucinda loved these events, but I would try to have hardened alters out so they could get exposed to people joyfully worshipping God. I wanted them to see there was an alternative to the dark world of the group.

The hardened alters would squirm in their seats and say they didn't want to be there, but I would catch them looking around with curiosity. One particular Sunday evening, after a time of worship and prayer, people were invited to come forward for personal prayer. I turned to the hardened alter sitting next to me and suggested we go up together for prayer.

Her hands were folded over her chest, and she adamantly shook her head.

"Come on, I think it would be good for you to find out what it's like when people of the light pray for you."

"I ain't goin' up for no prayer."

"Okay, I'll respect that."

"NanNan, can I get prayed for?" Child Lucinda unexpectedly burst out.

"Sure, let's go up together." I had no idea how this adult child would be received.

We waited in line for a few minutes until one of the people praying was free. I was very glad when I saw we were going to be ministered to by a man who was very powerful in God. I gently guided Lucinda over to him.

He took one look at Lucinda, and in a booming voice everyone could hear declared, "A trophy for the city." He prayed for her. I remember nothing of the content of his prayer. I was too busy contemplating his words.

What did they mean? A trophy is a prize, an award for a victory. Lucinda was going to be a prize for the city? What did that mean? Did it have anything to do with this battle we were fighting together? Was this an assurance that she would get the victory in this battle? One thing was certain: trophies and victories go together. Something inside me latched onto those words.

How could she ever be a trophy for the city if this group won her total allegiance? How would there be a victory unless she became unentangled from this satanic cult or drug ring or whatever it was? These were hope-giving words, and something deep in my spirit grabbed onto them. They became a life raft for me, and I would soon be holding onto them desperately.

CHAPTER 19

Krista

The next time I saw Lucinda in my office, I was feeling hopeful. After all, she was going to be a trophy for the city. The man who had made this booming pronouncement over her had a fine reputation as a gifted man of God. I felt I could trust his words. His words were hope-giving and life-giving.

So when Lucinda arrived for her appointment obviously distraught, I felt strong enough to remain level and not be pulled down. "Okay, Lucinda, I can see that you are not doing well. What's going on?"

Child Lucinda looked at the floor. Her hair fell across her face, which was buried in her hands. For a long time, she said nothing. Then she burst into tears.

I sat down next to her, putting my arm around her. "You need to tell me what is wrong."

"NanNan, they tried to take your bracelet from me. They said I had to give it to them. They said if I didn't, they would hurt me really bad. But I wouldn't do it. I told them they couldn't have it." She held up her wrist. There was the silver name bracelet I had given her.

"You were out with the group?"

She nodded.

"Did they hurt you?"

"No. They wanted to. They said they were gonna to take me to the room with the table, and when they were done with me, they were gonna to cut the bracelet off my wrist."

"But you still have it. They didn't get it."

"I was really scared. So when they took my arm to take me down to the room, I cried out to Jesus to help me. I didn't know what else to do."

"That was a good thing to do, Lucinda. Did he help you?"

"Yeah, he did. That fast, I was inside in the light, and someone else musta gone out."

I heaved a sigh of relief. "I'm so glad they didn't hurt you. The bracelet is just a thing that can be replaced, but I would have been devastated if they hurt you again." I was silent for a minute, wondering about the significance of the bracelet. "Why do you think they wanted the bracelet?"

"They said if I gave it to them, I'd be choosing them over you. I was so scared. I didn't want to choose them."

"I'm so glad you called to Jesus. You did exactly the right thing. If you are ever out with them again, call to Jesus. Maybe he'll pull you into the light like he did this time."

Lucinda nodded through her sniffles.

After Lucinda left, I contemplated what had happened. I remembered the note they had written me, offering me money to join them in working with Lucinda. They said they were interested in how the brain works under pain. Who were these people and what exactly did they want with Lucinda? At first, I thought they were a satanic cult. Then there was talk about them being a drug ring, wanting to use Lucinda's alters to make drug deals. Now they appeared to be interested in how the brain works, specifically how Lucinda's brain worked under pain. They obviously felt that her allegiance to me was an obstacle to their goals. Since they couldn't have my cooperation, they were hoping to win her over to their side.

While I was confident that child Lucinda would never give them her heart, I quaked at the thought of what they might do to try to win her over.

Then I remembered that phrase, *a trophy for the city*. If she was going to be a trophy for the city, somehow she would get unentangled from this horrible group of people. I needed to rest confidently in that.

*****

I was still spending time with the babies, Jacelyn and Erica. Jacelyn was now crawling around my office, much as Roxie had done. Erica was a true delight. She would look at me with eyes that sparkled, giggling and cooing and making baby babble. There were still times when they were tortured by the group, but invariably, as I held their head to my chest and they heard my heartbeat, healing would come, and they would bounce back to being winsome and endearing babies.

One particular session, Lucinda arrived looking very sad. "It's Erica. They musta really hurt her bad. She's not doin' good. She looks dead."

My heart was pierced by these words. I had such an affinity for this thirty-something baby. She was so innocent and full of life. The thought of the group inflicting unbearable pain on her was crushing. With a heavy heart, I called Erica out.

Her body lay limp in my arms. I held her head to my chest and prayed for God to do his healing work in her. For the longest time, there were no signs of life in her. When she finally stirred, she whimpered, then cried, then wailed and finally screeched like a dying animal. On and on it went. None of the others had ever displayed this much agony as they listened to my heartbeat for God to heal them.

I desperately sought to soothe and comfort her with my words, with my touch, with songs. Nothing stopped the agonized cries of this adult baby. Her body become rigid as the wails poured out of her. It seemed like an eternity before I detected her body relaxing. The intensity of her cries lessened. Gradually, the wails became whimpers, and the whimpers softened until she snuggled into me and fell asleep. I held her close to me and felt my own sense of total depletion. Would it ever cease to be this difficult to see these adult children in such distress?

As I watched her peacefully sleeping, I wondered why this had been such a difficult healing for Erica. What was different? Why did it take so long? Was I doing something different? Or was it the magnitude of what the group had done to her?

"Erica's okay now. God has healed her." Cinda interrupted my musings.

"Oh, Cinda, I'm so glad you're here. Why was this so hard for Erica? What did they do to her? Listening to her pain was almost unbearable."

"It is best you do not know what they did to her. The group is very angry that their plans are being thwarted. They are mad that Lucinda would not give them the bracelet. They are mad that Jacelyn and Erica and some of the others are babies. They are mad that you would not join them but continue to work against them. They are very powerful people who are used to having their way. They decided to teach the uncooperative parts and you a lesson by hurting Erica. They know that you have a soft spot for her."

"How do they know that?"

"The hard parts told them you really seem to like her."

I could hardly believe what I was hearing. I was speechless.

Cinda continued. "God saw how they tortured Erica. He was very angry. He has decided to intervene on behalf of Erica. From now on, unless she is out with you, she will be with me in the light. They will never be able to have her out again. She will be protected."

"Oh, Cinda, that is wonderful news. What about Jacelyn?"

"This is just for Erica. God knows what she endured last night. He will not permit it again."

I heaved a huge sigh of relief. To know that Erica would never again be tortured was such a relief. I silently thanked God for this special protection. But how I wished that protection could extend to Jacelyn and Steven and Sam and Lucinda. "Cinda, what can't that protection be extended to the others?"

"God's ways are not our ways. He has given Erica a special gift. We must be thankful for that and trust him with the rest."

I headed home that evening totally depleted by my time with Erica but also at peace. I certainly didn't understand God's ways in this matter, but I was grateful for Erica's special gift.

*****

I was truly not prepared for what surfaced in my next session with Lucinda. She arrived dressed in shorts and a T-shirt. We were well into the summer, so it would be a perfect day for a walk in the warm sun. The field across the street was now a full-blown construction site, so there would be no more walks in that field, but there was a nearby park that had a wonderful trail that followed a bubbling stream. I was still a bit unnerved by my last ordeal with Erica, so I decided a walk outside in the warm sun would be a nice break for both of us.

I was about to explain my plan to Lucinda, which I knew would delight her, but before I could get a word out, she jumped up from the love seat. "Where am I?" Another alter had appeared.

I hoped that I could quickly tend to this one so we could get to the park for our walk. "Hello. Have I met you before?"

The alter personality glared back at me. "Who are you?"

"I guess we haven't met. I'm your spiritual mother."

"What's a spiritual mother? And what am I doing here? Where's Linda?"

"Who's Linda? I haven't heard about her before."

"She's the one Nevil brought in to help with us. Nevil said he needed a woman for the little ones to attach to."

I mulled this over. A woman to attach to? I did not like the sound of this. "Why does he think the children need a woman to attach to?"

"Hell if I know. That Linda's a real twit. She tries to be all nice and sweet, but you can tell it's all an act."

I wondered how to draw this to a close so we could move ahead with the walk I had planned. "Can you tell me your name? That way I can call you out again, and we can get to know each other."

"I ain't got no name."

This sounded familiar. I remembered meeting Number Three. "Well, if you don't have a name, do you have a number?"

The alter personality looked startled. "How the hell did you know?"

"I met another one who had a number. What's your number?"

"That's none of your business. I gotta get outa here. You know too much." With that, this alter personality was gone.

I heaved a sigh and then stood up. Maybe now we could get on with my plans for a walk.

"Sit down. There are some things you need to know."

I instantly recognized Cinda's voice. "Okay, but I was really hoping to have a nice walk with Lucinda this afternoon."

"That will have to wait. It is time for you to know some things."

I confess I was slightly annoyed by this interruption to my plans. But I sat down to hear what Cinda had to say.

"You have encountered some of the numbered ones."

I nodded.

"You need to know about them. They are not like the other personalities who carry the pain of Lucinda's past. The ones with numbers were intentionally split off by this new group to be loyal to them. They intend to develop an army of numbered alters who will do whatever they're told. They got frustrated when you kept undoing what they were trying to accomplish with Roxie and Jacelyn and Erica." Cinda smiled. "Babies will not serve their purposes."

"They intentionally split them off? How could they do that?"

"Through inflicting pain. They discovered that Lucinda has an amazing ability to cope with inflicted pain by splitting. So they torture them until a part splits off. Then they give that new part a number and groom her to be loyal to them alone. It's the same thing Lucinda's grandmother did with the level that had all the *T* names. They were to be loyal only to her and the cult."

I sat very still, barely breathing. Cinda's voice sounded far away. I could not process what I was hearing. It felt like my mind had stopped.

Cinda continued. "That was what happened to Erica last week. They split off a part from her to use for their purposes, to be part of their army."

Slowly, what she said sank in. This heinous group was torturing Lucinda's alters to intentionally split off new parts, parts they would use for their own diabolic purposes. This was too much. I didn't know which was worse, that they could conceive of such a scheme or that they were actually carrying it out.

Everything inside me froze. I could barely think. I could not talk.

"It's okay. God knows what they are doing. He has a plan, and it is already in motion."

"What plan?" My voice was weak and quavering.

"Do you remember how things got scrambled before? Well, things got scrambled again. The numbered parts were only supposed to be out with Nevil and Linda. They programmed that into them. They were only to come out to the voices of Nevil or Linda and only when a code word was used. But they have found their way out with you."

"How did they do that?"

"That was God's doing. Now you need to undo what this group is doing."

"How am I to do that?"

"The first thing you must do is give each of them a name. They need to know that they are people, not robots."

That sounded easy enough. "Any name at all?"

"Whatever name God puts on your heart." Cinda continued. "Then start teaching them there is a whole world apart from the group. Teach them about God and his love for them. There is no power greater than God's love. As you do this, the work of this group will be undermined."

"That's the same thing I've been doing with all the alters who surface."

Cinda smiled. "So you know that you can do this. Win them over one by one."

I nodded weakly.

"You may go for your walk now. If a numbered one comes out with you, give her a name."

"After this news, I don't know if I have enough strength for a walk."

"Go. God will give you the strength you need."

So I called Lucinda back and told her we were going to the park for a walk. Her face brightened. We took my car on the short jaunt to the park.

There we followed the path, stopping to watch some ducks bobbing up and down in the stream, looking for food. I explained to Lucinda that when they stuck their heads in the water, tails pointing upward, they were looking for food.

"What kind of food is in the water?"

"Little bits of plants, maybe some bugs or little, tiny fish."

"Bugs. Yuck! Who would eat bugs?"

"A duck." We laughed and moved on.

I was still processing all that Cinda had told me. I had trouble keeping my mind on our nature walk, so I was a bit startled when Lucinda stopped. "Where the hell are we now?"

I collected myself and turned to this one that was out. Her jaw was set as she glared at me. "Are you the one that was out with me a little bit ago, the one that has a number?"

"Yeah. What is this place?"

"This is a park, and we are out in God's creation. God is the one that created everything there is, including you and me."

"God? Who's God? And he didn't create me. Nevil did."

"Oh no, Nevil didn't create you. Nevil just inflicted pain to split you off. God created you." I was surprised at my ability to be strong and sure of myself. Inwardly, I was still reeling from Cinda's revelations.

"I don't know what the hell you're talkin' about."

"You know, I don't know your number, but I don't have to know your number, because I'm going to give you a name. You are a person and not a machine, so you deserve a name."

The numbered part glared at me.

"Whenever I want to talk to you, I will call you out by this name." In my head I was searching around for an appropriate name for this part. Then it hit me, I will give these numbered ones names that connect to Jesus. There are any number of names that are derivatives of Christ. "How about Krista? Your name will be Krista. I think that's a beautiful name. It's good to meet you, Krista."

Krista continued to glare at me. Then she shouted, "I ain't allowed to have a name." And she was gone.

Lucinda looked at me. "Come on, NanNan. Let's see the rest of the park."

We walked down to the bridge, crossed over the stream, and headed back up the other side. Lucinda squealed with delight over the ducks and squirrels we saw, such a sharp contrast to the countenance of Krista.

I engaged with her the best I could, but inwardly, I was still recuperating from the bombshell that had been thrown at me.

*****

Knowing this group was purposely torturing Lucinda's alters to create an army was totally unnerving. By the time my next session with Lucinda arrived, I was still off-balance. Several late-night phone calls that failed to keep them from going to the group added to my distress.

Then, during our session, I had a limp, lifeless child to hold to my heart while God healed her. The healing took place quickly, but I couldn't help but wonder if this one had been tortured to split off a part. That question haunted me, leaving me emotionally empty.

As the wounded child ceased her whimpering and nestled down into me, I kept reminding myself that Lucinda was going to be a trophy for the city, trying to draw some encouragement from those words. As I held the child close, I watched her drift off to sleep.

As I studied her face, I became aware of a shift of personalities, the slight rolling of her eyes and fluttering eyelids. I watched to see what would happen. It seemed that another baby had come out. I wondered if it was Jacelyn or Erica. I waited to see if she would respond to me.

The little one opened her eyes and looked at me. There wasn't the same look of recognition that I usually received from the babies I knew. I looked into the eyes of this one and saw light, almost brilliant light emanating from her eyes. She looked at me and let out a soft coo. Then she smiled, a totally peaceful smile. She made soft baby noises, head snuggling into my breast, a bead of drool running down her chin. She, whoever she was, seemed completely content, filled to fullness.

I watched with fascination. Who was this child? Her eyes roamed the room, then focused back on me. I was mesmerized. The peace and contentment seemed to spill out of her and envelop me. We were locked in a moment of oneness. It felt like time stood still, that all eternity was somehow present as we gazed into each other's eyes.

"NanNan!"

"Lucinda, who was just out with me?"

"I don't know, but you got light again. Was it that angel?"

"No, it wasn't that angel. It was a baby. She seemed totally content, totally full, like her every need was met."

"I don't know who it was, but she musta rubbed off on you."

I laughed. "I guess she did. I feel full and content too. I'd love to know who she was."

"That was a gift from God to you. He knew you needed to be built up." It was Cinda.

"Cinda, who was that baby? I've never sensed so much contentment in my entire life."

She smiled. "That's the deepest Lucinda, her spirit, who receives everything she needs from God. She is totally content."

I cocked my head. "Really? Her spirit?"

"Yes, it's her child spirit. Everyone has a child spirit like that, hidden away deep within, a child who receives pure love from God. Most people are unaware of it, which is very sad. That child spirit receives pure love from God and is able to share that love with others. There is such a child in every person, no matter how broken they are outwardly. You have a child spirit like that. If you can find her, this battle will be much easier for you. Today, God gave you a glimpse of the eternal part of a person."

I sat very still. Had I really glimpsed the eternal part of a person? I felt like I was on holy ground. Quietly, I wriggled my feet out of my shoes. I had much to contemplate.

CHAPTER 20

Christine

Jacelyn and Erica continued to delight me. It was a special delight to be with Erica. Since she was now in the light all the time, I didn't have to contend with episodes of brokenness, which would sear my heart. One day I was playing with her, showing her a plush gray bunny with a blue bow on its neck, using the bunny to nuzzle her and talk to her. "Hi, Erica, I'm Mr. Bunny. And I like to snuggle little girls." I took the soft bunny and nuzzled it under her neck. She laughed with delight, reaching for the bunny and holding it close. "The bunny's soft, isn't he, Erica? And he loves you." I took the bunny and held it away from her. She reached for it.

"Buhhy," she said. Her attempt to speak was garbled, but I was sure of what she had said.

"That's right, Erica. This is a bunny." That was her first word. "You're starting to talk, Erica."

"Buhhy."

From that time on, Erica began to accumulate words at an amazing rate. Each time she was out, she would delight me with another word, including "mama."

Meanwhile, Jacelyn would crawl over to the edge of my couch, put her hands on the cushions, and lift her rear into the air, trying to stand up. She was further along in her development than Roxie had been when she integrated. I wondered how much longer before she would become one with Lucinda.

The day Jacelyn integrated, she had been crawling around the floor of my office, pulling toys out of the bottom drawer of a filing cabinet, throwing them around the room, and expressing herself with a litany of baby talk.

I sat on the floor with her, leaning against my couch. I reached for a simple children's book about Jesus and began to read.

Jacelyn reached for the book, trying to yank it out of my hands.

"Don't you want to know about Jesus? He loves you, Jacelyn. Look, here's a picture of Jesus." I showed her a picture of Jesus with children gathered about him.

"Yesus!" Jacelyn squealed.

"That's right. That's Jesus."

I pulled Jacelyn over to me and laid her head on my chest. She snuggled in while making baby babble, but in the midst of it, I heard the word "Yesus" several times. I held her until she fell asleep.

When I called Lucinda back, she looked up at me. She seemed especially peaceful. "NanNan, Jacelyn came into me. She's not there anymore."

I smiled down at her. "You are becoming more whole all the time." I thought back to Jacelyn's long journey with me, from the shell that was so hardened that the group wanted to use her to do drug deals. I remembered her crazed states when she was looking for a spaceship to take her away and when she painted their clothes dryer black. I remembered her being healed from drug addiction. I remembered her regression and development. She had traveled a long journey backward so God could heal her of all the atrocities that were done to her. She was a healthy baby when she merged back into Lucinda, free from all the brokenness and pain that marked her life.

I let out a long sigh. "God is truly doing an amazing work in you, Lucinda, healing you from the inside out."

Lucinda smiled. "Jacelyn was happy when she came into me. I can feel it."

I smiled too. And I wondered how much longer I would have Erica.

*****

Sam was still my inside help. When she could, she would draw close at the group and listen to what was happening. Several times, she was pulled out while doing this and became the victim of the group's activities, but she persisted in wanting to help me.

"They're really mad. They thought that by bringing a lady in they could win the little ones over. Ain't no way they're gonna do that because she ain't got the heartbeat. The last time they had Jacelyn out, they tried to get her to listen to Linda's heartbeat. Jacelyn just screamed."

"How do they know about my heartbeat?"

"Death told them that when you hold them and they listen to your heartbeat, they become babies. Then they think you're their mother. But they're really mad, because it ain't workin'. But I heard them say they have another plan. They said their plan to build an army of numbered ones is working real good, so this plan might work too."

The thought of another plan by this group did not sit well with me. I was almost afraid to ask and find out what diabolical scheme they had now concocted. I took a deep breath. "Okay, Sam, do you know anything about their new plan?"

"No, I don't, but I'll let you know if I find anything out."

"You are such a help, Sam. I don't know how I could ever do this without you."

"Well, you're helpin' us, so the least I can do is help you."

*****

It wasn't long before I met some new numbered parts. I gave each one a name that was a derivative of Christ: Kirsten, Kris, Christy. I wondered how many numbered parts there were and how many more such names I could come up with. I found myself jotting down possible names as they came to me. If the group was continuing to split off new parts, as I assumed they were, I might have to come up with other alternatives then derivatives of Christ.

I had no idea of the significance of meeting Number Twenty. She was about the fifth or sixth numbered part that revealed herself to me. The scrambling seemed to be working as more and more numbered ones found their way out in my office.

She seemed typical, a hard shell, totally devoted to the group. She looked wildly about my office. "Hey, you ain't Nevil. I work for Nevil." Her voice was loud. She almost seemed to be screaming. "I don't know what's goin' on. I'm only supposed to be out with them. This is the second time I been out when they ain't around. Nevil will be really mad if he finds out about it."

"Oh, have you been out with me before?"

"Hell no."

"When else were you out when Nevil wasn't there?"

"You ask too many questions." She spotted a picture of my new grandson on my bookshelf. "Hey, you got babies around here?"

"No, that's my grandson. They live in Vermont."

"Oh."

"Well, I assume you have a number. You need a name so you know you are a person, not a robot."

"We ain't allowed to have names."

"Well, I'm giving you one anyway. I will call you by this name whenever I want to talk to you." My mind was churning up the names that I had jotted down. I looked at her. She needed a strong name. "Christine," I announced. "Your name will be Christine. It means follower of Christ."

"I don't know what the hell you're talkin' about. I only got a number."

"Christine, you need to know you are a human being, God's wonderful creation, who deserves a name."

Christine glared at me. "Nevil better not find out about this."

Then she was gone.

*****

On a cold November evening, Kurt and Lucinda walked out of their city row home and headed to the nearby high school. They lowered their heads as they headed into the wind. Lucinda shivered inside her warm jacket. She was very excited to see her youngest son, Michael, make his debut as a high school wrestler. He was little and wiry, and even though he was just a freshman, he had landed a spot on the varsity team as a lightweight. After about ten minutes of trudging into the wind, they climbed the steps to the high school gymnasium.

The warm air of the lobby warmed their shivering bodies. They made their way across the lobby, crowded with teenagers and parents.

Upon entering the gym, Kurt spotted the section in the stands where the hometown fans were seated.

Lucinda followed as he made his way up the stands, greeting other parents dressed in school colors. Lucinda remained quiet. Before they left the house, Kurt had told her to not embarrass him by acting like a child. Lucinda sat down next to him, remaining very still, trying to hide that she was a child. As they waited for the match to begin, Lucinda looked about her and took it all in. There were so many people and so much noise. She started to feel a bit afraid.

Being a lightweight, Michael was one of the first wrestlers. Lucinda watched as he stepped onto the mat. There was a buzz in the stands as parents and schoolmates started cheering for him.

Lucinda watched her youngest son shake hands with his opponent. She was very proud of him. She felt a swell in her chest.

The match began. Fans screamed. Teammates chanted his name.

Michael and his opponent circled, each looking for an opportunity for a takedown. Michael lunged at the other boy's feet, grabbed his ankles, and pulled him down.

The fans around Lucinda screamed his name, cheering him on. One very overweight man was shouting his name in a loud and raspy voice.

It was too overwhelming for Lucinda. Her fear overcame her. Lucinda receded inside.

Another alter personality emerged. She looked around at the crowd, at the wrestling match, at the man shouting Michael's name. Where was she? Who were these people? Why was everyone shouting? Who was this man sitting next to her who seemed to be in a frenzied state?

Where were Nevil and Linda? She was only supposed to be out with them.

Number Twenty sat very still, trying to make sense of this chaotic scene.

When Michael won his match, such an uproar emerged that even Number Twenty was a bit shaken.

The man next to her jumped up and down, shouting, "He won. He won!" He shook his hands in the air.

Not knowing what else to do, Number Twenty raised her hands and shook them.

For the remainder of the match, she sat quietly and watched, wondering where she was and why she was there.

When the match was over, the man next to her stood up and made his way down the stands. About halfway down the bleachers, Kurt turned around, glared at her, and signaled for her to follow him.

Number Twenty, not knowing what else to do, followed him down, across the gym, through the lobby, and out into the cold night air. She followed him for several city blocks, walking a bit behind him. They arrived at a home in the middle of a block, and again, not knowing what else to do, she followed him in. She sat down in the living room and waited to see what would happen.

A short time later, Michael arrived home, all smiles and excitement over his victory.

The man slapped him on the back. "We'll order pizza to celebrate!"

Soon two other young men arrived. They congratulated Michael on his victory and listened as the man gave a blow-by-blow description, with some exaggerations, of how Michael had gotten the best of his opponent.

The pizza arrived, and they all chowed down with enthusiasm. Someone handed Number Twenty a slice.

She took the pizza, watched how they ate it, and followed suit. She had never eaten pizza before.

In time, the man announced that he was going to bed. He left the room and went up the stairs.

A short time later, the young men also went up the stairs, saying, "Good night, Mom," as they went.

Number Twenty sat on the couch and wondered what was going on. These young men addressed her as Mom. Was she their mother? Was this her house? Everybody acted as if she belonged there.

What about Nevil and Linda? Did she have two different lives? She slept on the couch that night, totally confused, but determined to figure this out.

*****

Number Twenty was awakened the next morning by the voices of the three young men, shouting back and forth to each other as they gathered their backpacks and books in preparation for school.

Michael was the last one out. He opened the door, slung his backpack over his shoulder, and looked over at her. "Bye, Mom. Thanks for coming to my match."

"Sure. I'm glad you won." She hoped that was an okay response. She didn't want these boys to know how confused she was.

After sitting still for a few minutes, examining the room she was in, she decided to do some digging. It appeared this was her house, these were her children, and that man was her husband.

She went upstairs and found the room he must have slept in empty. The bed was unmade, sheets crumpled, and a pillow lying on the floor. The man must have left before she was awake.

She opened the closet door. On one side of the closet were men's shirts and sweatshirts. On the other side were shirts that seemed more suited to a woman. She searched through them. She pulled one out and gulped. A dark-blue sweatshirt with a hood. Emblazoned across the front was a picture of a white tiger cub. She remembered wearing this shirt the last time she was out with Nevil. Everything seemed to indicate that this was indeed her home.

Next, she headed up to the third floor. These two rooms were filled with teenage boy belongings: sports paraphernalia, a guitar, sneakers, and sweatshirts littered the floor. The beds were unmade. A desk was covered with dirty dishes and empty soda cans. Her first instinct was to start cleaning up the mess, but then she remembered that she had some investigating to do.

She descended the stairs and went into another bedroom. This one was also a boy's room. On the dresser was a picture of Michael in a football uniform. But in stark contrast to the rooms upstairs, this one was neat as a pin, everything put away. All the surfaces seemed to be dusted. She opened the closet. The clothes were hung in a neat row. She chuckled to herself as she surveyed the room. "This must be Michael's room. He sure is fussy."

There was one more room at the end of the hall. She opened the door, took a step into the room, and stared at what was around her. Tall glass display cases were filled with large dolls with finely made clothes and innocent expressions. She peered closely at these dolls. Obviously, these were not children's toys. They were carefully arranged and well cared for. At the end of the room was a corner filled with lifelike baby dolls, some in cribs, some propped into sitting positions. Along the window were stuffed animals of many varieties: dogs, teddy bears, lots of monkeys, and a white tiger cub that matched her sweatshirt.

This room would have been the delight of any little girl. Was there a girl in this family that she knew nothing about? She went over to the white tiger cub and picked it up. Something about the animal resonated with something inside her. She held it close. As she did, she felt an inward presence draw near. It felt like a child's presence. She quickly put the tiger back on the windowsill. Now was not the time to get sidetracked.

She spent the next several hours carefully searching the house. She found boxes of photographs, which showed her as a younger woman holding babies. She found many pictures of those three young men, starting as babies and then as young boys, and finally as teenagers. There were many pictures of her with the man, one of which appeared to be a wedding picture. She was in a white dress; he was in a sailor suit. She found legal documents and discovered that together they had signed a rent-to-own agreement on this house.

She saw that her name was Lucinda, and his name was Kurt.

When she felt that she had enough information, she decided the house needed a good cleaning. If she was going to live in this place, it had to be neat and clean. As she cleaned, Number Twenty tried to make sense of her situation. If she was the mother of these boys, she needed to know what was expected of her.

For the first time, she began to ask herself about Nevil and Linda. Who were they, and why was she involved with them? Why did they call her Number Twenty when she had a name? Why did they hide from her that she had a life apart from them?

Nevil had said her job was to go inside and find the children, especially the babies, and push them out to be with him. She never questioned this. Never wondered why he wanted the children and babies out. She was told to do whatever he asked of her, and she was very compliant.

For the first time, she questioned his motives. What was he doing with the children and babies? He said he wanted them because the younger they were, the easier it was for them to be spilt. What did that mean?

Could Nevil be trusted? After all, he had hidden from her that she had another life. Did she really have to do whatever he asked?

She pondered these things as she cleaned until she lay down in exhaustion, falling asleep on the couch.

*****

It was Sam who emerged when she awoke. Sam looked around the room, surprised at how neat and clean it was. Child Lucinda must not have been out. She checked the time. The boys and Kurt would be home soon. She knew she had a counseling appointment late in the afternoon. She went into the kitchen, which was also spotless, and put some dinner in the oven. There would just be enough time to eat before Kurt needed to drive her to her appointment.

Sam arrived for her appointment, but Number Twenty quickly emerged. She was still processing the confusion she felt from her unexpected appearance at the wrestling match. When she was told her new name would be Christine, she wondered about the name, Lucinda, that had been on the legal documents.

Who was she? Was she Number Twenty who was to do whatever Nevil and Linda told her? Was she Lucinda, who was married to Kurt and had three boys? Or was she Christine? And who was this woman who was giving her a name?

The confusion was too much, and she receded back inside.

*****

Over the next couple of months, Christine would frequently be out in our sessions. She was sullen and detached. She eyed me suspiciously and offered very little information.

I had no idea that she was trying to figure out who I was in her life. I tried everything I could think of to engage her, things that had worked with the other alters. I spoke to her about Lu, how she came to trust me, and before she left, she told the others to listen to me, that I was there to help them. It seemed that all the others would respond to the name of Lu.

Not Christine. There was no recognition in her eyes. I assumed it was because she was split off after Lu had integrated. Lu meant nothing to her.

I reassured her she was safe with me, that I would not hurt her. I told her I was her spiritual mother. She was unmoved by this title. I tried to explain to her what it meant to be her spiritual mother, that I was there to teach her about God and his love for her. All to no avail. There was an impenetrable quality about her that left me frustrated.

At times, it was hard not to be short with her. I felt such a strong need to win her over, to pry her away from this evil group that had split her off for their own fiendish reasons.

After a particularly frustrating interchange with her, I threw my hands in the air. "I just don't know how to reach you!"

Cinda emerged. "You are trying too hard. All you need to do is love her. She has never known love before."

As usual, her words hit the mark. I hung my head. "I know. I'm doing a very poor job of loving her. I just get so frustrated when nothing I do works. I just want her to see the truth about this awful group."

"You are trying to do it in your own strength. Just let God's love flow through you. You must be patient. Everything is new to her. It may take time, but it will be worth it. Christine is very important. She is going to be a big help for you."

I took in Cinda's words. "Sometimes I feel so desperate to get them out of this group. I don't want it to take time. Then I get angry about this whole situation. I don't want them tortured anymore. Then I get angry at God, so I guess I try to make things happen, to fix the whole dreadful mess. I feel it's all up to me."

"You need only to love them. God will do the rest."

"Well, I wish he'd do it soon." I couldn't hide the rancor in my voice.

Cinda smiled. "Just remember God loves them and is working on their behalf. Everything has gotten scrambled, and Christine has found her way out with you."

CHAPTER 21

The Snow Angel

In the midst of a long, cold winter, I found joy in baby Erica and child Lucinda. Erica crawled about my office, laughing with delight at the toys I would strew across the floor. Her vocabulary grew. She even showed signs of wanting to get up onto her feet.

If I pulled her up and held onto her, she would teeter back and forth for a few seconds before she would collapse in a heap. "Up, up" she would squeal, wanting to again try her skill at standing.

How long before she integrates? I wondered.

Child Lucinda was both a joy and a challenge. She was so full of energy that she would wear me out. One cold Sunday afternoon, just after a several inches of snow had blanketed the area, I picked Lucinda up and brought her to my house. We had a deliverance session that evening, but I picked her up early so my husband and I could spend some time with her.

As we walked from the car to our house, Lucinda saw my husband shoveling snow. She ran through the snow to him, squealing with delight.

He playfully threw some snow at her.

She in turn, grabbed a handful and threw it back at him.

I watched as a snow war erupted.

As they chased each other about with handfuls of snow, I ducked inside to put on boots and gloves.

After I bundled up, I emerged from the house with the words, "Hey, Lucinda, let's build a snowman."

"A what?"

"A snowman. Come on, I'll show you."

Joby joined in as we rolled the snow about to form a large ball for the base. Lucinda watched with curiosity and then joined in the fun. When we had the traditional three balls piled on top of each other, I pointed to the small one on top. "That is going to be his head."

Lucinda cocked her head. "And that's his body." She pointed to the middle ball. "But where are his legs?"

"Snowmen don't have legs."

Lucinda squinched up her face as she contemplated this. "No legs? Then it's not a man. It must be an angel. Let's make her wings. Angels don't need legs because they fly."

Hubby and I smiled at each other and then went to work with her, forming, as best we could, a set of snow wings.

"She needs hair," Lucinda squealed.

After a moment of thinking, Joby shook his head with a satisfied smile. "I know just the thing." He marched through the snow to two large clumps of pampas grass that had not yet been cut back from the previous season. Their feathery fronds were still intact despite being partially weighed down with fresh snow. He pulled out his pocketknife and cut off a number of the fronds. Together we stuck them in her head, forming a soft wreath of curly hair. We all stood back and admired our handiwork.

"But where's her face?" Lucinda lifted her hands, palms upward.

"I'll get what we need for her face." I went to the house, emerging a few minutes later with the traditional carrot for her nose and some shiny decorative stones. We gave the snow angel eyes, a nose, and the standard buttons. Then we found some sticks, which we used to form her mouth.

"She's looking pretty good," Joby observed.

"But she needs one of those things over her head." Lucinda encircled her head with her fingers.

"You mean a halo." Now I was thinking hard. What could I use to make a halo? Some kind of hoop. But it would have to be gold or silver.

"I've got an idea." I headed back to the house and found an embroidery hoop that I hadn't used in years. I covered it with aluminum foil, grabbed a coat hanger, and headed back outside. I let Joby do the engineering as he attached the hanger to the hoop and stuck it onto the snow angel's head.

Lucinda clapped her hands. "She's a real snow angel!'

"One more thing." I headed back inside. I emerged with a trumpet, a Christmas decoration. We found another stick to prop up the trumpet.

"It's her arm," Joby said. Then he stuck another stick on her other side. "She needs two arms."

As the late afternoon sun receded, the three of us stood back and admired our handiwork. Hubby grabbed his camera and took some pictures. She was indeed a lovely snow angel.

"She's better than just an ordinary snowman," I observed.

"She's neat. She's the best snow angel ever." Lucinda was beside herself with excitement.

It was dusk now. A chilly breeze started to blow.

"Don't angels have candles?" Lucinda asked.

"We can give her a candle." I went inside and returned with a candle in a candlestick holder and some matches. I placed the candle on the ground in front of her and lit the candle. It was indeed a delightful sight. Just then, the breeze picked up and blew the candle out.

"Ooh," we all sighed, not wanting the moment to end. I reached for the matches only to be taken back by the candle relighting itself.

"How did that happen?" I exclaimed.

Lucinda squealed with delight. During the next few minutes, we watched in amazement as the flame repeatedly was blown out by the wind, but then relit itself.

Hubby, ever the science guy, tried to figure this out. Lucinda jumped about in excitement. I watched this unfold, not knowing what to make of it but enjoying every second.

Finally, the flame was blown out a final time. We all watched, but this time, it did not relight. Our magical moment was over.

At a later time, I told Cinda about making the snow angel, how it had been such an enjoyable and bonding experience. Then I explained to her the mystery of the candle relighting itself.

"Oh, God was just having fun with you."

Having fun with us? That jarred me a bit. It certainly shed a new light on this God I worshipped. In the midst of this horrible battle with this heinous group, in the midst of holding tortured, broken children, in the midst of wondering how long I could continue to fight this battle because I was so depleted, God took time to have fun with us? It seemed incongruous, yet somehow it felt so right simply because it was so unexpected. Fun in the midst of battle. The mystery of the divine.

*****

The snow angel.

The following week, Sam arrived for a session. I knew instantly that something was wrong. "What is it, Sam? You don't look too good."

Sam lowered her eyes. It was as if she didn't want to look at me. When she spoke, it was in a hushed tone. "They got Lucinda."

My heart skipped a beat. I tried to keep my voice level. "Oh no. She's been doing so well staying inside when she knew they were with the group. How did they get her? Didn't she know where she was?"

"Remember I told you that they had another plan. Well, it worked."

How could I forget Sam's report that they had another plan? I gulped. "What was their plan?"

Sam hesitated. "I think you'd better tend to Lucinda first. She needs you."

It seemed as if Sam didn't want to tell me about their new plan. "Okay, I'll have Lucinda out." I braced myself for what I was about to see. "Lucinda, can you come out?" Nothing happened. I tried again. "Lucinda, this is NanNan. You're at my office. You can come out." Again, nothing happened.

Sam spoke up. "I'll go in and push her out. I don't know if she's not hearin' you or if she's afraid to come out." Sam was gone, and Lucinda's body was in the *no one's out* trance that I had experienced so often in my early work with her.

I waited for about a minute until Lucinda's body fell sideways onto the couch and lay there lifelessly.

I moved next to her and pulled her toward me, trying to get her head onto my chest. As I pulled her toward me, her eyes opened, and I saw those deep pools of pain and brokenness that never failed to sear my heart. I desperately pulled her in and laid her head on my heart. This was child Lucinda, usually so full of life and light. I remembered her unbridled joy as she watched our snow angel take shape, her unadulterated innocence as she played in the snow. What had they done to her? How dare they try to destroy a pure child?

My heart broke as I clutched her and held her head to my chest. *Dear Lord, please let my heartbeat heal her. She doesn't deserve this.* I avoided looking at her eyes as I held her close, but when I thought I detected her stirring, I sneaked a peek.

Tears flowed from her eyes. This was followed by the most dreadful wails interspersed with cries of "No, Mommy, no, Mommy."

I tried to soothe her with soft touches and whispers. The wails and cries went on and on. I tried to make eye contact with her, hoping to bring her out of her memories, whatever they were. But it was as if she did not see me.

Finally, the wails and cries lessened, until she was softly whimpering. At that point, she looked into my eyes, her eyes still pools of pain. "NanNan."

I could barely discern her voice, but I knew she saw me. I gently rocked her back and forth until she fell asleep.

A few minutes later, I called Sam back. "What did they do to her?" I wasn't sure I wanted to hear the answer.

"The usual. They stuck things up her." I didn't want to ask what things.

"But how did they get her out? She knows not to come out to any voices other than mine."

"That was their new plan."

"What do you mean?"

"They had a tape recording of your voice. They used it to pull her out. They used the ones you made for them a long time ago."

My heart skipped a beat.

Those recordings I had made for Lucinda, soothing and reassuring words, meant to comfort her when I could not be with her. That they had used these tapes for such heartless reasons infuriated me. I said nothing but stewed inwardly.

"But that's not all. There was more to their plan."

"Oh?" I wanted to put my hands over my ears and scream for her not to tell me. My heart was pounding.

"Her mother was there."

"Her mother was there?" I couldn't believe what I was hearing. "What was her mother doing there?"

"The group got her to come help them."

"What? Her mother participated in torturing her? How could she do that to her own daughter?"

"Remember when they offered you money to help them?"

"You mean they paid her?"

Sam nodded.

"How do you know that?"

"After they were finished with Lucinda, I drew near the surface to see if I could help her. I saw them hand her a bunch of money."

I was stunned. This was too much. Her own mother participated in torturing her daughter for money. I didn't know which was worse, that she was part of this scheme or that she did it for personal gain.

"It didn't work when they tried to get Linda to be our mother, so they thought that we might be drawn to our own mother, that if we attach to her, they can get us away from you. But the problem is, she ain't got the heartbeat. They might think it's gonna work, but it won't. The others…they still want a mother, but they're looking for the one with the heartbeat. They've given up on their own mother."

Another infernal plan. When would it all end? Lucinda's mother lived in a constant state of poverty. How much had they paid her? How much would be enough to participate in torturing your own daughter?

I realized that dwelling on this would only fill me with contempt for this woman. Instead, I said a silent prayer thanking God for the gift of my heartbeat.

*****

The next time I saw Lucinda, she was subdued. When I asked about her experience with the group, she shuddered. "I didn't know my mom would be there." Her eyes filled with tears. "Why don't she love me?" She wept for a few minutes, tears streaming down her cheeks.

I held her hand, wishing there was something I could say to ease her pain.

When she finally spoke, I could barely hear her. "They hurt me again, but the really bad part was seeing her. They even had her do it some, stick things in me. I kept asking her to stop, but she just kept doin' it." She looked at me with those pain-filled eyes. "All I ever wanted was a mommy to love me. Why don't she love me?"

I had no answer for her. We sat in silence for several more minutes.

Finally, I spoke. "It breaks my heart that you had to go through that."

"I'm sorry, NanNan. I heard your voice, and I thought you were there. Once I saw my mom, I got all mixed up. I didn't even remember to call to Jesus to help me, like I did last time they had me out."

Anger rose within me. How could this group be so fiendish? And how could her mother be so heartless? I wanted to throw something across the room. Silently I prayed. *Help me, Lord. I want to respond to Lucinda in a positive and constructive way.*

While I tried to collect myself, Lucinda said, "NanNan, I'm sorry. I don't want you to be so sad. I'm so glad God gave me a spiritual mommy who won't hurt me. Thank you for being my spiritual mommy."

Her comments totally disarmed me. The anger melted away. "I'm just so sorry you had to go through all that. I hurt because someone I love is hurting."

Lucinda threw her arms around me. "I love you, NanNan. You're the best spiritual mommy ever."

I laughed in response. "I'm not perfect, but I do want the best for you."

Lucinda planted a big kiss on my cheek. "Let's do something fun."

Amazing! Lucinda was bouncing back from her dreadful ordeal. Her resilience was astounding.

"I have some very good news for you." Cinda looked at me with those peaceful eyes. "God saw what happened to Lucinda. He saw what they did and felt Lucinda's pain. You know, the pain of having her mother be part of the group was worse than the physical pain. God has had enough. From now on, Lucinda will be protected. The group will never again be able to get her. They will try, but she will be protected in the light. They think they have found a way to have her out, but it will never work."

I wanted to jump up and down and cheer. "Thank you, thank you, Cinda. Now both Lucinda and Erica are protected." I paused for a moment. "But what about the other children. Will they be protected?"

"It's just for Lucinda. And Erica too. They will still be able to get the others."

I felt my heart sink. "Why can't he protect all the children? They don't deserve to be tortured, either." I was indignant.

"God's ways are not our ways. He is giving a special gift to Lucinda. For the others, he has given the gift of your heartbeat."

I wanted to rejoice, but simultaneously, I was crestfallen. Child parts would still be tortured to split off new parts. Sometimes I did not understand this God I worshipped. He would not tolerate them inflicting such pain on Lucinda or Erica, but he would tolerate it for the others. "I don't get it, Cinda. Sometimes I just don't understand God."

"He is giving you and Lucinda a gift. Receive it with gratitude. And you need to trust him with the others." Cinda departed.

"NanNan, what can we do that's fun?" Lucinda's eyes were once again full of life.

"First, I have some great news for you. Cinda told me that from now on, God is going to protect you. The group will never be able to get you out again, no matter what they try."

"They'll never get me again?"

"Never."

Lucinda clapped her hands. "What about the others?"

"This is just for you. The others will still have my heartbeat to heal them."

"Oh, I wish it was for the others too."

"So do I. I guess we just have to trust that God knows what's best. Now let's have some fun."

I put on some music, and we danced about my office as we chanted, "No more group, no more group." Despite my many questions, I was able to rejoice.

CHAPTER 22

Christine's Child

As the weeks went by and the winter snows gave way to blustery March winds, the battle to free Lucinda from the group wore on. There were still late-night phone calls, broken children to be healed, and hard, angry alter personalities to be broken down so they might become children.

I fought to keep my head above water. Child Lucinda and Erica, who was now toddling about, were my bright spots. They gave me hope that this whole process was actually moving in a positive direction.

More and more of my time, both in sessions and on the phone, was being spent with Christine. I soon began to understand that she took in everything I said. Even though she was usually hard and abrasive, she was like a sponge. Nothing got by her. She watched and absorbed everything I said and did.

When I would hit her impenetrable walls, I tried my best not to react to her, but my frustration often spilled out in harsh words. Despite that, she began to consider the things I said and to question the group herself.

The first indication that Christine was beginning to trust me came when she explained in detail her role with the group. Nevil realized that she was strong enough and crafty enough to go within and find others that she could push out to be with him. He was especially interested in the babies and would send her on missions to find them and bring them out to him. She dutifully obeyed him and basked in the praise he would give her. When she shared this with me, I explained to her exactly what Nevil wanted with the babies.

"Christine, do you realize what he is doing with the baby parts? He tortures them until the pain is so unbearable that they split off another part."

"How would you know that? He says he's using them to understand how we work. He's fascinated by us. He says we can be a whole army just by ourselves."

"I know what he's doing because I hold the babies after he's tortured them. I see the pain in their eyes and hear their cries. Trust me, he is ruthless and up to no good."

Christine considered what I told her and decided to search this out on her own. After she had forced a baby part out to be with Nevil, she drew close enough to the surface to be able to detect what was going on. She could see his cruel acts and even feel some of the pain the baby was experiencing. For the first time, she began to question Nevil and his motives.

She was no longer blindly obedient.

*****

Child Lucinda peeked out from within. She saw the boys tussling with each other as they got their books and put them in their backpacks. "Bye, Mom," they shouted as they swung open the front door. They ran down the front steps, still gently pushing and shoving each other.

The house would be empty. She wanted to come out and play. There was that room upstairs filled with dolls and stuffed animals and coloring books and crayons. She had so much fun in that room, but it had been a while since she had played there.

She wasn't allowed to come out whenever she wanted anymore. A new one seemed to be in charge now, and when that new one was out, it felt like she hit a wall if she tried to emerge. She didn't know where this one came from, but she knew NanNan called her Christine. Maybe if she tried to talk to her, she would let her come out to play.

Christine, Christine, she said in her inner world.

"Whad'ya want?"

Can I come out to play? I don't get to play in my doll room anymore.

Christine knew the group was supposed to pick her up at nine o'clock. She was also beginning to understand that this group was not looking out for her best interests. She saw how Nevil tortured the babies and decided she didn't want to be part of that.

What would happen if she didn't go today, if they came to pick her up and no one came out to meet them? There were some inside that would respond to a phone call from them. Certain words would bring them out, and they would robotically respond to what they were told to do.

Christine rolled this around in her head. She was strong enough to keep Lucinda in, but not those who were being drawn out by a hypnotic suggestion. But if Lucinda was out, and she was right behind her, maybe the two of them together would be strong enough to block the others. Christine thought it might work. "Okay, Lucinda. You can come out to play."

Lucinda burst into the room, excited to be out. "Thank you, Christine. Let's go to the doll room. You can play with me." She excitedly ran up the stairs.

She opened the door to the doll room and looked about with childlike wonder. The babies…she saw the babies and made a dash for them. "The babies missed me while I couldn't get out," she explained to Christine. "They need me to play with them and take care of them." She gathered several of them into her arms. "They're hungry. Nobody has been feeding them. I'll get them breakfast in the kitchen."

With baby dolls clutched to her chest, Lucinda scampered down the stairs and into the kitchen. She sat each baby at a chair around the table and darted to the refrigerator.

Oh no, Christine thought. *She's gonna make a mess.* When Lucinda reached for some eggs, Christine burst out. "You can't play with the eggs. Give them some cereal instead." She took a box of Cheerios out of the cabinet and set it on the table. Then she receded.

"Okay, they like cereal too." Lucinda found a bowl and poured some Cheerios in. She found a spoon and began to feed each one, Cheerios spilling off the sides of the spoon and onto the table and floor.

Inwardly, Christine rolled her eyes, thinking of the mess she would have to clean up. But she and Lucinda needed to be side by side, not allowing any space for other parts to come out.

The phone began to ring.

Lucinda was immersed in her play, seemingly oblivious to the ringing phone.

Christine wondered if it was the group. It was a few minutes past nine. She felt some pressure from the inside, as if someone was pressing to come out. She stood her ground next to Lucinda, who told the babies it was time for their baths. Christine let Lucinda go back upstairs and into the bathroom, clutching the three baby dolls.

The phone stopped ringing. When Lucinda turned the water on to fill the tub, Christine reached out and turned the spigot off. "Just pretend there's water in the tub." Very quickly, she resumed her place right next to Lucinda.

The phone rang again. Christine felt an inner pressure seeking to push her out of the way.

Lucinda took the clothes off the babies. "You're all so dirty because nobody gave you a bath while I couldn't be out." Once their clothes were off, strewn randomly across the bathroom floor, Lucinda dumped the dolls into the bathtub and proceeded to go through the motions of washing them. Then she grabbed a towel off the rack and wrapped it around the three babies. "You look so clean now. After we put your clothes on, you can play." She sat on the bathroom floor, and looked at all the doll clothes, wondering which ones belonged to which baby.

That one wears the blue-and-white dress, Christine whispered to her.

"Thank you, Christine." With Christine's help, she dressed the babies.

Christine was so close she began to share in Lucinda's child-like innocence. There was something compelling about it, a freedom Christine had never experienced. The world seemed simple and uncomplicated. She was just in the moment, caught up in the experience of dressing the three baby dolls. Christine wasn't aware of it, but her own inner child was accessing the moment. Christine even asked Lucinda if she could play with her again. *This is fun.*

But she was jolted away from her moment of child joy by the sudden sound of banging on the front door. It was a loud and insistent banging.

Christine knew it was the group, very angry because no one had emerged from the house and no one had answered the phone. On and on the banging went.

Lucinda seemed oblivious, totally immersed in her play. The dolls were dressed, and she was heading down the hall to the doll room.

Christine maintained her station right next to Lucinda, not allowing a crack between them.

Voices inside said they had to get out…someone was here for them…they would be in big trouble if they didn't go.

Christine stood firm.

Lucinda was down on her knees with crayons in hand, telling her dolls it was time to color.

Next Christine heard banging on the back door, the same loud, insistent banging. She stood firm despite the inward pressure to give way. After an extended period of time, the banging ceased, and the house was once again quiet.

Christine let out a sigh of relief. It was the first time she defied the group. She had a mind and will of her own. That felt very powerful. Maybe she didn't have to live two different lives. Maybe she could have a life here with her three boys, without the group.

She thought about Matthew, Mark, and Michael. They were *her* boys, and she felt a stirring inside—such a strong connection with them. They meant a lot to her, much more than the group ever would.

This was the life she wanted. She wanted to be their mother.

"It's time for your nap now." Lucinda placed each doll into a crib. "Night, night. Mommy will see you when you wake up. I love you."

Christine smiled to herself. Whatever a mother was, that was what she wanted to be.

*****

The next time I saw Christine in my office, she was her usual hard and impenetrable self. I had no idea that inwardly something had shifted. When she walked in my office door, she lowered herself onto my couch, arms firmly crossed in front of her. I braced myself. Dealing with the hard Christine was exhausting.

I tried to find my most calm and soothing voice. "Good afternoon. I assume this is Christine?"

She nodded. "Yeah, it's me."

"It seems that you are the one who comes to sessions most of the time now. You must be out a lot."

Again, she nodded.

"Are you the one who's taking care of things around the house and tending to the boys?"

"Yeah, that's me. The others are useless. Especially that Lucinda. If I'm not out, the house is a mess, and the boys run wild. I'm the only one who can keep things running smoothly." After a moment of silence, she resumed. "One thing about the group is that everything is structured and in order. I like that."

"So, you're still going to the group?"

"Yeah. The other day, Lucinda and I were able to block the others from going, but the next morning they got us. But I was able to pull one over on Nevil. He's such a twit. He didn't even know what was happening." Christine forced a laugh.

"What did you pull over on him?"

"He wanted us to bring a baby out to him. But I showed him." There was evident pride in her voice. "Instead of pushing a baby out, I came back out and acted like a baby. He thought if he hurt us enough, we'd split. But he couldn't get me to split. He was really mad. I just kept thinkin' about actin' like a baby and trying to keep him fooled. When he was stickin' stuff up me, I tried to not be there, to not feel the pain, and to keep actin' like a baby. He couldn't figure out what was goin' wrong. You know, you were right. They used me to get the babies, but no more. They're just little babies. They don't deserve that. I'll take it for them."

I looked at Christine, sitting there with arms folded, encrusted with self-protecting walls. I was truly amazed. Underneath all that armor was a will and a heart I had not seen before. She had willingly endured the pain to protect the babies. And she had fooled Nevil in the process, enduring the pain in such a way that she had not split.

Admiration welled within me. "Christine, that is truly amazing, that you sacrificed yourself on behalf of the inner babies."

"Well, you do what you gotta do." Her arms were still folded.

Obviously, she was not about to let her walls down with me. "You're like Lu. You're a protector."

"I don't know who the hell Lu is, but yeah, I'm a protector, and Nevil's not gonna hurt those babies anymore, not on my watch."

*****

The weeks wore on, and Lucinda's parts still found ways to go to the group. I still held broken children who had been wounded at the group to let them hear my heartbeat. At times I was so agitated that I was tense and could not relax and let the children settle in to receive their healing. When the healing would not come easily, my agitation often increased, and I became cross and irritable. When this happened, Cinda was likely to appear so she could have a few words with me.

"You are trying too hard. You are trying to make the healing come in your own strength. You cannot heal them. Only God can. You need only to love them. As you allow God's love to flow through you, the healing will come."

"But how can I relax when I see that pain in their eyes and hear their cries of distress?" The tone of my voice screamed out my exasperation.

"You need to stop looking at the pain and remember the wonderful gift God has given you. This time of letting them hear your heartbeat is not just for them. It's for you too. You will be built up as you see God at work. And God will use this time to bring you and your spiritual daughter closer together."

I let out a long sigh. "I know you're right. God seems to work most powerfully when I feel the most love for them. But sometimes, I just can't get there."

"Take this time to enjoy your spiritual children."

So I tried again, seeking to keep my focus off the pain and on God's healing power. I sought to find gratitude in my heart that God had given me this amazing gift for their healing. I tried to yield my heart to God to allow his love to flow through me.

Sometimes I was not able to move beyond my own outrage that God allowed them to be hurt at all. But at other times, as I held these broken children, I found that place of rest and could trust God to do his work. I could feel deep love for these children and know that God's loving power was pouring through me.

After one such time, I had a wonderful surprise. The healing had unfolded quickly, and the newly healed child was sleeping in my arms. I waited for Lucinda or Christine to come out, but neither one appeared.

Instead, the one out looked at me and said, "Spiritual mother."

I looked back at her, studying her face, trying to discern who this might be. "That's right. I'm your spiritual mother. And who are you?"

She smiled at me. Then she giggled. Finally, she said, "It's Heather."

"Heather! The one who wrote me the note to warn me about this new group and then went away?"

She nodded, still smiling.

"Where were you, and why did you come back?"

"Well, after I wrote you that note, I knew I couldn't bear being part of another group. So I went as far inside as I could possibly go. And I hid there."

"I'm so glad to see you, Heather. And thank you for that note. Without it, who knows how long it would have been before I figured out what was going on."

"Are they still going to the group?"

"Yes, they are." I regretted that I had such bad news for her.

"Oh, I thought maybe they weren't going anymore. I felt something so strong coming through to me, even where I was hiding way in the back. It felt so good and warm. I didn't think we could feel anything that good if they were still in the group."

"That was God's love and healing power coming through me to heal the one who had been hurt. God gave me a wonderful gift to heal those who have been hurt. It comes through letting them listen to my heartbeat."

"Oh, so that was what I felt. I always knew your heartbeat was very powerful."

"That's because God uses it. It's nothing I'm doing, just cooperating with God."

Heather smiled at me. "Can I hear your heartbeat?"

"You certainly can." I pulled Heather's head down onto my chest.

"Bump, bump," she murmured, as she listened.

I remembered how resistant she had been to any signs of love or affection, and how reluctant I had been to tell her I was her spiritual mother. She was the first to hear me use that term. We both had changed. As I held her, I felt such a strong connection to her, and I was so grateful for the note she had written. "Heather, I am so grateful for you."

She smiled at me again. "Bump, bump. Bump, bump." She was becoming more childlike, even baby-like. Gradually, she drifted off to sleep.

My heart was full as I gazed at her.

After a few minutes, Lucinda burst out. "NanNan, who was that out with you?"

"It was Heather. Remember when she had you bring me her note that warned us about this group?"

"Oh, it was Heather. I'm usually in the light and don't know what's happening out here, but I felt myself being pushed out to where the others are. Then I could feel the warmth coming through. I knew it was from your heartbeat, so I came close to the surface so I could feel it better. I got real close to Heather and saw that she was getting littler and littler. Then she was just a baby, and that's when she came into me."

"She came into you? You and Heather are one?"

Lucinda nodded.

I gave Lucinda a spontaneous hug. "She told me she went away and hid so she wouldn't ever have to go to this new group. Now she's part of you, so she will be protected with you. Maybe God honored her willingness to go against the others and write that note."

"God's power was real strong tonight. I could feel it."

I laughed. "It makes such a difference when I can relax and trust that God knows what he's doing. When I'm mad because they got hurt or when I'm trying to make it happen myself, it's just not the same. As usual, Cinda is right."

"That's cause she's from God."

"She does have amazing spiritual wisdom."

*****

As the spring progressed, I saw significant forward progress in Christine. She still wore that tough outer shell. At times, it seemed I would never be able to penetrate her defenses. I tried my best to not react to her, but something about that impenetrable shell could bring out the worst in me. Perhaps it was my own battle-weary state that left me with few resources to draw on. There were times I felt like a total failure as a spiritual mother, at least when it came to Christine. I could tell from the moment I laid eyes on her if I was going to encounter an impenetrable wall. Then all my fortitude drained out of me, and I would silently pray for strength. I did not yet understand how much Christine tapped into my own personal need to excel.

But sometimes, in my moments of greatest exasperation, she would say something to let me know that all was not lost. One day she arrived for her session, sat down with arms folded, and glared at me. I braced myself as she began to talk.

"That idiot Kurt. He thinks he can just push me around. When Lucinda's out, he gets her to do whatever he wants. Then he thinks I'm the same. But no one pushes me around. Nevil thinks he can push me around too. But I'm not impressed with either of 'em. Nevil thinks I'll go in and get the babies for him. No more. I just pretend I'm the baby. I think he's beginning to catch on, but hell, I'm not changin' what I'm doin', no matter what he says. In fact, I have a plan that will really drive him crazy."

"Oh? And what is your plan?"

"I'll go in and get the babies and bring 'em out to you. That way they can hear your heartbeat. It'll make 'em stronger."

"You would do that?"

"Hell yeah. I know you don't wanna hurt 'em. And they always seem better after hearin' your heartbeat."

So that session, Christine pushed out a baby to be with me. After the baby had fallen asleep, Christine emerged. "I did somethin' different this time. I came close while the baby was out with you. I wanted to see what the big deal was with your heartbeat." Her voice had softened.

"And what did you experience?"

Christine was quiet for a moment. When she spoke, it was with a hushed tone. "It was warm. And peaceful. I ain't ever felt anything like that before. It was gentle, but at the same time, it was very powerful. I don't get it. Where's that power come from?"

"It certainly wasn't from me. That was God's power coming through."

"You talk a lot about this God. You know, the group talks about power too. But their power is different. It's gettin' people to do what they want by being bigger, richer, meaner."

"You're right. God's power is different. He never forces himself on anyone. He doesn't want to push you around. He wants to you to freely choose him."

"Another thing I noticed."

"What's that?"

"When I got close to hear your heartbeat, I started to feel like I was little. I remember one other time I felt like that. When I was close to Lucinda, the day we kept them from goin' to the group, and Lucinda was playin' with them dolls, I started to feel like a little child playing. It scared me. It didn't scare me so much this time."

I couldn't believe that Christine was being this vulnerable with me. "It seems you have an inner child too. You know, we all do."

"Well, don't tell nobody. I can't be little and weak."

"Okay, I won't tell. Thank you for being so honest with me."

When Christine left my office that day, I felt renewed. Maybe we were getting somewhere after all.

CHAPTER 23

Coming Home

I sometimes wondered how Christine could be so abrasively hard and yet, at the same time, so spiritually receptive. Her impenetrable exterior remained intact, which proved to be a constant challenge. That hard Christine, the protective outer shell, was simply her defense, meant to keep others at a distance. It was very effective. My usual response was to put up my own walls. There would be tense interactions between us, and she would retreat into sullen silence.

I wondered if I was causing more harm than good, and I'd throw up my hands in exasperation. I certainly was not modeling the love and acceptance of Jesus.

But during the course of several weeks, she made three giant steps forward. She revealed the first one to me at the end of a session when I had spent most of my time with a broken child who had been wounded by the group. I tried to follow Cinda's advice of focusing on the gift of healing rather than the child's pain and to receive spiritual renewal for myself.

Once the child was sleeping peacefully and I felt I was in a place of peace, I called Christine out.

She looked up at me from her position in my arms. Then she bolted upright. "Were you with one of them babies?"

"Yes, I was. She seems to be healed now."

"I don't know how they got her. It wasn't when I was with them. They must have found another way to get them children out." Christine seemed agitated.

"It's okay, Christine. I trust you are doing everything you can to protect the little ones inside."

"You ain't mad at me?"

"No, I'm not mad." I was relaxed, not in the tense state Christine so often evoked.

"But I didn't do my job."

"I didn't assign you that job. You took it upon yourself."

"I thought you were counting on me. You sure are different than Nevil. He gets really mad if you don't come through, don't do your job."

"I'm not interested in controlling you to do what I want. In the light, people are free to make their own choices."

"You know, I been thinkin' about what you said about your God—that he waits for us to come to him. That sure is different. I even told Nevil I want to learn more about your God. Boy, did that make him mad. He said that your God is a pussy. I said, 'Maybe so, but I felt his power and it's stronger than anything I ever felt.' He told me I was an idiot, that if I stick with them, I can become rich and powerful. I told him I didn't care about his money. He could take it and shove it."

"That's the Christine I know. Doesn't take crap from anyone." I laughed. "But seriously, Christine, I'm so glad you are open to finding out about God. He is the most powerful force in the entire universe. Let me read something to you from his book, the Bible."

I pulled my Bible off the shelf and read to her from Genesis 1.[6] "In the beginning, God created the heavens and the earth." I read to her about how, with a spoken word, he brought into existence light and sky, the seas and dry ground, plants and animals, and finally, men and women. "He created it all, Christine, including you and me."

"But the group said they created me, so I belong to them."

"No, they didn't create you. They applied enough pain to one of the other parts that you split off. But they did not create you. They had had no control over what you were going to be like. God

[6] Genesis 1:1 (NIV).

ordained that. He gave you an incredible strength of personality because he has his own purpose for you. He is just waiting for you to accept it."

"Really? God has a purpose for me? I'll have to think about that."

"Christine, God says that if you seek him with all your heart, you will find him. Just keep seeking." Inwardly, I was rejoicing. Christine was seeking after my God. Despite my feeble attempts to be her spiritual mother, she was moving forward.

*****

Christine's next giant step forward came the following week. I was on the phone with her, late at night, hoping to keep her from going to the group. She was especially talkative that night, so I let her ramble on about the boys, about Kurt, about her frustration with living two different lives. "I don't wanna to go to the group, but someone else takes us there, and then they call me out. They want me to do stuff for them, like keep track of how much money is coming in from their drug sales. They have people out on the streets sellin' the stuff, and they want to make sure that all the money gets back to them. And they're always checkin' to make sure that no one's pinchin' the bags."

"What does that mean?"

"It means they take a little bit out of each bag. They either want to sell it separately and keep the money for themselves, or they want to use it themselves. The group don't tolerate anyone doin' that. They want all the money comin' back to them."

"Exactly what kind of a group is this? Is it a drug ring, or a satanic cult, or what?"

"It's both them things. They also got this interest in cloning."

"Cloning? That's bizarre. Why would they be interested in cloning?"

"Hell if I know. It's mostly Nevil and the others from England. They say they want to clone me, to create a whole army of people who can split like I can. They are fascinated by me, by the way my brain works. Sometimes I think Nevil is obsessed with it. Some of the others get mad at him for spending so much time with us. He says he's creating an army just with us. He wants to create all these hard ones who will do whatever he asks them to do."

"That doesn't sound much different from what your grandmother tried to do."

"I don't know anything about that. I wasn't around back then. But Nevil wants me to be part of his army. I think he knows he don't have me like he used to. And he blames you. 'That damn counselor of yours. Once she got her hands on you, you changed. What does she have that's so exceptional? Stick with us, and you can become rich.' Like I care about his damn money. But I told him he'll never get us away from you because you're not just our counselor. You're also our spiritual mother. And there's power in that."

My heart skipped a beat. "You said that, Christine, that I'm your spiritual mother?"

"Yeah, I know that's who you are. I've drawn close to hear the heartbeat. I know how it affects all them babies and children."

I was ecstatic. Christine acknowledging my role as her spiritual mother seemed highly significant. When we hung up the phone, I prayed for God to protect them from going to the group. I also prayed for Christine to continue moving forward in her spiritual quest.

*****

The next time I saw Christine, my jaw dropped. "What happened to you?"

Christine lowered her eyes and turned her face from me. She sank down onto my pastel love seat, head turned away.

"Look at me, Christine."

Slowly, she turned her head toward me, eyes still lowered. Her upper cheeks, beneath her eyes, were red—extremely red, like she had fallen asleep under a sunlamp. The rest of her face looked normal. "What happened to your face?"

She responded in a hushed tone. "The group did it."

"What? What did they do to you?" My voice had a hard edge.

Christine seemed unusually subdued. She squirmed a little. She obviously didn't want to offer an explanation for the crescent-shaped marks on her upper cheeks.

I tried to soften my voice. "Christine, you know I'm your spiritual mother, and I'm here to help you. Hiding things from me will not solve anything."

She was silent awhile but finally said, "They were really mad that I wouldn't push the babies out to them. They figured out what I was doin', pretending to be a baby. They said they had ways of makin' me cooperate. I told 'em that I didn't care what they did, I wouldn't push 'em out."

"So what did they do to you?"

"Well, first they tied my hands behind my back. Then they took me to this room. They made me sit down on this chair and tied me to it."

I didn't want to hear anymore, but after telling Christine not to hide anything from me, I knew I had opened the door and had to listen. I took a deep breath. "Then what did they do?"

"They took this tape and taped my eyes wide open. I couldn't blink or nothin'."

I was horrified.

"Then they turned me to face this great big light. They turned the lights in the room out and then turned that light on, adjusting it so that it went right into my eyes. It was really bright. My eyes burned, and there was nothin' I could do to stop it. They kept askin' me if I would push the babies out now. I wouldn't say nothin'. They were gettin' really mad, but I wouldn't say nothin'. One of them said they'd better stop because my skin was burning. Finally, they told me that if I didn't push them out, they would do this to me again. Then they turned the light out. They took the tape off my eyes and untied me."

"Did they do it to you again?"

"No. They said they would have to let my skin heal before doing it again."

"How could you stand that light in your eyes?"

"I just kept goin' inside myself."

"Was another part out to take the pain?"

"Hell if I know."

I looked at Christine's eyes. "They could ruin your vision by doing that. Can you see okay?"

"Yeah, I can see, but my eyes really hurt after they were done."

"And what about the burns on your skin?"

"It hurts like a bad sunburn."

"Didn't Kurt and the boys ask about what happened, why you have these burn marks?"

"Yeah, they asked. I just told 'em it was sunburn."

"You don't usually get a sunburn in just one spot. They believed you?"

"Yeah, they believed me."

The burns under her eyes, and only under her eyes, were very real. I didn't want to believe her story, that she had been tortured in this way. But I had no other explanation. I felt sick in the pit of my stomach. Could this really have happened? Could these people really be that heartless? But these were the same people who put knives inside her. So yes, they could be that heartless.

Maybe Christine and Lucinda were delusional. This group did not really exist, except in their own mind. It was all part of their mental illness. Maybe Christine somehow burned her own eyes to give credence to her story. Maybe she was the one who sent me that note offering me fifty thousand dollars to work with them. Maybe I had become part of her grand delusion.

I toyed with this idea. But then I considered the deep pools of pain in the eyes of the tortured children. Could she have manufactured that? I tried to imagine how Christine could have inflicted those burns on her own face. The delusion theory had its own drawbacks.

I simply did not want to believe this all could be true, that this person I loved was regularly being tortured. Tears welled in my eyes. I did not like the pain this brought to my own heart.

"I don't know how you endured that. I'm sorry you had to go through it. I just don't understand why God has allowed it."

"Well, you know, the more they do stuff like that to me, the more I realize they got ain't no power. They can't make me do what they want. The real power...well, I felt it when them little ones were listening to your heartbeat, and I drew close. There was real power there. That's the power I want."

"I pray you will find the real power. The power of love is the greatest power. And I believe you are well on your way to finding it." It seemed incongruous that our session ended on a positive note." Despite the horror I felt at what had been done to Christine, I was able to smile at her, not failing to notice the red crescents on her cheeks. "You just never know how God is going to be working."

*****

It took me several days to shake the sick feeling in my stomach. I again wondered if I was suffering from secondary post-traumatic stress.

The burns on her cheeks gradually faded. I was glad when I did not have the continual reminder of what this nefarious group had done to her. I tried to bolster my spirits by reminding myself that she seemed to be dead serious in her quest to learn about God.

In our personal lives, my husband and I had become deeply involved in the movement praying for our city. We attended regular prayer gatherings where Joby often led worship with his guitar. At these prayer gatherings, we learned about a two-day conference coming to our city. It was led by a group known as Eagles' Wings. We decided to attend, and I wondered if this might be a positive experience for Christine.

When I approached her with the invitation to join us, she seemed hesitant but said she would think about it. Several days later she agreed to go. "But if I don't like it, I'm leavin'. And don't expect me to talk to people I don't know."

I agreed to her conditions, wondering how she was going to respond to an experience filled with Christian worship and teaching. Perhaps this would help her in her quest to learn about God.

Looking back on that conference many years later, I distinctly remember three things. First was the unbridled worship. Christine agreed I could have Lucinda out for some of the worship, and I watched as she entered in with childlike exuberance. She was completely unfazed by the people around her who might have thought it odd for an adult to be so authentically childlike. She danced and she sang and she laughed. She waved worship flags as she jumped up and down. My heart was full as I watched her. She exuded unrestrained child joy.

The second thing I remember was the Scripture verse that was emphasized throughout the conference. Before it was read the first time, the speaker said for everyone to pay close attention because this verse expresses of the heart of God. We need to appropriate it for ourselves. "This is what the sovereign Lord, the Holy One of Israel says. 'In repentance and rest is your salvation, in quietness and trust is your strength, but you would have none of it.'"[7]

When I heard it read, I knew that verse was for me, that somehow I needed to find that quietness and trust if I was going to be strong for this battle that besieged me. Way too often, I was drowning in discouragement, in anger, in hopelessness, in weariness. Every day I was fighting to keep my head above water.

The third thing I remember about the conference was Christine. Much to my surprise, she became fully engaged, especially in the worship. Years later, she revealed to me how deeply she was affected by one of the worship leaders. I was aware that she bought his CD, but I had no idea how this man's worship touched her heart.

The intimacy of his worship caught her attention—the closeness he seemed to have with God. She specifically cited a song called "Draw Me." This song drew her into the beginnings of her own relationship with God.

---

[7] Isaiah 30:15 (NIV).

"When I got to the conference, I was so confused. I felt like I lived in three different worlds: the world with the group, the world with Kurt and the boys, and then there was my world with you, at your office and goin' to deliverances. Where did I belong? Where was my real home? Somethin' about his worship drew me to another home, a home with God. By the time the conference was over, I felt like I had finally found my real home, where I really belonged. And it was none of them other three places. My real home was with God. And I knew that home was a safe place."

Even though it was years before Christine revealed to me the depths of what she experienced at that conference, I drew encouragement from her positive response to it and the beginning of her interest in Christian worship music. Perhaps it was best that Christine said little to me about what truly transpired in her own heart. I suspect I would have expected to see dramatic changes in her and been very disappointed when that did not happen. But within, Christine quietly embraced my God.

She came into the light, and at last, she found her true home.

CHAPTER 24

Finding Joy Again

As the months continued to wear on, I continued to wear out. Seeing the pain in the eyes of the broken children never got easier. I still spent many nights on the phone, hoping to spare them from the ordeal of going to the group. I was often sleep-deprived. Somehow I managed to stay focused at work and be present for other people, but knowing Lucinda might be with this group, even as I was counseling others, was never far from my mind.

The contentious nature of my relationship with Christine was not alleviated by her new relationship with God. This wore on me, and I wondered why it was so difficult for me to maintain my equanimity with her. I frequently found myself in tears. How much longer could I endure?

At this time, Cinda's role in my life started to change. Her focus had always been on Lucinda and her many parts and helping me navigate my role as their counselor and spiritual mother. Now she seemed more concerned about my emotional and spiritual condition.

After a particularly difficult session with Christine, the hard and abrasive Christine, Cinda emerged. "I know this is difficult for you, but God would not have called you to this without giving you everything you need. He has a word for you. After Christine leaves, I want you to read this Bible verse and then pray about it. Ask God to speak to you through it. Now write this down: 1 Peter 4:12–13." Inwardly I smiled at her quaint way of giving me the verses, saying "one Peter" as opposed to "first Peter," as is our custom.

As soon as I was alone, I pulled my Bible off the bookshelf and thumbed to the reference Cinda had given me.

> My dear friends, do not be surprised at the painful trial you are suffering, as though something strange were happening to you. But rejoice that you participate in the sufferings of Christ, so that you may be overjoyed when his glory is revealed.

I reread these verses several times, letting the meaning sink in. The passage reminded me that I am not the first one to have suffered for Christ. I thought of many who had gone before me, great martyrs of the faith who gave their very lives in the service of Christ. I felt a bit sheepish. It seemed that all I did was complain about how hard this was for me, and truth be known, my suffering was minimal. Is it possible I could learn to rejoice in the midst of these sufferings? I realized I had a long way to go.

I silently prayed and confessed to God that I had fallen far short of his standard. I asked him to teach me how to rejoice rather than complain. I let out a long sigh. "Now give me strength for the battle. On my own, I'll never make it, but with you, all things are possible."

*****

Christine continued to join us as we went to the various prayer gatherings in our city. She seemed to be a bit more receptive to these events. I was always glad to have her with us on these Sunday nights. It spared me spending late nights on the phone with her, and it gave me the peace of knowing that she was with me and not that heinous group.

After one such gathering, we were returning to my house. It was a late spring night, and the sky was clear with a crescent moon providing a sliver of light. We walked from the garage to the house, Christine following me, when her husky voice pierced the silence. "Look at that!"

I twirled around to see Christine darting into our backyard, gazing upward. I followed her gaze skyward. There I beheld a streak of light crossing the sky. What was it? I'd never seen anything quite like this. My heart pounded. My first instinct was to drop to my knees, in awe, in reverence, in fear. But my knees never made it to the ground. My mind was working overtime. There must be an explanation for this. Perhaps it was a vapor trail from a jet, illuminated by the moon sliver. Yes, that must be it.

Then it was gone. The sky was black. There was no streak of light. Had I imagined that streak of light? Was my mind playing games with me? I looked over at Christine, standing in the middle of my backyard, still gazing upward.

"Wow, that's amazing!" was all she could say.

"Do you still see it? I saw a streak of light, but now it's gone."

"You can't see it?" Her head was tilted back, eyes fastened on the sky. "It's not just a steak of light. Those are angels."

I walked over toward Christine. Maybe her position in the yard enabled her to see it.

"What did you see?" I instantly recognized Cinda's calm voice.

"I saw a streak of light."

"What was your reaction?"

"My first instinct was to drop to my knees."

"Why didn't you do that?"

"I don't know. I guess I wanted to make sense out of it, figure out what it was."

"Did you figure it out?"

"Well, I thought maybe it was a vapor trail from a jet, with the moon illuminating it."

"Is that what you think it was?"

"I thought maybe it was, but then it wouldn't have disappeared so suddenly. And Christine could still see it. So no, I guess it wasn't a vapor trail."

"Do you understand what happened?"

"No, I don't understand any of it."

"You should have dropped to your knees. That's what your heart was telling you to do. But instead, you went to your head to try to figure it out. God wanted to give you a glimpse into the heavenlies, to see his holy angels. But you can only see them with your heart. Christine could see them because she stayed in her heart."

"But Christine is uneducated. She isn't trained to use her head to understand things. It's second nature to me." I wanted to justify myself.

"Your mind is a wonderful gift from God, but your mind needs to serve your heart."

"I don't get it. I can't just shut off my mind."

"What was your first reaction when you saw it?"

"Awe and wonder, maybe a little fear. No, a lot of fear."

"Is that why you went to your head, to make it more manageable, less fearful?"

"I'm not sure. I guess so."

"That's what people do. There's nothing wrong with it, but if you had stayed with your first reaction and dropped to your knees, you would have been like a child, lost in the wonder of it all. You know, you all have a child within, not just Lucinda. Your child would have seen the world as a child does, and you would have seen God's angels. You need to find your child. Going to your head keeps you from experiencing her."

I felt a bit sheepish.

"Next time, go with your heart, not your head."

I spent a lot of time thinking about what Cinda told me. I could believe I had an inner child. I had already figured out that we all are like Lucinda, with outer protectors that we think will keep our more vulnerable child part safe. While Lucinda looked to her angry, fighting instincts to protect, I looked more to my mind to be my protector. But I had not connected the dots, that this child part is key to our spirituality.

If I had dropped to my knees, admitting my fear, as well as the awe and wonder of the moment, if I had been a child at that moment, rather than analyzing the situation, I would have had a glimpse into something awesome. Somehow my mind got in the way of all that. I had much to think about.

*****

In the heat of summer, my struggles continued. I have vivid memories of driving to work with tears streaming down my cheeks as I cried out to God, "I can't do this, I can't do this, I can't do this." That had become my personal mantra.

It had been almost three years since Heather had written me that ominous note warning me about the new group. Three years of broken children, three years of late-night phone calls, three years of emotional wear and tear.

I pulled into my parking place at the office, crying hysterically, knowing that in a short time I needed to be counseling other people. Somehow I managed to wipe the tears away, stuff all those emotions into the recesses of my psyche, and walk in with a smile on my face. I found it amazing that nobody seemed to notice it was all a big front, that the smile was but a thin veil hiding a cauldron of brokenness and seething emotions.

Cinda was coming out with me more often, inquiring into my emotional state. At times I broke down and cried my heart out to her. She would hold me close and tell me that she was praying for me, speaking to God on my behalf. I thought it was interesting that an angel would pray. "We communicate with God too. We are always in touch with him."

After a particularly difficult session, after I had held another broken child, Cinda emerged to tell me God had answered her prayers. "He knows how deeply it affects you when you see the broken little ones, especially when you look into their eyes. He has heard your cries and my prayers. From now on, things are going to be different. When the little ones get hurt at the group, they will still be healed, but they won't come out to you. Your heartbeat will still heal them, but the healing will come through Christine or Lucinda or Erica. They will listen to your heartbeat, and God will draw the broken one so close that she will be able to hear it. The healing will still come, but without the broken one being out. That way, you will be spared seeing their pain."

I felt strangely humbled by this, that God was so clearly concerned about my emotional well-being. "God is doing that for me?"

"Yes, God is doing this for you. He knows how difficult this has been for you. He also sees your faithfulness. You keep going even when it is difficult. When you fall down, you get back up and keep moving forward. God is pleased with that."

"It seems all I do is complain. I am truly amazed that God sees anything positive in me. It's very humbling."

"God knows what you need. Just receive this gift with gratitude."

"Thank you, Father, for this gift, that I won't have to look into the eyes of broken children anymore." A tear spilled over my eyelid and down my cheek. I was truly touched.

"You have lost your joy. The journey has been so difficult for you. You are carrying a heavy load. He wants to restore your joy. Next time you see them, I want you to spend time with Lucinda and Erica. Find joy in being with them."

*****

The following session, I took Lucinda to a nearby lake that was inhabited by a large population of ducks and geese. I had tucked away in my purse a plastic bag filled with bread scraps. Every child enjoys feeding ducks.

Child Lucinda was beside herself with excitement when she saw them. "Look, look! All them ducks. Let's play with them!" She went running right at them with a childlike gait. It never ceased to amaze me that she was so genuinely a child. As she ran toward them, the ducks turned around and waddled off to the lakeside, plunging into the water. Lucinda stood on the shoreline in dismay. "Don't they want to play with me?"

"I think you scared them by running after them. We need to wait until they're ready to come out of the water."

Meanwhile, several big old Canadian geese came out of the water and charged toward Lucinda, snapping at her and making mad goose noises. Lucinda ran back toward me and hid behind me. "Why don't they like me? I won't hurt them." She was near tears.

"It's okay, Lucinda. They are like your parts inside. They are just protectors because they think you might hurt them."

One goose let out a vicious sounding hiss.

"I'm scared. I want to go in."

"Okay, I'll have Erica come out. Erica, do you want to come out and be with NanNan?"

That quickly, Lucinda was gone, and gentle Erica emerged. I didn't get to be with Erica very often anymore; there just wasn't enough time, so it was a delight to have her out. In contrast to Lucinda's childlike exuberance, Erica had a sweet, gentle personality.

She peeked out from her position behind me and saw the goose. She stood motionless and smiled. The goose looked back at her, right at her. Erica put her finger in her mouth and looked up at me.

"That's a goose, Erica."

"Goo." She watched the goose with curiosity.

The goose moved toward her, close enough that I could have reached down and touched him.

Erica smiled again.

Then, a parade of ducks and geese made their way out of the water and waddled over to Erica, surrounding her. There were white ducks and mallards, and one mama duck who was followed by a trail of babies.

"Look at the baby ducks, Erica."

She pointed to the trail of little ducks. "Babies."

I watched this unfold, amazed that these creatures were so drawn to her. "Let's feed the ducks, Erica." I reached into my purse for my supply of bread scraps.

I watched in amazement as Erica gave pieces of bread to the ducks, each one taking the scrap gently from her hand. There was no fighting among the ducks, no competing for the bread scraps as had been my previous experience. There we were, surrounded by ducks and geese, Erica smiling and making soft cooing noises.

I decided to call Lucinda close, so that she could partake in this experience. "Lucinda, I want you to come close to Erica, and join with her while she's feeding the ducks." I watched closely to make sure that Lucinda would not burst out. "Don't come out, Lucinda. Just come close."

When the bread scraps were all gone, Erica handed me the empty bag, still smiling with delight. I felt so much fullness and inner warmth as I stood with Erica and we watched the ducks, one by one, descend to the lakeside and splash into the water.

"Watch how the ducks swim, Erica. God made them with special feet that help them move about in the water."

Erica watched with curiosity. "Goo." She pointed to one of the geese.

"Has your joy been restored?" It was Cinda.

"That was amazing, Cinda, the way the ducks and geese were drawn to Erica. I've never seen anything like it."

"That's because I was right behind her. They were seeing God's light. Remember how the monkeys at the zoo responded to Lucinda? It was the same thing. God's creatures are drawn to the light. But what about you? Have you found joy again?"

I realized that the fullness I had experienced earlier was joy. "Joy is a feeling of fullness, isn't it? Yes, I felt joy today. Thank you for helping me find that joy. It's been a long time."

Cinda smiled. "You need to take time to enjoy your spiritual children. It will help you be strong for the battle."

That night I pondered what I experienced. To see those ducks that ran from Lucinda turn around and amiably meander over to Erica, surrounding her with a cloud of feathers, was surreal.

The monkeys at the zoo had been drawn to Lucinda, staring right at her as she peered into their cage. Then I recalled the streak of light in the sky that I saw just a few weeks earlier. These were not your average, everyday happenings.

I had lost sight of all the remarkable ways God was at work. All I was able to see was the daily struggle. All around me were indications of the divine hand on Lucinda, directing and guiding her healing path. Indeed, I believed that I communicated regularly with an angel of light, sent to Lucinda in all her darkness to help her find wholeness.

Was Cinda truly an angel of light? Was it really her light that drew these creatures to Lucinda and to Erica? If that was the case, then I was in the midst of something so crazily aberrant that I was either hopelessly deluded or seeing the divine at work in ways that few ever get to see. It was humbling; it was scary. It was strangely exhilarating that I should experience all this.

There is much at work in the universe that seldom meets the eye. I never asked to be in this, in the midst of this, but here I am. Now, with your help, Lord, let me go on to fight this battle. And let your joy be my strength.

After I prayed this spontaneous prayer, a smile rose within me. For the first time, I understood the meaning of that Bible verse: "The joy of the Lord is your strength."[8] No wonder Cinda wanted me to find joy again.

*****

I wish the joy I found that afternoon could have lasted indefinitely.

While I didn't have to see the eyes of the broken children, I still knew they were being tortured. I still struggled with Christine's abrasiveness, and she responded with the conviction that I preferred to be with Lucinda.

She was right. Lucinda was a delightful child, while Christine was one tough cookie. She still took on the group in her own way, refusing to push the inner children out to them and sometimes taking the torture in their place. While I admired her grit and her will-

8 Nehemiah 8:10 (NIV).

ingness to sacrifice herself, I also found it hard to feel close to her. The tough exterior was abrasive.

When Christine would arrive for an appointment, I would quickly size her up to determine if she was going to be impenetrable. Sometimes she was, and at these times, we were likely to clash.

I am by nature a rather placid soul, so I found my own behavior to be out of character. What was happening to me? Who was this intolerant person I was becoming?

I didn't like this new me, and much of my anger was being turned upon myself. "I can't do this, I can't do this, I can't do this," I would cry out between sobs and tears. Where was the joy? I often felt nothing but discouragement and depletion.

Occasionally, God broke into my emotional malaise in unexpected ways. Once I attended an event at church with a visiting pastor. At the end of the evening, I went forward for prayer. I needed help to hold the course in this battle.

When I approached this pastor for prayer, he stepped back, looked me in the eye, and said, "You can do it, you can do it, you can do it." He took a deep breath and repeated himself. "You can do it, you can do it, you can do it." On and on he went, repeating this over and over and over again.

It seemed that for every time I had said *I can't do this*, he told me I could. This man knew nothing about me, certainly nothing about the battle besieging me. Yet his simple words went right to the heart of the matter.

Yes, I could do this. God had called me to it and was reminding me I could do this. I took these words of encouragement as straight from the heart of God. I girded my loins and returned to the battle reassured that I could do it.

CHAPTER 25

The Limo

The roller-coaster ride continued. As the summer progressed, I watched through my office window as a new building took shape across the street. That summer, there were no wildflowers to enjoy, only piles of bare dirt and stretches of building debris thrown about haphazardly.

As the summer drew to a close, I noticed those piles of dirt started to take on a life of their own. The forces of nature cannot be stopped. Weeds pushed through the mounds of dirt, adding the warmth of green to an otherwise barren landscape. It was good to see the sun reflecting off the blanket of green that emerged.

That day, Christine arrived for her appointment in a particularly jovial frame of mind, smiling as she walked in. She was now the alter that was out the vast majority of the time. In many ways, this was positive. Christine was very capable and made sure everything ran smoothy at home. I no longer wondered how child Lucinda managed to run a home and parent three teenage boys.

When I saw Christine smiling, everything inside me relaxed. Perhaps I would not have to deal with the contentious Christine that day.

"Wow, you shoulda seen our street today. It was crazy."

"What happened?"

"Well, the group decided they were going to pick me up in a limousine."

"What, a limo?"

“Yeah, a limo. They have a number of ’em, ya know. They thought they would be the big shots and pick me up in one. That was just dumb.” Christine chuckled. “First of all, you know how narrow our street is.”

I certainly did know. Picking her up at her home could be a real logistical challenge. The local people called these narrow city streets half streets, a term I had never heard until I moved to this area. They were all one-way streets. With cars parked on both sides of the street, there was barely room to maneuver an average-sized car down the block. I couldn’t imagine what it was like with a limo.

“Well, they could barely move it down the block, and then, all the neighborhood kids saw it. A limo in our neighborhood? Most of them kids had never seen one before. They swarmed out of houses all over the block, shouting to each other to come see the limo. I heard all the commotion and looked out the second-floor window. Kids were everywhere, even climbin’ on the hood. The driver put down his window and started yellin’ at ’em, but they didn’t pay no attention. There was no way they were gonna move that car. So that gave me time to hightail it outa there. I went out the back door and ran down to my sister’s house. So the group didn’t get me today. I couldn’t believe how stupid they were, bringin’ a limo into our neighborhood.”

I laughed along with Christine, envisioning the scene she described. Who were they and what were they doing with limousines? So many questions and so few answers. “That was pretty stupid, trying to bring a limo down your street. But even more important, their mission was aborted. They didn’t get you today. For that I am truly thankful.”

*****

The next time Lucinda arrived for a session, it was child Lucinda. This surprised me since Christine was now in charge most of the time. Lucinda followed me down the hall and into my office, toting a stuffed monkey.

I knew the second I laid eyes on her that this was not Christine. "Is this Lucinda?" I asked once the office door was closed.

"Yeah, it's me, NanNan."

"You brought something with you."

Lucinda held up the plush brown monkey. He had an orange hat perched on his head and a cock-eyed expression. "I was in the store with Christine and saw this monkey. I told Christine I wanted it. It made me think of the monkeys we saw at the zoo. They were so neat."

I smiled, remembering her fascination with them. "You really like monkeys, don't you?"

"I do like them. And I'm not the only one. Every time I hold this monkey, I feel another child getting close."

"Oh? Who do you think she is?"

"I don't know, but she cries a lot. I think when she sees the monkey, it helps her feel better."

"Has she been with the group?"

"I don't think so. I think she's sad about somethin' else."

"Is she close to you now?"

"Yeah, she is."

"Let me see if I can draw her out with the monkey." I took the monkey from Lucinda and held it directly in front of her. "Hello. I'm Mr. Monkey, and I love children. I love it when children hold me close. Would you like to come out and hold me close?" I took the monkey's soft arm and rubbed it against her cheek. "You can come out and hold me." Nothing happened.

"She's really close, NanNan, but I think she's scared to come out."

I continued the monkey monologue, making the monkey jump and dance.

It took quite a while, maybe fifteen minutes, until there was a clear shift of alters. I observed this new one. She looked very timid. I handed her the monkey.

With trembling hands, she took it and pulled it in close.

After a few minutes, I said, "Hello, what's your name?"

There was no response, only a fearful look.

"It's okay. There's no one here to hurt you, and you can hold the monkey as long as you want."

She held the monkey close and buried her head in its fur. A tear trickled down her cheek.

"What are you sad about?"

She said nothing but tightened her grip on the monkey.

After a few minutes, she was gone, and Lucinda, with all her lack of inhibitions, squealed with delight. "She really liked the monkey. She felt better when she was holding it. I think that helped her, NanNan."

"Do you know anything about her?"

"Only that she liked the monkey."

"There was a connection." Christine had emerged. "I got close when that child was out. I could feel it was more than just a child liking a toy, like Lucinda does. It was deeper. There was a connection with the monkey."

I wondered about this. What could the connection be, and was it significant? I let out a long, satisfied sigh. It was so good to have a therapy session that wasn't consumed with the group.

"Is there a way you can protect this one from the group?" I asked Christine. "She seems so innocent. I'd be crushed if they got her."

"I'll do my best. That damn group."

I smiled at Christine, knowing for certain that we were on the same team. Despite her abrasiveness, I knew her heart was good.

*****

Perhaps my desire to protect this new child kept me focused on her. I suggested to Christine that she bring the monkey to each session so it could be used to bring the child to the surface. We tried to bring her to the surface with Christine out and holding the monkey, but met with little success.

I kept asking for the child who liked to hold the monkey, but there was no response. "What do you think the problem is, Christine?"

"When you call for that child, there's all this commotion inside, and I hear someone saying, 'She's not in the system.'"

"That seems like an odd thing to say. What do you think it means?"

"I think the problem is me. I'm new to them ones inside since I was split off by the group. They don't know who I am, and I don't think they trust me. That's not the first time I heard them say I'm not in the system. Maybe if you have Lucinda hold the monkey, it'll work better."

It felt good to be working with Christine and not against her. "Good idea. Let's try that."

It worked like a charm. With Lucinda out and holding the monkey, the new child drew close, and after a little coaxing, she came out to hold the monkey.

I tried to engage with her, but she stayed focused on clinging to the monkey, tears making their way down her cheeks. It took several sessions, but in time, she let me sit next to her. My goal was to get her to listen to my heartbeat. Perhaps that would bring healing to whatever pain she carried.

The day I pulled her head down to hear my heartbeat, chaos erupted.

She bolted upright and stared right at me. A deep, guttural voice erupted from within her, speaking in a harsh-sounding language.

I looked into her eyes and saw that heinous look of evil that I now knew was the darkness within her. They did not want her to hear my heartbeat. Even though I had encountered darkness in this manner before, I found myself shaking. I did not want to take this on alone. "In the name of Jesus Christ, King of kings and Lord of lords, you get back down. You are to leave this child alone because she has a right to receive healing from her traumas." My voice sounded a lot stronger than I felt.

That quickly, the child was back, clinging to the monkey, but looking especially frightened.

I spoke soothing words to her and then called Lucinda back.

"What happened, NanNan? Everything was all crazy inside. There were monsters there, and they were really mad."

"I'm not sure what happened, but I think it's time to take this new child to see Paul and Adele. She needs deliverance. The darkness did not want her to hear my heartbeat, that's for sure."

"Whatever you did must have been very powerful. They turned and ran."

"It wasn't me they were afraid of. It was the name of Jesus."

"Wow, I saw it all." Christine emerged. "That darkness acted like they were all big and tough. But when they heard the name of Jesus, they were useless. He's got the power, not them."

I nodded. "Thanks for helping out with this new child, Christine. If darkness is all stirred up, we're on the right path."

*****

So there were times when Christine and I were able to work together. That gave me hope. But at the same time, I was fighting a new battle—within myself. I wondered if all this could possibly be true. Was there really a group routinely picking up Lucinda and using her for evil purposes? Was all of this a delusion of a mentally ill mind? Was I wearing myself out fighting a battle that did not even exist?

I considered this possibility from every angle. Each time I did, I found that all roads took me back to one place. Cinda. If Cinda was truly an angel of light, she would speak only truth, and I could trust that all this was real and true and solid. If, however, she was not an angel of God, then everything would collapse. Like pulling out a bottom card from a house of cards, it would all come tumbling down.

But if Cinda wasn't an angel of light, what was she? I surmised four possibilities.

Perhaps she was just part of Lucinda's mental illness, part of her paranoid delusion. The main problem with this possibility was that Cinda was so eminently sane. She was consistently calm, reasonable, and lacking in defensiveness. When there was nothing but chaos among Lucinda and her alters, Cinda would emerge with a peaceful presence, unalarmed and filled with insight. How could someone with such severe mental illness also maintain such sanity? Indeed, her level of sanity far surpassed my own.

So maybe she's not just part of a delusion, but is actually a genuine alter personality who embodies all that is best about Lucinda. Indeed, for years that is what I took her to be: Lucinda's internal self-helper, an alter personality whose role is to be a guide on the path to healing. That made sense to a certain point. The problem came because Cinda herself claimed to be an angel from God. Then she was either a deluded self-helper or a deceitful self-helper. In either case, deluded or deceitful, she could not be a very good self-helper, since she was not rooted in truth and reality.

So then I wondered if perhaps she was made up by Lucinda, to draw me in, to gain my sympathy and allegiance. I didn't think she would have made her up with malicious intent, but perhaps out of her own need, she created this pseudo-alter who I later came to believe was an angel. But this possibility had serious drawbacks. Lucinda was uneducated and unsophisticated. She had little, if any, theological or biblical understanding. Cinda, on the other hand, could quote the Bible chapter and verse and showed great depth of theological insight. How could Lucinda make something up that had far greater understanding and wisdom than she herself had? You cannot make up something that is greater than yourself. That is a logical impossibility.

So there was one last possibility. Perhaps she is an angel of darkness masquerading as an angel of light. The Bible tells us that Satan himself can masquerade as an angel of light.[9] Of all the possibilities, this one seemed the least convincing. First of all, I had been at a deliverance when Paul had tested her, as the Bible instructs. "By this you know the spirit of God: every spirit that confesses Jesus Christ has come in the flesh is of God, and every spirit that does not confess

[9] 2 Corinthians 11:4.

Jesus Christ has come in the flesh is not of God."[10] I was right there when Paul asked her if Jesus came in the flesh.

There was not a moment's hesitation as she proclaimed, "Absolutely, he came in the flesh." No spirit of darkness would ever proclaim that. But beyond that, Cinda consistently pointed beyond herself to Jesus as God's son and God as the loving heavenly Father. She warned against worshipping her and humbly confessed that she was only a messenger. Darkness, on the other hand, seeks all the adulation it can get.

No, I knew that whatever she was, Cinda was not a fallen angel.

Round and round this would go in my mind. Who was Cinda, and could I trust her? I reviewed many events that had no explanation if she was not an angel: Dr. Kirkly's response to her simple message, Barbara's remarkable healing after a single encounter with her, animals being drawn to her light, her explanation for the streak of light in the sky. These were things I had seen with my own eyes. She must be the real deal.

I would end up reassuring myself that she could be trusted, she was indeed an angel from God. But I found that going through this mental process filled me with anxiety. It was one more thing to wear me down.

*****

On a late summer afternoon, Joby and I made our way down Lucinda's narrow city side street to pick her up for a deliverance session. She quickly emerged from her home and jumped in the back of our car.

When we arrived at Paul's home in the country, it was dusk. His golden retriever, Buddy, barked out a warning as we parked the car. Lucinda had been out on the ride down and eagerly jumped out of the car, toting her stuffed monkey. She had become very attached to Paul and Adele and looked forward to seeing them.

---

10 1 John 4:2–3 (NKJV).

We entered by the side door, and they greeted us warmly. Paul asked about the monkey. "Did you bring someone with you, Lucinda?"

Lucinda held up the monkey. "I like monkeys, so I asked Christine to buy this for me."

Paul and Adele smiled kindly as they admired her monkey.

Joby pulled out his guitar and tuned it. We had developed the practice of worshipping before our sessions. We sang several worship songs, Lucinda waving a worship flag and dancing about in a child-like way. After several songs, Paul prayed a short prayer asking for God's guidance as we sought deliverance for Lucinda.

"So who are we going to work with tonight?" Paul looked to me for guidance.

"There is a child alter who is very attached to the monkey Lucinda brought. We'll use the monkey to draw her out. I believe that she is ready to be delivered."

The deliverance process flowed smoothly that night. Once the child was out, she allowed me to sit next to her. When I pulled her head down to hear my heartbeat, darkness showed itself just as it did at my office.

Paul took charge, ordering the darkness to leave since it had no ground: the child did not ask it to be there. Lucinda and Christine were on the inside telling it to leave in the name of Jesus. With little resistance, the darkness left.

Then I could pull the child's head down to hear my heartbeat. She resisted a bit at first, but soon she settled in, relaxing and making cooing noises. We watched as she slowly regressed until she seemed to be a small infant, making raspberry sounds with her tongue and smiling contentedly.

Lucinda emerged. "NanNan, she came into me. I was right behind her when she was listening to your heartbeat. I could tell she was getting real little, then she just came into me."

"Another integration! Deliverances and integrations are getting so much easier. Did she have any pain when she came into you?"

"She did at first, when she first heard your heartbeat. I could tell she was real sad, but then she just got quiet and still and came into me."

"Do you know what her sadness was about?"

"I got some pictures from her. They weren't good." Lucinda became very quiet.

"Can you tell us about the pictures?"

Slowly, Lucinda began. "She was lookin' at somethin'." Lucinda shuddered a little. "It wasn't very nice. It was little and all bloody. It was floatin' in a toilet." She shuddered again. "You know, NanNan, it kinda looked like a…a…"

"What did it look like, Lucinda?" I reached over and took her hand.

"It looked like a…monkey."

A heavy silence settled over all of us.

"Then she took a towel, got it out of the toilet, and wrapped it up. Next, she put it in a suitcase with all these other clothes. What was it, NanNan?" Lucinda looked at me with tear-filled eyes.

I looked around at the others. "Do you think she had a miscarriage?"

"It certainly is a possibility," Paul said. "It would explain the child's attachment to the monkey."

"We're not sure, Lucinda, but she might have been carrying a baby in her womb which didn't survive."

Lucinda gave me a puzzled look.

"But whatever happened, she has been healed from it. She was totally at peace when she became part of you. God healed her, and she will no longer be sad because of what happened."

Lucinda wiped a tear away. "I just wish I didn't have to see her pictures."

There was a heaviness in the car as we drove home that night. Lucinda's description of what she saw had affected both my husband and me. Lucinda kept asking questions about what was floating in the toilet. I tried to explain to her that sometimes when a mother is carrying an unborn child, the child is not able to survive, and the baby will be expelled from the mother. Lucinda didn't understand this, and she kept saying that it looked like a monkey.

After several minutes of silence, Lucinda began to talk again. "I'm getting more pictures, NanNan. I don't understand them."

"What are you seeing, Lucinda?" I was afraid she was seeing more deeply disturbing images.

"She's outside now. And she don't feel so sad. She's skipping. She's in this place where there's lots of people walking around. And she's walking on boards. There's all these boards on the ground and railings along the side. On the other side of the railings is lots of water. Everybody looks happy, and she feels happy too."

"It sounds like she's on a boardwalk at the seashore."

"I don't know what that is."

"It's a place where people go to vacation. Are you seeing anything else?"

"Well, she's walkin'. There's lots of pretty colored lights all around. She's lookin' at them and they make her feel happy. Then she goes into this place with lots of toys. She goes to this shelf and pulls down a monkey. It's a monkey, NanNan! She puts her hand inside it and makes it move its arms and head."

"It sounds like a puppet."

"Yeah, it's a puppet. Then she goes to this lady and gives her some money to buy it. Then she goes out to the place with the boards. Now she's really happy."

"Did it look like the monkey you have?"

Child Lucinda thought for a moment. "No. It was white. My monkey is brown."

"That's unusual…a white monkey."

"All I know is that she was happy."

"Well, I'm glad she has some good memories too." I was relieved that these new pictures were not so disturbing.

Christine emerged at this point. We explained what had happened at the deliverance session and asked if she had any insights into the pictures Lucinda saw.

She shook her head. "I wasn't around for any of that. But I do know that the child had a strong pull toward the monkey. She felt connected to it."

We turned onto the half street where she lived. We slowly made our way between the parked cars on either side. Suddenly, Joby stopped the car. "Well, look at that." He pointed ahead to the left side of the street.

We all peered forward into the darkness. There, parked across from Lucinda's house, was a limousine, a long black limousine. I could see a man sitting in the passenger seat wearing a hat. The brim was pulled down, hiding his face.

He straightened up, and then the limo pulled out of the parking space with as much speed as possible under the crowded conditions.

I was dumbfounded.

"It's that damn group. They were probably waiting for us to come out." Christine was obviously agitated.

"Do we dare drop you off? Will they come back for you?"

"No, I don't think they'll be back. They got outa here in such a hurry. I think they were rattled that you saw them."

"How would they know who we are? We're just a car coming down the street."

"Oh, they know a lot about you. They probably know your car."

I shuddered inwardly. "Are you sure you will be okay? What if they come back for you?"

"I'll be fine. They got outa here so fast. I don't think they'll be back."

"Well, I'll call when we get home, for my own peace of mind."

Christine got out of the car. We watched her fiddle with her keys and open the door, then disappear into her home.

My heart pounded. I turned to Joby. "I cannot imagine what a limo was doing sitting on this block and then taking off like that when we arrived. The only explanation I can think of is that there really is a group."

We drove off but circled the neighborhood several times, looking for any signs of the limo. We saw none. So we headed home, but the limo quelled my doubts about the reality of this group, at least for a time.

CHAPTER 26

Healing My Heart

Over the next several weeks, Lucinda disclosed some more pictures that she was receiving from the integrated child. Together we pieced together what must have happened. Most of these new pictures involved Marilyn and Jimbo, an interracial couple she lived with in her early teens.

It seems that Marilyn was infertile and desperately wanted a child. She encouraged Jimbo to take advantage of Lucinda, hoping she would conceive. When she did, Marilyn was ecstatic, thinking that she would be able to raise the child. In her elated state, she allowed Lucinda to go on a trip to the shore with some friends. Normally, Marilyn watched over her vigilantly, but her friends convinced her, and Marilyn reluctantly agreed. At her friends' urging, she even gave Lucinda some spending money.

When Lucinda returned from their excursion, Marilyn unpacked Lucinda's suitcase. She found the monkey puppet sitting on top. Next, she found the towel carefully wrapped around the fetus. She unwrapped the towel and stared at the bloody remains. She realized what had happened and that her dream for a baby was crushed.

Unable to face her heartbreak, she erupted into the only emotion she allowed herself to feel—anger. No, this was more than anger; this was rage. She screamed for Lucinda to come upstairs.

When Lucinda appeared in the doorway of her bedroom, Marilyn turned on her with vicious words, ranting and raving that Lucinda had killed her baby. She grabbed an electrical cord, which was on the top shelf of the closet, and began to wildly swing it at Lucinda, striking her on her legs, on her back, even on her face.

Lucinda cowered in a corner, protecting herself with her hands.

"You took my baby from me," Marilyn screamed over and over again as she lashed Lucinda with the electrical cord. Finally, Marilyn exhausted her rage and left the room.

When Lucinda was convinced Marilyn would not return, she crawled over to the bed with the open suitcase. She reached up and took hold of the monkey, pulling it close to her breast. Then she lay down on the floor, burying her head in the puppet monkey's soft fur. In time, she fell asleep.

When Lucinda shared these memories with me, tears trickled down her cheeks. "She loved that monkey, NanNan. When she held it close, she felt better."

"Well, I'm glad she had the monkey to comfort her."

"She didn't have it long, NanNan."

"What happened?" I wasn't sure I wanted to hear.

"She's outside on the sidewalk, and she's holdin' the monkey real close. Marilyn comes out of a house and sees her."

"Lucinda, don't be such a baby. You're acting like you're two years old. Give me that monkey." Marilyn had reached over and grabbed it out of her hands. "Now act your age."

Young Lucinda wanted to scream at her, *Give me back my monkey*. But fear of Marilyn's rage gripped her, and she stood in silence.

Marilyn spotted a young man walking with his young daughter who was about three years old. She went over to him and held the monkey up. "Would your little girl like to have this monkey?" She knelt down so the child could see it. "Would you like this monkey?"

The little girl nodded eagerly.

Marilyn stood up. "You can have it for two dollars."

The man reached into his pocket and took out his wallet. He handed Marilyn two crisp one-dollar bills.

With a satisfied smile, Marilyn handed the monkey to the child, who was delighted.

The child alter watched this transaction. She saw the little girl and her father walk down the street with the child happily toting her monkey. She felt a stabbing pain in her heart. That puppet monkey was her only source of comfort in the midst of the confusion and trauma of having miscarried a child. Tears welled up. *Must hide the tears, must hide the tears.* She felt a pull from inside herself. Another alter personality emerged, and that child receded into the depths of Lucinda's subconsciousness.

It was more than twenty years before this child surfaced again, pulled forward by Lucinda's stuffed monkey. For over twenty years, she had been trapped inside with these horrific memories of miscarrying a baby, being beaten with an electrical cord, and then having Marilyn sell her only source of comfort. But that was how Lucinda survived these events. The traumatized child disappeared inside along with these memories, all buried deep within her subconscious.

I looked at child Lucinda. "I'm sorry you had to experience all that."

"It's okay, NanNan. Them pictures make me sad, but I know that Jesus healed that one. She don't have no pain anymore."

I smiled. "And now she is part of you, so you are becoming more whole."

*****

With the child who had been attached to the monkey now healed and integrated, I once more turned my attention to the battle with the group and my contentious relationship with Christine. Although Christine and I could connect against our common adversary, the group, we were often at odds with each other.

Her abrasiveness was a continual challenge for me. Even though I told myself that this was just her outer defense, I was unable to graciously endure the hardness until she let the defenses down and showed her true self. My defenses would go up, and I would respond with an icy tone of voice. This convinced her that I preferred Lucinda over her.

She felt that nothing she did could endear her to me and that Lucinda would always be my favorite.

I felt that nothing I did with Christine was right and that I was failing miserably as her spiritual mother.

One day Cinda addressed this with me. "Do you know why you have such a hard time with Christine?" She did not wait for an answer. "Christine connects to your own broken inner child. Your child cannot tolerate failure in any form. She feels she will only be loved if she excels." I considered her words. "I will pray for your inner child to be healed. When I am with you, I am going to place my hands on you and pray for your child. She needs to know that she is loved regardless of her successes or failures."

In my heart, I knew Cinda was right. I was raised by highly accomplished parents who expected nothing but excellence from me. I knew that the crux of my struggle with Christine was that I felt like a failure with her, that nothing I did could break down her walls. But I had not considered that the child within me was carrying deep childhood wounds and fears, fears of failure, fears of weakness, fears of showing my more vulnerable emotions.

I presented to the world a placid and contained exterior, an exterior that was being worn down by this grueling battle with the group. Those hidden emotions were surfacing and, at times, spilling out onto Christine. I was tired of this scenario. It only contributed to the tension between us. If God wanted to heal this broken child within me, I was all in.

The first time Cinda laid her hands on me and prayed for me was a hot August night. Joby and I had taken Christine to one of our city prayer gatherings. Christine had sat with arms folded, and I was frustrated that she was showing no interest in the worship or prayers that were being offered. She refused to let Lucinda out because she didn't want to be embarrassed by her childlike behavior.

We returned to our home afterward and sat on our front porch. Christine agreed to let Lucinda out to have a dish of ice cream with us. After we had finished our ice cream, Cinda emerged. "It is time to pray for you. You are very frustrated with Christine, and your child is close. I want you to lie down on the ground, face down."

We spread some pillows from the porch furniture on the hard tile floor. I lay on these pillows, face down, while Cinda and Hubby knelt on either side of me, hands on my back. Cinda prayed, "This child needs healing. Somewhere, way back, she was left alone and was overcome with panic and fear, and she is still frozen there." Although I had no remembrance of such an incidence, I felt no need to question or protest. I tried to receive all that God might have for me. Cinda continued her prayer. "Father, heal this child from that emotional trauma."

I clearly remember the touch, the feel of four hands on my back, a gentle, loving touch. I sensed that the power was not in the words, but in the touch. It was comforting, reassuring; but it was also powerful. I wondered if this is what Lucinda's parts felt when I held them. As Cinda prayed, I felt a calm arising within me, spreading throughout my inner being. There was a stillness within, unlike anything I had ever experienced before. I felt totally still within. After Cinda had finished praying, I just lay there, basking in the new place of calm.

Finally, I spoke. "I feel so peaceful. Was my child fully healed?"

"She was healed from that time of feeling left alone."

"Do I have parts like Lucinda?"

"No. Your child is not separate. But you did not receive the comfort you needed when you felt all alone. Tonight your child received comfort, and now you are at peace."

"Is this how Lucinda's children feel when I comfort them?"

"Yes. Perhaps God wants you to know in a new way how powerful comforting touch can be."

In the weeks that followed, I was aware of a place of stillness within me. If I paused in my day long enough to focus, I could access that stillness. It was a great comfort to me. It gave me hope and a new confidence in God's healing power.

This was the first of a number of times that Cinda prayed for me, always with touch and always with the focus on my inner child. I had not realized how I had hidden away the broken part of myself, the quiet, sensitive child who felt that the only way to be loved was to excel. I learned at an early age to hide my weaknesses and present to the world a facade of calm indifference. I found that if I engaged my thinking, I could hide in my head as a way to keep the inner emotions at bay.

Christine was the catalyst that broke down that facade and exposed the hidden brokenness and cauldron of boiling emotions within. I was not that different from her. My outer shell might have been more refined, but like Christine, I hid my true self with a protective outer layer. I was now in the process of learning to access the true emotions hidden by my placid facade.

*****

Unfortunately, Cinda's prayer for me did not alleviate the tension with Christine. I might have found a deep calm within, but Christine's brash hardness still rankled me. I desperately wanted to accept Christine as she was, but her hard exterior aroused a sleeping giant in me.

But occasionally, something would bring us together. The day she told me about a great fiasco with the group was just such a time.

It was one of those nights when Cinda told me they were going to the group and I needed to hang up the phone. Reluctantly, I told Christine that it was time to hang up. I prayed for her first, asking God's protection on her. I also made a point to tell God I was not happy with his plan.

Before we said goodbye, Christine told me that the group had some important people visiting. "I don't know who they are, but they said I'd better be there."

I certainly didn't like the sound of that, but reluctantly I hung up the phone.

When she arrived for her appointment the next day, she was all smiles. A wave of relief swept through me. Whatever happened the night before couldn't have been too terrible, and I would not have to deal with the contentious Christine.

She seated herself. “You shoulda seen it. They made fools of themselves.”

“What are you talking about?”

“Remember I told you they had all these important people visiting? Some of them were from England and some from other countries. Some of them looked Arab. I knew they were gonna be there, so I decided I was gonna stay real close to the surface so I could come out if they were hurtin’ the children or doin’ somethin’ else real bad. So I could see it all.”

Who were these people that they had all these foreign connections? I wondered.

Christine continued. “They were supposed to show them how they were building an army in us, all these hard parts that would do anything they were told to do. They had all their numbered parts ready to show off.” Christine started to laugh, a loud, hearty laugh. It was infectious.

“So what happened?”

They started callin’ them out.” Christine laughed again. “When they came out, they were just babies! Every one of their numbered parts came out as a baby. They kept tryin’ to get them big, but nothin’ they did worked. They made fools of themselves. They were so mad. I think maybe these bigwigs were supposed to give money for what they called research. Boy, they sure didn’t get any money.”

I pictured the scene in my mind, and I began to laugh with Christine. “Were the numbered parts babies, or did other babies from inside come out?” I asked between giggles.

“I don’t know. I just know that they made total fools of themselves.” Together, we held our sides and laughed. When our laughter finally subsided, Christine spoke first. “Ya know, I was mad when you said you hadda hang up last night. I could tell you didn’t wanna do it, but I felt like you was desertin’ me. But it was worth it to see what happened. They were so embarrassed. And ya know, I thought it was really funny that they always wanted me to bring the babies out to them, but I wouldn’t do it. I’d just pretend to be a baby. Once they figured out that’s what I was doin’, they’d get so mad at me. But this time, they only wanted the hard parts, and guess what they got. This time they got the babies!" Christine started to laugh again.

"There is an irony there. You know, I was mad too. Not at you, but at God. But I guess he had a plan that we would never have guessed. Do you think they will give up on making an army now?"

"I don't know. Nevil don't give up easy."

"Well, at least this was a major setback for them. And it felt good to laugh with you." Sometimes we were on the same page.

Before she left that day, Cinda came out. "God had the victory last night. Christine saw the humor in what happened. He wants you to see it too. I have a Bible passage for you. I want you to read Psalm 37:12–17."

I walked over to my bookshelf and pulled out my Bible. I turned to the book of Psalms and began to read aloud. "'The wicked plot against the righteous and gnash their teeth at them, but the Lord laughs at the wicked.'" I stopped and chuckled. "I guess God was laughing last night."

"Yes, he was. Now keep reading."

"'The Lord laughs at the wicked, for he knows their day is coming. The wicked draw the sword and bend the bow to bring down the poor and needy, to slay those whose ways are upright.'"

Cinda interrupted me. "Does this sound familiar? This powerful group is coming against Lucinda, who is just a poor, broken person. Now keep reading."

"'But their swords will pierce their own hearts and their bows will be broken.'"

"That is God's promise to you. Now go on."

"'Better the little that the righteous have than the wealth of many wicked; for the power of the wicked will be broken, but the Lord upholds the righteous.'"

"I want you to meditate on these verses. This is God's word to you in the midst of this battle. The victory is assured."

I took a deep breath. At that moment, I was encouraged. I spent the next several days memorizing these verses. With this assurance that God would have the victory, I felt renewed and ready to press on.

*****

Several nights later, I was on the phone with Christine. We were talking about the fiasco with the group, still enjoying its comic nature. There was an openness between us, no tension. Walls were down. Christine began to open up. "Ya know, God showed me somethin' the other night. I ain't ever had him show me anything before."

"What did he show you?"

"It was a picture. No, more than a picture. It was like a movie. I know it was from him. God was handin' a baby to you. I just saw his hands, but he handed this little baby to you. I realized somethin' then, that you are my spiritual mom. I always felt like we was this team fightin' the group, fightin' evil. But when I saw that, I realized that's not what I want. I'm tired of bein' a team fightin' the group. I just want a mom to come home to. That's all I want. Will you just be my mom?"

There was a tenderness to Christine's voice and a simple childlikeness. I had never heard her talk like this before. It was very disarming. I was moved. "There is nothing I'd like more than to simply be your spiritual mom. I'm tired of fighting this group too."

"I realized somethin' when I saw God givin' you that baby. I realized that God took us, all of us, from the hands of evil and put us in your hands, even when we was just an infant, even when we didn't know you yet. And I realized that he has protected us all along, even when bad things happened to us when we was just children and even now when the group gets us. Like the other night. He was protectin' us."

As I listened to Christine, I felt my heart being touched. It was like every wall that I had constructed to protect my own heart came down. I realized how many walls I had built to protect myself from the pain of broken children, to protect myself from the horrors of this group, to protect myself from Christine's brashness. I was protecting myself and not allowing God to be my protector.

"Christine, I'm no different than you. I have been protecting myself too, building walls. I've built walls with you because I feel like I continually fail you as your spiritual mom. I've built walls to protect myself from the pain of this battle. I'm encamped behind my walls rather than letting God be my protector." Tears welled up, and I quietly wept. Deep sadness surfaced, a sadness laced with honey. It was very deep and very painful, yet somehow very sweet. It was sweet because I knew God was in it.

Then I felt God speak to my heart. *I'm not asking you to battle this group. Let me do the battling. You just be her spiritual mom and trust me with everything else.*

"Well, Christine, let's see if we can start anew. This time, we'll let God do the battling. He will be our protector, and you will be my spiritual daughter."

CHAPTER 27

Dominique

"Where's my star?"

I had been holding Lucinda close to hear my heartbeat. The latest wounded victim of the group was behind her, receiving healing. As Cinda had promised, I no longer had to hold the broken children who had been tortured. Instead, I would let Lucinda or Christine or Erica listen to my heartbeat while the broken child would draw close and receive healing from within. It made the healing process so much easier for me. Not having to see the brokenness in their eyes, not having to hold a lifeless body gave me a bit of emotional distance from the reality of their pain. I looked down at Lucinda and realized she was no longer out. The eyes I was looking into were not broken, but they had a faraway look.

"Where's my star?"

"This must be Dominique. I haven't seen you in a very long time."

I remembered back to nearly a decade earlier when my work with Lucinda was so much easier. There was no group, there were no tortured children, and there was no contentious Christine to drain my resources. Instead, there was a stream of hardened alters who shared with me tales of horror. But these were tales of long ago, not present realities.

Those alter personalities came in layers (or levels, as they called them). Alters from levels one and two carried the memories of family incest. Level three was composed of alters that her grandmother groomed to participate in her satanic cult. All of these alters had names that began with the letter *T*, except Dominque. I did not know much about Dominique because you could not converse with her. She would stare into the distance with a blank expression and say, "Where's my star?" That's as far as the conversation went. Mentally, she seemed to be absent.

And now, Dominique had reappeared. I wondered if she had been out with the group. I could not imagine that the group would have much use for her, except as another victim to torture in hopes of splitting her.

Dominique looked at me with her faraway eyes.

"Do you remember me, Dominique? I'm your spiritual mother."

"Where's my star?"

"NanNan, who was out with you? She feels really cold." Lucinda had emerged.

"It was Dominique, one of the ones from your grandmother's cult. Was she the one behind you getting healing?"

"Yeah, but even when she got better, she felt really cold. There's somethin' wrong with her."

"I agree. It's like she's only partially present. I sure hope the group doesn't get her again."

Lucinda nodded in agreement.

*****

The next time we met for a session, Dominique came out while Lucinda and I were coloring. I knew a switch had taken place when Lucinda dropped her crayon in the midst of drawing her signature bumblebee angel.

She looked up at me with faraway eyes and said, "Where's my star?"

I picked up a blue crayon and drew a star on a piece of paper.

She picked up a red crayon and drew a rough circle around it. "There's my star."

Were we making progress? At least she was interacting with me a little.

Then she said, "Where are the children?" with her quiet, expressionless voice. This was the first time she had ever spoken about something other than her star.

"What children are you looking for?" I asked.

She did not respond.

"Dominique, let's go sit on the couch. I would like you to hear my heartbeat." I got up and took her hand, tugging it gently. I sat on the couch, gently pulling her toward me.

She slowly got up and came over to me.

Again, I gently pulled her hand and patted the seat of the couch. "Come and sit down."

She sat down next to me. "Where are the children?"

"I don't know what children you're looking for. But come lay your head on my heart." I pulled her head toward me.

She was amazingly compliant, certainly not the norm for Lucinda's alters. She placed her head on my heart, and I rocked her gently. After a few minutes, she sat up. "That's very strong."

"That's God's power you're feeling."

Her eyes fixed on one of the paintings Lucinda had done of her imaginary world of escape. It depicted a woodland stream disappearing into the horizon. A few tears collected along her lower eyelids. For the first time, she was showing emotion.

"NanNan, what's happening? There's a lot of growling inside." Lucinda had emerged.

"Dominique is starting to interact with me. I guess darkness doesn't like it."

"What's she sayin'?"

"She wants to know where the children are."

"She must be talkin' about the children she has with her inside. I think she's collecting broken children because she wants to help them."

"It seems Dominique is starting to awake from her stupor."

"I think it's your heartbeat. It's wakin' her up."

*****

My next encounter with Dominique began with letting her listen to my heart. After a few minutes, she sat up. "Where are the children?"

"I understand you have some children around you."

Dominique looked at me. Her eyes did not look quite as vacant as I remembered. "Where's the room?"

"What room?"

"The room where the children can be safe. They need a room."

"It sounds like you want to help the children."

"They need a room."

Again, I noticed Dominique looking at the picture of Lucinda's world. "Do you like that picture?"

A tear made its way down her cheek. "I wanted to go too. She left me."

"Who left you?"

"Lucinda left me. I wanted to go too."

"Oh, I think I understand. When Lucinda went away into her world, you wanted to go along. You wanted to leave this world too."

Dominique quietly wept. "She said there would be no pain where she was going, and there would be a Mommy to love her. I wanted to go too."

"You have a spiritual mother now. You don't need to go away. Besides, Lucinda's world ended up being filled with darkness. She learned that she needs to stay in this world."

"Where's the room? They need a room."

Dominique was certainly making visible progress. She was conversing; she was feeling her emotions. She was wanting to help the children. It also seemed she was more closely connected to Lucinda than I had known. Indeed, she knew Lucinda's plan to escape into her fantasy world. I wondered what this connection might be.

*****

Against this backdrop, things began to deteriorate with Christine. Even after our intimate conversation when she shared with me the vision of God handing me a baby, even after our agreement to let God do the battling while I was just her spiritual mom, even after the tenderness of that conversation, we seemed unable to get our relationship on a smooth course.

We relived the same scenarios over and over. Christine's tough exterior touched something deep within me, a sense of failing to connect meaningfully with her.

When she detected my walls going up, she was convinced that I preferred child Lucinda over her. She felt that I never forgave her for the times when she had pushed out the children, including Lucinda, to be with the group.

We would exchange harsh words with each other, and I would throw up my hands in exasperation. My level and placid nature was caught off guard by these more volatile expressions. I didn't like this person who responded with so much emotion to Christine.

Who was this new me? Where did she come from? I didn't like her, but I seemed unable to find that even keel that had characterized most of my adult life. After a clash with Christine, I would turn on myself, berating myself for my inability to respond to her with equanimity.

"I'm tired of this roller coaster. Just when I feel that Christine and I are making a new start, everything comes crashing down, and we're at each other again. When will it end? This is the hardest thing I've ever done. I can't do this!" I vented to Cinda. She listened patiently while I cried copiously. "I am worn out. This up and down, up and down is more than I can bear. I want off this roller coaster!"

Cinda maintained her ever peaceful demeanor. Finally, she spoke. "You are not on a roller coaster. You use that expression a lot. It is time for you to view this differently. You are not on a roller coaster. You are on a journey. On a roller coaster, you have no power over where it will take you. You are on a journey, and you can choose each step you will take. A journey also has ups and downs, but you have the power to choose where you are going. And while a roller coaster just keeps going in the same loop, a journey has a destination. You are going somewhere. I want you to stop thinking that you are on a roller coaster. You are on a journey, and you have the power to choose where you are going."

Cinda's words stopped me in my tracks. I thought about the image of a roller coaster. She was right. Once you're on the ride, you have no power. You can only hang on until the end. Cinda was suggesting that I have some say in where we were headed. Maybe I needed to stop feeling at the mercy of the forces around me—the group, the broken children, Christine's brashness—and choose to take steps in a positive direction.

I grabbed a tissue and wiped my eyes. "Okay, I'm on a journey. I will try to make positive choices and head in a good direction. I am not helpless in the midst of all this."

Cinda smiled at me. "I know that this is not easy, but God chose you to be her spiritual mother from the foundations of the earth. He would not have chosen you if you did not have what it takes to complete this journey. God does not make mistakes."

I smiled weakly. "God has more confidence in me than I have in myself."

"He sees how you don't give up. When you fall down, you get back up and continue the journey. He is pleased with that."

It amazed me that God could be pleased with me. But I took Cinda's words to heart and once again resolved to move forward in the battle.

*****

The next time I saw Lucinda, she reported that Dominique had gathered quite a few children. "She wants to help them, NanNan. She don't want them to be out with the group. I don't want them out with the group either. Can we stop the group from getting them?"

"We can't stop what happens when they're at the group." I tried to keep the image of the journey in my mind. What positive choice could I make in this moment rather than feeling at the mercy of this heinous group? "Why don't we pray and ask God if there is a way to protect these children?"

"Okay, NanNan. God, we don't want the group to get these children. Dominique is trying so hard to take care of them. Is there anything we can do?"

A few minutes of silence followed. I marveled at Lucinda's childlike faith. I tried to still my mind and listen inwardly for any direction God might give.

"NanNan, I think God wants them to hear your heartbeat."

"Okay. Who should be out?"

"I think Dominique should be out, and then I should be right behind her, and then the children."

"Is God telling you all this?"

"I just feel it inside."

"Okay, then let's do it. Dominique, this is your spiritual mother. Will you come out with me?"

"Where's the room?" Dominique was out.

"You're still looking for a room for the children. It's so good that you want to take care of them. But right now, I want you to hear my heartbeat." I gently pulled her head down to my chest.

Dominque compliantly lay her head on my heart. She smiled slightly as she listened.

"Okay, Lucinda. Bring the children close." Dominique lay very still. I rocked her gently, looking at her vacant eyes.

Occasionally, her eyes would meet mine. She would look directly at me for few seconds before turning her eyes away. I was surprised that she lay so still.

"That is very strong, but it's not scary," Dominique murmured in her monotone voice.

"That's because God loves you. He wants to heal you, not hurt you."

I continued to gently rock Dominique. Then I began to softly sing to her. "Jesus loves me, this I know, for the Bible tells me so. Little ones to him belong. They are weak, but he is strong." Several times, I heard a soft cooing sound coming from her. I wondered if she was regressing into babyhood. After about fifteen minutes,

Dominque was fast asleep. I held her as she slept, wondering if I should call for Lucinda or wait for her to emerge.

"NanNan." I looked down at Lucinda, who had indeed come out. She looked sleepy. She rubbed her eyes. "NanNan, you shoulda seen it. All them children came around me. We heard you singin', and we heard the heartbeat. God's power was really strong. It was gentle, but strong. And then, one by one, each of them children got real little, like babies, and they came into me."

"They came into you?"

"Yeah, I took all them parts. Your heartbeat got them real little, and then they came into me. And last of all, Dominique came into me."

"Dominique came into you?"

"Yeah, she got real little too. And then I took her."

"How do you feel, having taken all those parts?"

"I feel a little funny, like I'm littler than I really am. But your heartbeat healed them, so there was no bad memories. At least not yet."

"Wow, this is amazing! And now we don't have to worry about the group getting those children. God answered your prayer." I felt like I was on a mountaintop. The image of the roller coaster flashed through my mind, up and down, up and down.

No, this is not a roller coaster. This is a journey. Lucinda and I took the step to ask God for direction, and he answered us in an amazing way. This is a high point on the journey, but it did not merely happen to us.

I tried to ground myself in this new understanding. Then I prayed aloud. "Thank you, Lord, for this wonderful healing and for honoring Lucinda's prayer, and for this time of refreshing on the journey."

"Amen!" Lucinda chimed in. "And thank you that none of them children will be hurt by the group."

I nodded in agreement. "Lucinda, I got the sense that there was a connection between you and Dominique. She knew your plan to run away to your imaginary world, and she wanted to go with you. Do you feel a connection with her?"

Lucinda squinched up her face. Then she shook her head. "I don't know, NanNan. I can barely remember going away into my world. I don't know if there was a connection. I do know she went into me real easy."

"Well, I guess the mystery is unsolved. The important thing is that she is now part of you. You are more whole than ever."

"And the group won't get her or those children ever again."

CHAPTER 28

Ruthie

Christine and I still clashed, but I steadied myself with the new perspective of being on a journey. I was not at the mercy of external forces pulling me up and down.

About this time, Christine began to report in her sessions about a new friendship. She first encountered Ruthie at church.

Ruthie had seen the incident when child Angie had skipped down the aisle after watching the children's choir sing, only to be told by another woman to act her age. She had seen the wounded look in Angie's eyes, and her heart was touched. She began to look for Lucinda at church, but when she saw her, she detected the steel walls of Christine, not the childlike exuberance of Angie. This puzzled her.

Her curiosity led her to strike up a conversation with Christine. She found her to be closed and unapproachable, but she remembered the innocent child she had seen, so she persisted. In time, Christine opened up a little, sharing with Ruthie that she was in counseling and had come from a very abusive background. Christine began to sense that this woman's kindness was genuine and that she could be trusted.

I first met Ruthie when Christine brought her to a session. She wanted me to help Ruthie understand her multiplicity. Ruthie entered the room with a smile and sat down on my couch next to Christine. I judged her to be a few years younger than I. She was professionally dressed in a blazer and tailored pants. Her dark hair was short and cut in layers. She wore small gold hoop earrings and a gold chain around her neck. She looked to be the consummate professional.

I asked her questions about herself, wanting to know more about this woman that Christine was starting to trust. Anyone who could penetrate Christine's walls had either a heart of gold or a determination of steel. Maybe both.

"So tell me about yourself, Ruthie. I've been hearing a lot about you from Christine, but she hasn't said much about your background."

"Well, my faith is very important to me, so I'm at church every week. I noticed her long before I actually started talking to her. But you asked about me, not Christine. Well, I'm a physical therapist by profession. I've been at it for about twenty-five years. I love my work. It's what I was meant to do, to help people who are broken get mended. Maybe that's why I'm drawn to Christine." She let out a nervous laugh. "I'm divorced, have been for a number of years. I tried everything I could think of to save our marriage, but when I knew for sure he was cheating, I couldn't do it any longer. We never had any children, partly because I was so involved in my career, partly because the marriage was never on solid ground." She let out a long sigh.

"Is that a disappointment for you?"

"Yes, it is. I always assumed I would have a family. I do like children. They're so innocent and spontaneous. I think that's why I was drawn to Christine. After church one day, I saw her skipping down the aisle, looking and acting exactly like a child. It was totally disarming, and when I heard some old curmudgeon of a lady tell her to act her age, I wanted to belt her. I thought her childlikeness was beautiful. I haven't seen that side of her since. Christine thought you could help me understand all this."

I liked this woman. She was warm and insightful, and I would catch her looking at Christine with fondness. I thought of all the caring, motherly women that Lucinda had drawn to herself through the years. Some of them, like the teacher Miss Kindle, had been positive influences. Others had left her wounded and broken. I hoped Ruthie would be a positive person for her.

I spent the rest of the session giving Ruthie a crash course in dissociative identity disorder. I explained that she had seen two separate personalities: Angie who was a little child in every way except her body, and Christine who was a protector, so she could be very tough.

Ruthie laughed. "Yes, she can be tough, but I also see that under that she has a heart that is as big as this." She spread her arms wide to show the size of Christine's heart.

I nodded. "And you know, under all that toughness, Christine also has a broken child, but she's very invested in keeping her hidden."

Christine squirmed a little when I said this.

"Oh, I've caught a few glimpses of that child. I know she's there."

Christine squirmed again.

So my session with Ruthie went very well. She was receptive and eager to learn. And I could see that there was a dogged determination about her. She would not be easily discouraged.

*****

Over the next several months, this friendship grew. Christine even confided in her about the group. Ruthie was horrified and wanted to know if she could do anything to help. So once again, Christine brought her in for a session.

When they entered my office, Christine fell back into her usual spot on my pastel couch. Once again, Ruthie sat down next to her. I noticed that Ruthie would occasionally reach over and touch Christine on her arm or leg in a reassuring way. Christine seemed to accept this.

Ruthie began. "Christine and I have been spending a lot of time together. We've been going to yard sales on Saturday mornings and then out to lunch. One Saturday, Christine took me to her house to see her doll collection. Oh my, I've never seen so many dolls, and they are just beautiful. Next week she wants to take me to the doll store where she used to work so she can show me some of the dolls she would like to add to her collection.

"As we do these things together, she's been opening up to me, telling me a little about her past and how the two of you discovered that she had been raised in a satanic cult. But she keeps adding that she was not around when all that happened, and she really doesn't know much about it." Ruthie shook her head. "I'm not sure I really understand all this. So I asked her why she wasn't around." She looked over at Christine and patted her leg. "What she told me next was just too much. She said that several years ago one of the alter personalities had joined another group, and she came from that group, that they tortured one of the parts to split off a new part, and that new part was her. Then she says they still go to that group. It's all so unbelievable. You seem like a reasonable person. What's your take on all this?"

"First, I want to say that Christine must really trust you if she shared this much. And yes, it is unbelievable. There are times I question if it can all be true. But I have seen the burns on her face from the lights they used to torture her. I have held the broken children after they have been in their clutches. I have seen the limousine they sent to pick her up late one night. As fantastic as it is, I believe it is all true."

"If it's true, what can I do to help?"

"Being her friend is so important. She is trusting you with her story. Continue to build this relationship. Help her to grow spiritually. She is very young in her faith."

"But why would God allow all this to happen to her? It just isn't fair."

"No, it isn't fair, but his hand is on her and has been from the beginning."

"Hello, Ruthie." Cinda was now addressing Ruthie.

I instantly recognized her voice and demeanor. What do I do now? Do I tell Ruthie that an angel is addressing her? Ruthie had said that I was a reasonable person. Would that assessment stand if I told her she was talking to an angel of light?

I began to speak, not sure exactly what I would say. "Ruthie, this is Cinda." I hesitated. "You are very honored that she is speaking to you."

"Oh, she must be one of Lucinda's personalities."

"Not exactly."

"Then what is she?" Ruthie cocked her head.

"Remember I just told you that God's hand has been with her from the beginning?"

Ruthie nodded.

"Cinda is one of the ways he has been with her."

Ruthie looked puzzled. I took a deep breath. If Cinda was going to talk to her, she might as well know who she was talking to. "It seems that God sent one of his angels to be with her from the time she was very young to protect her, to guide her, to help with her healing process. That angel is Cinda."

Ruthie said nothing. There was a heavy silence.

"She's right, Ruthie. I am a messenger from God. And he has sent me to speak with you."

Ruthie was truly speechless.

"God has seen the way you have sought out Christine, the way you have accepted her and not been dissuaded by her walls of protection. He saw the way you prayed for her the other night, with pleading and tears. God knows you are strong enough to stand up to her when she needs to be confronted. He is calling you to a very special ministry with her."

"But how do you know? I mean, about my prayers the other night? I was all alone in my bedroom when I prayed for her."

"God saw you and heard your prayers. But you didn't know that you are to be part of the answer to those prayers. You are to be part of the team that is going to help free her from this group."

Now I jumped in. "You mean she is going to get out of this group?" My heart raced. I was elated.

"God wants her freed from this group. It may take more time, but God wants to set her free."

I was almost giddy with excitement. "This is the best news ever."

Cinda turned to Ruthie. "I want you to go home and search your heart. God is not calling you to an easy task. Search your heart to see if you are willing to accept this call from God."

Ruthie was again speechless. Finally, she nodded. "I feel overwhelmed by all this. And you must be an angel because you knew about my prayers."

"What happened?" Christine had returned. "I was inside and couldn't even get close to coming out. The way was blocked completely. That only happens when Cinda is out."

"Yes, Cinda was out. Ruthie had her first encounter with an angel. I'll let her tell you about it on your way home. But one great piece of information the angel gave was that God plans to free you from the group." I got up and went over to Christine. She was not one for hugs, but I hugged her anyway. "I feel hopeful and renewed by what has happened here today."

Ruthie and Christine walked out my office door together. Ruthie was quiet while Christine kept asking her what had happened.

I sank down in my chair and prayed, thanking God for the hope that I felt. Perhaps this battle with the group was coming to an end.

*****

I wasn't surprised when Cinda came out at the end of our next session to discuss this new turn of events. She looked directly at me with her clear eyes and a very serious look. "Ruthie has accepted the call to be part of the team helping Lucinda. She feels deeply connected to Christine, and being part of the team resonates with her. She couldn't imagine saying no. Now, I have something important to discuss with you. You know that you are on a journey, and you can make choices about where you want this journey to go. God is opening the door for you to have some help. He knows how difficult this has been for you. Christine is learning to trust Ruthie, so God is opening the door for Ruthie to be with her some evenings, so you can have a break. But God won't open that door unless you agree, since you are her spiritual mother."

I was not surprised by Cinda's words. I was hearing a great deal about Ruthie from Christine, and I sensed an intensity when Christine talked about her. They were getting close, and Ruthie seemed able to navigate Christine's abrasiveness with much more grace than I did.

Cinda continued. "I have talked with Ruthie and have told her that her relationship is to be only with Christine. Under no conditions is she to have Lucinda out. Lucinda has bonded with you, and she would not understand having a relationship with Ruthie."

I took all this in. The thought of having open evenings without late-night phone calls sounded wonderfully freeing.

"Christine has confided in Ruthie about how she feels you favor Lucinda over her. It is good for her to have a relationship where she will not feel in competition with Lucinda."

Now I wanted to scream. It angered me that Christine thought this about me. How can you compare a relationship with a five-year-old to a relationship with an adult? Christine portraying me to Ruthie as openly preferring Lucinda made me very uneasy.

"Well, what do you think? Do you want to open this door?"

"Is this what God is calling for?"

"He is calling for this if you agree to it."

I certainly didn't want to stand in the way of God. And I needed help to carry the load of this battle. I was emotionally worn down. "If God has opened the door, I will walk through it."

"Very well. Take tonight off. Ruthie will spend the evening with Christine."

It was such a relief to have an enjoyable evening with my husband, to go to bed at a reasonable hour, and to have the peace of knowing that Christine was protected from the group.

I tried not to think of her complaining to Ruthie about me. If she did, she did. *Having someone to help me carry the load is going to be a good thing,* I thought to myself as I drifted off to sleep. I slept well that night.

*****

The day that Cinda told me that it was time for Ruthie to join our deliverance team, that she needed to learn about deliverance, I nodded compliantly. I suspected this was the next step. As I interacted more with Ruthie in this new setting, I began to see that she was not one to take a back seat. She wanted to be by Christine's side at all times, and I was starting to feel crowded out. I noticed that she was starting to call herself Christine's "auntie," and I wondered who had given her this title.

I struggled within myself to accept that Ruthie seemed able to do what was so very difficult for me, to accept Christine with all her hardness and to see beyond that protective exterior to not only her big heart but to the broken child within. There was a connection there, and I wondered where I fit in.

At one of those early deliverance sessions, we were dealing with a masculine alter named Jay. He was a cult alter, groomed to serve the purposes of the satanic cult. He was hard and nasty and very uncooperative. Typically, we would spend time listening and seeking to find the chink in his armor, the place where we could get him to let down his walls and admit to his brokenness.

Every so often, the darkness within surfaced, giving us that evil look and growling at us.

Paul took charge, ordering the darkness down in the name of Jesus. Then we refocused on Jay, pointing out to him how darkness had to submit to the name of Jesus.

This agitated Jay, who screamed at us. "I don't belong here. Let me go. I have more important things to do."

Paul, Adele, Ruthie, Joby, and I all looked at each other. What were we to do now? We seemed to be getting nowhere.

Paul broke the silence. "His darkness is very strong. It seems to be impeding him from moving forward at all. There is a very strong hold there."

Ruthie's words tumbled out of her. "That's because this isn't any ordinary spirit. It is the spirit of all the groups in the city."

Her words hung in the air. Something within me acknowledged the truth in her words. I remembered when years earlier, Lucinda told me that her grandmother, who was the priestess of their cult, was a very powerful force in the entire city. To free Lucinda from this spirit might release a hold that darkness had on our entire city.

I turned to Ruthie. "How did you know that?"

"I don't know. It was just there in my head."

We closed the deliverance session at that time. We all agreed that we were not yet ready to tackle this spirit. And certainly, Jay was not ready to be delivered.

*****

Many changes were happening. Ruthie's involvement with Christine was increasing, and she was spending much of her free time with her. As a result, there were not many nights when the group had her. For this, I was truly grateful.

I still had occasional late-night phone calls, usually when Ruthie was attending church events; but for the most part, my evenings were free, and I was returning to a normal sleep schedule.

Even more important, Christine was safe in the evenings. She was even spending nights at Ruthie's apartment. But of course, Ruthie had to work during the day, so days became the primary time when the group would contact the parts they had groomed to respond to their phone calls.

Once they had one of these parts on the phone, it was a simple matter to get them to come with them. But I was well aware that it was often a week or more between the times when they had her. At last, it felt like their hold on her was starting to break. For this reason, I was truly thankful for Ruthie.

Another significant change was that Christine's place as the host personality, the one that was out the most and carried on the continuity of her life, was being cemented into place. Lucinda, who had this role from the time I had known her, who had probably had that role since she first suspected that Kurt was cheating on her early in their marriage, was now a child, maybe five years old.

Lucinda never had the strength of personality Christine had. For our first seven years together, Lucinda had been drowning in suicidal depression, wanting to give up on life, lamenting that she never had a mother to love her and desperately looking for someone to fill that role. She found motherly women to cling to in hopes that they would fill up her empty places.

Even though Christine also struggled with depression, she hid it well, presenting to the world a no-nonsense, take-charge personality. She was strong and commanding and kept her broken inner child well hidden. In many ways, she was fearless, unafraid to stand up to anyone, and always up for a challenge. She was not intimidated by the group or their threats. She kept her broken side well hidden and seldom showed vulnerability.

I found this very frustrating. As her therapist, it was my job to give her a safe place to let her walls down. I had been able to do this with Lucinda. But Christine was another story. My frustration with her frequently spilled out.

Ruthie, on the other hand, seemed to have endless patience with her, and Christine was more likely to let her walls down with Ruthie. I'd remind myself that Ruthie was fresh in the battle, not worn down by months...years...of battling.

But the more attached Christine became to Ruthie, the more I had to fight my own sense of failure. At times, I resented Ruthie. I fought my own inner battles, reminding myself that the group was the enemy, not Ruthie. The things that surfaced in me were not pretty, and I did not like the person I was becoming.

Another significant change was within her marriage. Lucinda had always tolerated Kurt's controlling ways. At times, he would become violent with both Lucinda and the three boys. There were many ugly fights. When Kurt attacked the boys physically, protector personalities would surface, putting themselves in front of the boys and absorbing the blows. Sometimes she would turn on Kurt, exchanging blows with him. Lucinda hid this from me. She believed Kurt when he told her that if she left him, he would get the boys because of her mental illness. Despite all the dysfunction, she truly loved her boys and did not want to lose them.

However, Lucinda was no longer the personality whom Kurt interfaced with. He had to deal with Christine. From the beginning, she had no attachment to Kurt. Once she figured out that they were married and that these boys were their children, she wondered why Lucinda had ever married him. She felt a strong attachment to the boys immediately, but Kurt…well, he was just someone she had to tolerate.

Kurt kept at his usual methods of controlling Lucinda, but they were no longer effective. Lucinda was well aware that she could not support herself, that being able to maintain employment with her mental illness was very unlikely. "I'm leaving and I'm taking the boys with me" was his standard threat. When Lucinda heard this, she would meekly give in to whatever Kurt wanted.

Now, when he made such threats, Christine's standard response was, "There's the door." If Christine feared his leaving, she did not let on. This befuddled Kurt.

After one such encounter, he looked at his wife, standing tall, arms folded in front of her. "Who are you?"

"Someone who can take care of myself and doesn't need you."

This troubled Kurt. He was losing control of her, but he had no idea how to rectify the situation. He had never made much effort to understand her mental illness. He knew there were alter personalities, but it never occurred to him to have an honest conversation with his wife about the changes that were occurring.

Perhaps it was his fear of losing her and being left alone that motivated him to start searching for relationships on the Internet, which was a relatively new innovation in 2003.

*****

Changes were also occurring for me. I was seeing a great deal less of Lucinda. As Christine rose to prominence, Lucinda seemed to fade into the background. Gone were the days when Lucinda would show up at my office. I only saw her if I intentionally called her out.

She spent a good amount of time while inside in the light. There, she would be bathed in the light and love of God.

Often, she would be "taking parts," as she called it. Personalities that were healed by listening to my heartbeat would be integrated into her. While this turn of events was positive, I did miss child Lucinda, so full of life and spontaneity.

Another change that occurred was that I felt less and less like her therapist. The kind of therapeutic work I had done for over a decade with Lucinda was much more difficult with Christine. She was deeply invested in keeping her brokenness hidden. Her walls of protection often kept our sessions on a more superficial level.

I began to wonder who I was in her life. Maybe I wasn't to be her therapist anymore, just her spiritual mother, helping her grow in her faith. Was it time to terminate our counseling sessions? I toyed with the idea, but I also sensed that without the structure of regular sessions, Christine would start to decompensate. That is, she might become unbalanced. Despite her exterior presentation, there was still a great deal of brokenness within.

As Ruthie increased her involvement with Christine, I had to do some deep soul-searching. Ruthie was not going anywhere. She was in this for the long haul. Somehow I had to make room for her, even as she seemed to be taking over everything. Ruthie was not one to hold back. She learned quickly and seemed to understand and appreciate Christine in ways I did not.

I needed to stop feeling outdone by her. I needed to see her as my ally, not my competition. And perhaps Ruthie needed to be more of a team player. But my immediate goal was seeing Lucinda freed from this group. That trumped everything else. If Ruthie could help with that, I was all for her involvement.

CHAPTE29

Christine Remembers

Many years later, Christine filled in for me some of the intrigue that occurred in the group during the last months of her time with them. She had chosen to be very secretive about much of what was happening. It was more than a decade later that she explained it all to me.

"There was a divide in the group. They were mostly a drug ring, but there were a few of them, mostly the ones from England, who were interested in my ability to dissociate and split. Nevil was the main one. He was sure he could learn a lot from us…about how the mind works. He was always talkin' about that army he wanted to build, an army of parts who would take orders and do whatever he told them. They were supposed to have no emotions, no anger, no fear, so they would do risky things. They would be like robots. At first, the others went along with him, but the longer it went, and the less success he had, the more the others thought he was wastin' their time and money. After that fiasco when only the babies came out to them bigwigs from other countries, they were about done with him.

"Then he decided he had to win me over to his side, to bring me on board. He wanted my loyalty. The first thing he did was to try to make me feel important by givin' me responsibilities, tellin' me I could be a big help to him. He was all interested in how my mind works. He had figured out that I have pretty much of a photographic memory."

I nodded as I listened. I was well aware that Christine had an extraordinary memory. She could recall events detail for detail with amazing accuracy, even many years later. She said it was as if she could see a movie playing in her mind of past events. Despite her lack of education, she had an outstanding ability to remember numbers. When she finally got her own checking account, she would remember every detail of it, without recording a single entry. At any point in time, she knew how much money was in her account and any outstanding checks. Never once did she bounce a check. This always amazed me.

"So Nevil started to let me see their books and tell him if anything didn't look right. He did this in secret, knowing the others would not tolerate me knowin' all that stuff. I was always stunned by how much money went through that operation. Nevil started to explain to me how their operations worked, how the drugs got into the country, mostly hidden inside the walls of coffins. They were tied into some of the funeral homes in the area. He let me know which ones. I thought he was stupid to trust me with all that information. But he was obsessed with me, and he thought it would win me to his side.

"When I still wouldn't cooperate, he kept remindin' me I was an important part of them now, tryin' to build me up, make me feel important. By now, the others were gettin' suspicious of what he was doin' with me, and he didn't want me lettin' on how much I knew. So he tried to bribe me. If I kept my mouth shut, he said he would give me fifty thousand dollars. I told him to take his money and shove it. He thought I wanted more, so he asked me how much I wanted. I just laughed in his face. He was stunned. In their world, anybody could be bought. He didn't know what to do with me."

I marveled at the moxie this woman had. Christine could be positively fearless. She was not intimidated by anybody.

"Then Nevil tried a new tactic. He said that unless I promised to keep my mouth shut, he would go after Kurt, that he would mysteriously die of an accident…or just disappear. Again, I just laughed at him. 'How soon can you do it?' Nevil couldn't believe me. I guess I sounded very hard-hearted, but I had no attachment to Kurt.

"Then Nevil started tellin' me he had a family, and if I let on how much I knew, his kids would be fatherless, and it would be all my fault. He knew I had a heart for children, and I knew how ruthless the group could be. I wouldn't put anything past 'em. So I decided I wouldn't tell, but I didn't let him know that.

"Next, knowing my heart for kids, he decided he would go after my sons. He showed me pictures he had of 'em, mostly taken outside my house. That scared me, but you better believe I didn't let on. By that time, I was startin' to learn some things about God, so I prayed that they would be kept safe. I told Nevil that my God would protect my boys. He said that my God was a myth. I told him God was way bigger than him, that he could wipe all of 'em out. I kept remembering all the times you told me there is somethin' bigger than me, bigger than all of this." She waved her hand in a broad sweep to indicate all that was around her.

"Then Matthew got a notice in the mail sayin' he won a brand-new car. He was supposed to go to this place at a certain time to get the keys. He was just learnin' to drive then, so he was all excited. He showed me the notice. I knew right away he didn't win no car. The group was behind this. I kept tellin' him it was a scam. I was afraid they might use the opportunity to kidnap him...or worse. I wouldn't let him go. 'You didn't win no car. You didn't even enter a contest, so how did you win a car?' I made sure he didn't go. He was so mad at me, but I just kept tellin' him that the whole thing was fishy. I think on some level he realized that.

"Then I think Nevil and the others close to him decided it was my allegiance to God that was the problem. They decided I needed to renounce God. If I did that, then you and Ruthie—by this time they knew all about Ruthie too—then you and Ruthie would leave me, and I'd have no one helpin' me. And then, they could get me whenever they wanted. So they kept sayin' that God is nothin' but a myth, and I need to renounce him. I just ignored 'em. Or I'd say, 'Why would I renounce God to give allegiance to puny little people like you?' Boy, did that make 'em mad.

"Finally, they showed me pictures of the boys, one of Matthew on our porch holding that damn brochure about the car, one of Mark with some of his friends down the street, and one of Michael with his girlfriend. They said if I didn't renounce God, their lives were in danger, that they knew where to find 'em. Now I was really scared. I love my boys. I'm a protector. Everything in me was shakin'. Everything in me wanted to save my boys. But then I thought, *Even if I tell 'em I renounce God, they still might kill my boys. I can't trust 'em.*

"Oh yeah, there was one other thing they wanted from me. They wanted me to renounce God, and they wanted access to the parts. They just wanted to use me for their own demented purposes. It took everything in me, but I asked God to protect my boys, and then I told them that I would not renounce God."

As I listened to her story, those many years later, I felt so proud of her. Christine had a strength of character that astounded me. She risked her own sons to take a stand for God and not become a puppet of the group. She would not give in to Nevil and his cohorts, and she would not renounce her God. I looked over at her, tears collecting in my eyes. "Now that is walking in faith! You really trusted God. I am so proud of you, Christine. You truly are a woman of God."

Christine acknowledged my comment with a nod. "It was the hardest thing I ever done. But I knew there was somethin' bigger than them. So I accepted God over evil. And God was with me. Me and my boys are all still here today."

"I guess that settled things with Nevil. You were not going to give in to them."

"Well, they weren't quite ready to give up yet. They made one last attempt."

"And what was that?"

"Florida."

I shuddered inwardly as I remembered their family vacation in Florida.

CHAPTER 30

Florida

Christine had just returned from her Saturday morning outing with Ruthie. She had bought some baby clothes at a yard sale and was very excited to see how they looked on her baby dolls. She swung open her front door to see Kurt with a big smile on his face. He was holding a paper. It seemed to be some sort of brochure.

"You know you always wanted to go to Disney World? Well, I think we can go." He held up the paper and shook it. "This is great! I found this paper on our front door. There's a condo in Orlando for rent. It's only $900 for a week, and that includes all meals and use of all the resort's activities. All we'd have to pay for is our gas to drive there."

Christine grabbed the paper. "Let me see that." She scanned the color brochure showing a swank-looking vacation community and the inside of a spacious condo. "This can't be just $900. Somethin's not right."

"Oh, don't be such a killjoy. With our tax refund, we could do this. Think how excited the boys will be."

"What about our neighbors? Did any of them get one of these?" She swung open the front door, leaned outside, and checked the doors of the houses on either side. Then she peered across the street to see if there were brochures on any of those doors. "Kurt, none of our neighbors have a brochure. Why would we be the only ones?"

"I don't know. Maybe they put them on doors randomly."

"Kurt, why would anybody try to market their high-end condo in our neighborhood? This is the hood, or just one step up from it. This whole thing don't seem right to me."

"Well, I'm calling the number to find out more."

Christine did not like the sound of this. Nothing seemed to add up, and deep inside, she wondered if the group was involved. But why would they offer them a cheap trip to Florida? She shook her head and headed upstairs to try the new baby clothes on her dolls.

A short time later, Kurt came running up the stairs. He was very excited. "I got it. I got the condo! I can't wait to tell the boys we're going to Disney World. We have it for a whole week in August."

"What were the hidden costs?"

"No hidden costs. The guy said the people who were going to take it backed out, and now they just want to find someone to stay there and cut their losses."

"But why did they put the brochure on our door?"

"I don't know. I didn't ask. He said all we have to do is bring the money the day before we leave and pick up the key."

"Pick up the key where?"

"It's about fifteen minutes from here, in the suburbs." He told her the name of the area.

Christine gulped. The area described was not far from where the group had their headquarters. "I don't think we should do it. Sounds like a scam to me. Who ever heard of picking up a key for a place in Florida in a state hundreds of miles away?"

"What would you know about renting a place in Florida?"

The sound of the front door opening caught their attention. Kurt yelled down the stairs. "Who's home?"

"It's me, Michael."

Kurt went flying down the stairs. "We're going to Florida! I just rented a place near Disney World. We're going in August."

"Really? That's so cool. Wait till Matthew and Mark hear about this!"

Christine heard the excitement in Michael's voice. Didn't every kid want to go to Disney World? What were the chances that her children would have this opportunity? And truth be told, Christine had an inner child who was rising up within her.

Disney World? She was going to Disney World? She had a large collection of Disney movies and loved them all. She would be able to have every child's dream, a trip to Disney World. That well-hidden inner child was surfacing.

*****

On a hot August morning, Kurt wedged suitcases into the rear of his outdated station wagon. Christine opened the front door, hauling a cooler filled with drinks and sandwiches. "Is there room for this is the trunk?"

"No way," Kurt replied. "I can barely squeeze in our suitcases. That birdcage takes up so much damn space. You'll have to put that on the floor of the back seat. Michael's the smallest, so he can sit with it under his feet."

"Hey, Mom, I can't find my iPod. I can't go without my tunes." Mark, leaned out the doorway of the house. "And is there room for my guitar?"

"There's no room for your guitar unless you want to strap it on the roof. And I last saw your iPod on the kitchen table."

"There's no way my guitar's going on the roof."

"Then the guitar stays home," Christine said with finality.

"Aw, that stinks." Mark disappeared back into the house in search of his iPod.

"That boy is so unorganized," Christine mumbled as she shook her head.

"I'm ready. When are we leaving?" Michael emerged, neatly dressed in a matching athletic shirt and shorts. He was sporting brand new sneakers, which matched his clothes. A backpack was slung over his shoulder. "I have everything I'll need for the trip in here." He jiggled the backpack. "Got my music, some snacks, a bottle of water, and some comic books. I'm ready to go."

"That's great, Michael. Your brother should be half as organized as you are," Christine said.

The door swung open again. This time both Mark and Matthew emerged. "Found my iPod." Mark waved it in the air.

"Are you ready to go, Matthew?" He also had a backpack. It was going to be crowded in the back seat.

"Yeah, I'm ready."

"Then pile in, and I'll get Sonny. Michael, you sit where the cooler is, since you're the smallest."

The boys pulled their teenage frames into the car with some good-natured pushing and laughing. "I don't see why I've gotta sit where the cooler is," Michael grumbled.

"It's because you're a squirt." Matthew laughed at Mark's comment, while Michael pulled his legs up to his chin.

Christine reemerged from the house, carrying a cardboard box filled with bird food, several swings that would be hung in the cage, and a cloth teepee where Sonny liked to sleep. "Where does this go?"

"It'll have to go at your feet." Kurt opened the passenger side door.

Christine leaned over and carefully placed the box on the floor.

One last time, Christine went back into the house. When she appeared again, there was a small sun conure sitting on her shoulder. His brilliant golden hues stood out against her black T-shirt. She locked the door, rattled it to make sure it was locked, then headed for the car.

She climbed into the passenger seat, Sonny still on her shoulder.

"I can't believe we're taking that bird." Matthew rolled his eyes in the back seat.

"He's part of the family," Christine replied.

"Hey, Dad, did you get the car's air conditioner fixed? It's hot already, and we're headed to where it's gonna be even hotter." Mark, squished in the middle between his two brothers, fanned his face in an exaggerated way.

"The air conditioner is not fixed," Kurt said with irritation. "I couldn't do both that and this trip."

All three boys let out a long, loud groan.

"Open your windows. The breeze will feel good," Kurt said.

Down went the back windows.

Christine took Sonny and stuck him inside her shirt, his head just peeping out over the neckline. "He'll be safer there. We don't want to lose him out a window."

Kurt pulled away from the curb. The old brown station wagon made a loud roar as they pulled down the street.

"Dad, when are you going to get that muffler fixed?" Michael lowered his head, embarrassed by the attention the car was drawing. The other two boys waved goodbye to neighbors on their porches. Sonny let out a loud squawk.

"We look like the Beverly Hillbillies." Matthew peered over the back of the seat and saw the box of bird paraphernalia at his mother's feet.

"Nah, we're the hillbillies from the hood," Mark said.

Christine enjoyed their banter. They were excited. She was too. But an ominous feeling lurked in the background. To have obtained this condo for so little just didn't add up.

*****

Kurt turned the car down a stately boulevard lined with palm trees. Manicured flower beds filled with brilliant hues lined each side of the road. The car windows were still down. Sonny was still tucked inside Christine's T-shirt. The heat was oppressive, and everybody was tired and grumpy.

"The place should be at the end of this road," Kurt said.

All three boys straightened up and peered down the road. They came to a small gatehouse with a guard sitting inside. Kurt pulled the car up to the window. "We've rented a condo for the week. Here's all the information." Kurt handed the guard a small piece of paper.

The guard scanned the paper. "Oh yes, sir. We've been expecting you." Just follow this road to the fork and then bear to the left. Your condo is on the second floor, second building." The guard opened the gate for them to proceed.

They followed the road to the fork and went to the left. The road curved around a slight embankment and up a gradual incline. When they reached the crest of the incline, all five of them simultaneously gasped. They looked down on a magnificent display of coral-colored buildings with glistening white balconies. At the center of the complex was a gracefully curved swimming pool and large deck lined with towel-draped chaises. In the front of the complex was a large pond surrounded by reedy grasses. In the center of the pond was a stately fountain surrounded by a circle of smaller fountains. Sinewy water birds on stilt legs stood among the reedy grasses. At the outer edge of the property were basketball courts and shuffleboard courts. A skateboard park was off to the left. A winding walking path connected all the buildings and outdoor activities.

"Us hillbillies from the hood have struck oil," Mark exclaimed.

"This place has everything!" Matthew said.

"Let's go see our condo." Michael bounced in his seat. "We're gonna really live it up. I can't wait to try the skateboard park."

A few minutes later, Kurt swung open the front door of the condo. A blast of cool air from the air-conditioning met them as they stepped inside. "Wow! This is quite a place." Kurt gave a low whistle.

The five of them wandered from room to room, taking it all in. They had never seen such luxury: king-size beds, sunken bathtubs, panoramic views of the pool and a nearby lake.

Matthew wandered into the kitchen. "Look at this. The fridge is totally stocked. So is the freezer. Look here. There's steaks in the freezer. We're gonna be eating steak this week."

"And look at this!" Mark had opened a closet in the living area. "They've got all kinds of movies and game systems with all kinds of games. And look at the size of that television! Who needs Disney World? We can spend our vacation right here."

Michael joined him as they checked out the game systems, arguing over which one they should set up first.

"Yep. I told you we were going to have a great vacation." Kurt turned to his wife. "And you said there was something fishy about this."

Christine said nothing. That uneasy feeling was no longer in the background. She may not have been sophisticated, but she knew that rented condos do not come with fully stocked refrigerators. She headed out to the car to retrieve Sonny's cage. Just as she was reaching the car, her newly acquired cell phone rang. She thought it would be Ruthie calling to see if she had arrived safely in Florida. "Hello."

An all-too-familiar voice with a British accent said, "Welcome to Florida."

Christine stopped dead in her tracks. She instantly hung up. Her insides were shaking. The group was behind this. But why?

*****

Kurt woke everyone up early the next morning. "We've got to get to the time-share in about an hour. It'll take us about twenty minutes to drive there."

"I don't see why we hafta go," Matthew said. "You can go without us."

"No, if we want to get five tickets, we hafta have five people there. So get moving."

Christine emerged from the master bedroom, having showered in the most luxurious shower she had ever experienced. There were nozzles everywhere. She wasn't sure if she enjoyed being sprayed from all angles or not.

Hearing Kurt waking the boys up, she remembered how angry he had been when he discovered how much tickets for the Disney parks cost. He had thrown his hands up in disgust. How could he ever come up with that much money? Christine wasn't sure how he discovered that if they attended a time-share presentation, they could receive free park tickets. His plan was to attend the time-share presentation their first day in Florida, then they could go to the parks the following days with a break or two between park visits.

"Remember, Kurt. We're not gettin' no time-share. We're just there for the tickets." Christine feared that Kurt might be drawn into an agreement they could not afford.

"I know, I know. Now let's get moving."

The presentation was high pressure. Surely, only a fool would pass up an opportunity like this. They were shown pictures of time-shares perched over pristine beaches, by secluded mountain lakes, in the hearts of modern cities, all spacious and luxurious. And all this could be had for a modest monthly sum. They were taken through a sample unit with a large balcony overlooking a small, serene lake. Yes, they could vacation this way every summer.

Every time another person signed a contract, bells would ring and cheers would erupt. Christine could see that Kurt was getting drawn in. Each time the salesman made a better offer, Christine barked out, "Nope, can't afford it." Then Kurt would give her a dirty look.

An hour and a half later, they emerged from the time-share presentation with Disney tickets in one hand. In Kurt's other hand was a signed contract. All the way back to their condo, Kurt raved about taking vacations like this every summer.

Christine rolled her eyes. "I can't believe they let you sign that contract without a credit check. We can barely make our mortgage payments. How are we going to pay for a time-share too?"

"Aah, we'll figure it out."

Christine folded her arms. "They weren't gettin' my name on that piece of paper. When you can't make them payments, they ain't comin' after me." Christine may have lacked formal education, but she was no dummy. She had a knack for understanding numbers, and she knew those numbers did not add up.

In several months' time, Kurt figured out that he could not pay both the mortgage and the time-share. He let the time-share payments lapse. When ominous letters arrived threatening legal action if he did not pay, Kurt ignored them. He figured they couldn't repossess the time-share. What could they do to him? In time the letters stopped coming. But Christine fumed every time she thought about the money they wasted on the few payments he did make.

Sometimes Christine felt as if she would be better off without Kurt. She was confident in her ability to manage her own life. But she loved her boys. Above all else, she did not want to lose them. At times, she was surprised by how intensely she felt the desire to mother them.

No, she could not leave her boys, so she tolerated Kurt and stayed in the marriage.

*****

Kurt now had firmly in his grasp five tickets to the Magic Kingdom and five tickets to Universal Studios. That night, over a steak dinner, the family planned how to use their time.

Truth be told, the boys would have been happy to stay at the resort. They had discovered a large arcade filled with the latest games as well as pool, foosball, and air hockey tables. The swimming pool was large and had several amazing waterslides, not to mention bikini-clad girls slathered in suntan lotion, gracefully dangling their limbs over the edges of the pool.

Michael had visited the skateboard park, far more sophisticated than any he had ever seen before. Top-of-the-line skateboards were for rent. He could show off his skills to an admiring flock of "little rich kids," as he called them. The resort alone was enough of a vacation site for them.

But Christine's heart was set on seeing the Magic Kingdom. Despite groans from the boys, they agreed to begin there. Then they would take a day off before and after visiting Universal Studios. That way, the boys would still have plenty of time to enjoy the resort.

Christine had trouble sleeping that night. The child in her couldn't quite believe that she was going to see the Magic Kingdom. The hardened outer shell that encrusted Christine's psyche was starting to crack.

*****

Early the next morning, the old brown station wagon pulled into the parking lot at Magic Kingdom. Christine began to catch a glimpse of the magnitude of the Disney complex. After parking the car in one of many lots, the five of them found their way to the tram that would take them to the park's entrance. The tram was packed with families. Excited children of all sizes peered forward, hoping to catch a glimpse of the Magic Kingdom. After a short ride, the tram stopped in front of the gates where long lines formed. The five of them joined a line.

Christine looked around at all the children laughing and smiling. Some were literally jumping with excitement. She envied the freedom they had to just be children. Inwardly, she felt like jumping with excitement too. But she knew that above all else, she must not let herself become a child.

She took a deep breath and erected a solid, impenetrable wall to keep all those inner children at bay. Lucinda was in the light, well protected from any input from the outer world. She would not feel the pull to come out. But Christine wasn't so sure about the other children within her. She was especially unsure about her own inner child. She felt excitement rising within. She was about to enter the Magic Kingdom, every young child's delight.

She must remain an adult.

The family passed through the ticket gate. At that moment, her new cell phone rang.

Kurt glared at her. "You and them damn women. You can't even be away from them for a week."

Christine noted the call was from Ruthie but didn't answer. She didn't want Kurt to be mad and ruin her Magic Kingdom experience.

There were people everywhere, all headed in the same direction. Keeping one eye on the boys, she followed the crowd, not sure where she was headed. Then she became aware of stores on either side of the wide entryway into the Kingdom, stores filled with Disney souvenirs. She wanted to break away from the crowd and rush into these stores. She knew there would be so many things there that she would like, dolls and stuffed animals and trinkets of all kinds.

No, she must stay adult and keep an eye on the boys.

The crowd started to spread out a bit. She turned her eyes away from the stores, knowing she could come back to purchase souvenirs on their way out. She looked straight ahead, and then she saw it: the famous castle at the end of Main Street. Her eyes became glued to it.

A little girl next to her begged her father to lift her onto his shoulders so she could see the castle. Christine wanted someone to lift her up too so she could take it all in. They were truly in the magical place called Disney World. The castle was everything she had imagined it would be, only more so, bigger and brighter and more beautiful.

She started to skip with excitement, only to pull herself up short. No, she couldn't do that. *Must stay an adult, must stay an adult.* She felt the pressure of little children wanting to burst out, to dance and jump with delight. *You must stay in. You can look, but you can't come out.*

With her iron will, Christine pushed all those children back.

Christine's day at Disney World was alternately filled with child delight and rigid self-containment. Part of her longed for the freedom to just be a child who could enjoy this world of fantasy, but part of her knew her boys needed an adult mother. She did not want to embarrass either them or herself by being the true child she was.

Later that evening, after being enchanted by the famed light parade and fireworks over the castle, they stopped at the souvenir stores. Christine could hardly contain herself. There were so many items she wanted to purchase. Each child inside was vying for attention, saying what they wanted.

With her limited amount of spending money, she tried to please each voice within her. When the family finally left the park, she carried two large bags, filled with memories of their day at the Magic Kingdom. Every item in those bags was suitable for a child. Her boys teased her about her purchases, but it was good-natured, and she didn't mind.

But Kurt's sarcastic comments rankled her. "When are you gonna grow up? What adult buys that kind of stuff?"

She held her tongue, but inwardly she seethed.

She diverted her thinking to how well she had kept those inner children at bay. To the best of her ability, she had remained an adult during the entire day. Yet there were still moments when she felt true child delight, when inwardly she had clapped her hands in excitement.

Her day at the Magic Kingdom had been a success.

*****

Several nights later, Christine's phone rang late at night. Kurt lay next to her, snoring loudly. Christine grabbed the phone and held it to her ear. A voice with a British accent said a single word. It was repeated several times. Someone came forward and said, "Yes, sir."

"You are to be outside your front door in ten minutes. You must be there."

The one who was out hung up the phone, got out of bed, and found the clothes Lucinda had worn that day. She dressed and went to the front door. She quietly unlocked it and slipped outside.

A few minutes later, two men emerged from the darkness. They stood on either side of her. "Come with us."

She walked with them to another condo in the same complex.

Once they were inside, several other men and a woman joined them. One of the men said, "We're so glad you made it." They escorted her outside to a car. The one who was out compliantly went with them and got into the back seat.

A familiar man with a British accent seated himself next to her. Then the car drove off.

Inwardly, Christine became aware that someone else was out. Using her iron will, she began to push her way through. She was surprised at how difficult it was to break through to take charge of her body. At last, she was able, with a burst of energy, to get out. The first thing she was conscious of were voices, voices with British accents. Then she became aware that she was seated. She tried to peer around her to see what was going on. Gradually, her surroundings came into focus. She was in a large room like a warehouse.

She recognized Nevil. He was sitting next to her on a folding chair. Several people were facing them and firing questions at Nevil. She saw fear in his eyes. She had never seen that before.

She wondered where she was and why she was here.

"How much did you tell her? How much does she know?"

Nevil said nothing.

"Answer us. You do realize you have betrayed us. You let her see our finances. Your life is on the line, mister."

Finally, Nevil spoke. It seemed to burst out of him. "I had to do it. I had to win her over. It was the only way I could build the army. If she was one of us, she'd cooperate."

"You and your damn army. Do you realize you have put our entire operation in danger? What if she goes to the police? What if she tells her counselor or that other friend of hers and they go to the police? We're thinking we may need to move our operations to a new location. All because of you and your damn army."

Christine connected the dots in her head. The higher-ups in the group were afraid Nevil had told her too much about their finances and inner workings. She sensed both she and Nevil were in danger.

Nevil protested. "I did nothing wrong. Do you realize how much she can help us once I have that army in place? Those damn parts are fearless. They'll do anything we ask."

"We're tired of hearing about your army. When you went to show it off, all that came out were a bunch of babies. You made fools of us. We've had it with you, Nevil. And we've had it with your army. Now how are we going to keep her quiet?"

Christine listened to all this, and fear crept in. What about her boys? Would they try to use them to keep her quiet? Were they in danger? Would they threaten them to subdue her? Did they have them now? She strained her ears to hear any sound of their voices. She tried not to panic. Finally, she blurted out, "Do you have my boys?"

All eyes turned to her. "Who is this? Nevil, who is this?"

Nevil knew Christine was the only part who had any concern for her boys. "It must be Christine."

Now she was barraged with questions. How much did she know? What did Nevil tell her? What had he showed her in the books? What does she know about them?

Christine said nothing.

"Tell us, or we'll end your life. You will mysteriously disappear. We'll dump your corpse in the ocean where you'll be eaten by sharks."

Christine still said nothing. Her heart was pounding. She feared she was going to die, but even more, she feared that her boys would be dragged into this.

Nevil spoke up. "I just tried to befriend her so she would cooperate. She doesn't know that much."

Christine could sense the fear in Nevil's voice. She was afraid too, but with that iron will, she pushed away the fear and folded her arms as if to say, *You can't push me around.*

Once again, they barraged her with questions. "And what about that counselor of yours? And that other lady? How much do they know? What have you told them?"

Christine let a slight smile cross her lips, as if she was enjoying some inner secret. But she said nothing.

For the next several hours, they tried to pry information from them, using every threatening tactic they could think of. At one point, they brought out a body bag and told Christine she was leaving the building in it.

Nevil started to break, but Christine sat with her arms folded and said nothing. By now she was convinced they did not have her boys. If she died, she died. As long as her boys were safe, she knew they could not break her.

Perhaps it was their fear of what she might have told her counselor and Ruthie that kept them from harming her. But in the end, one of them turned to the others and said, "We can't break her. This is useless. We'll deal with Nevil, but she's like a stone wall. She is like the others inside her. She has no fear. We can't break her. Take her back."

As the sun was rising, Christine was dropped off at the resort entrance. She returned to the condominium. First, she checked on each of the boys to make sure they were soundly sleeping. Then she quietly crawled into bed.

She wondered if Kurt knew she had been away. And she wondered if this group would ever leave her alone.

She slept until past eleven the next morning. When she emerged from the bedroom, she found her boys playing video games. She went into the kitchen where Kurt was drinking coffee, not the low-end store brand he usually drank, but Starbucks. He looked over at Christine. She could tell that he had been brooding. She said nothing as she searched for a bowl and a box of cereal. She sat down across from him, cereal in hand. There was a tense silence.

Finally, his thoughts burst out. "Where the hell were you last night? I know exactly where you were. You were on the phone with them damn women. This is supposed to be our vacation. But no, you have to bring them along too."

Christine said nothing. It was best he thought that was the reason for her absence. If he knew about the group, he would probably do something rash. She finished eating her cereal and left the room. Again, she felt caught in the middle of three worlds: her life with Kurt and the boys, her clandestine life with the group, and her life with Ruthie and her counselor.

Sometimes it felt like the three worlds were colliding.

CHAPTER 31

Break Up

Later that day, Christine called me and told me about her experience with the group. I was horrified. "They threatened to kill you?"

"Yep. They said if I didn't tell them all I knew, I'd be history."

"But they let you go?"

"Yeah. They know too many people would try to get to the bottom of it if I disappeared."

"Weren't you terrified?"

"I started to get scared, but then I pushed all the fear down. I guess that's somethin' all of us can do."

"But why did they want you in Florida?"

"I think they have some kind of big operation down here. A lot of drugs come in on boats. And I think they thought if they could get me away from you and Ruthie, I'd break."

"They sure underestimated you."

"As long as I knew my boys were safe, I was okay."

"When will this group ever leave you alone? Can't they see they'll never get their army?"

"Most of them have had it with the army. It's mostly Nevil, and I think he's in big trouble with them."

I felt sick to my stomach after we ended our conversation. Was her life really in danger? Did they really lure her down to Florida to pry information out of her? Who were these ruthless people, and to what extent would they go to accomplish their ends? And could it really all be true?

I contemplated this question. But how else could I explain this trip to Florida at all? A week at a luxury resort for only $900? With a fully stocked refrigerator?

These questions swirled through my head as I sat in church that next Sunday. Christine's family was on their way home. Tomorrow, I would see her in my office. I couldn't bear the thought that I would once more be battling this group.

Having Ruthie in the picture certainly helped relieve some of the burden, but she brought another set of struggles. I felt so resentful of the way she had waltzed in and so easily connected with Christine. She was now calling herself Christine's mother. She had gone from auntie to mother. If she was her mother, who was I?

I was her spirituel mother. That was different, but once again, I felt myself being squeezed out by Ruthie. I did not want to feel that way. I wanted to be a team with her, working together for Lucinda's healing. It was easy to be down on myself because I could not graciously accept Ruthie.

All these thoughts spun through my head as I sat in church. It felt overwhelming. How could I continue this journey? Inwardly, I cried out to God. *You've got to help me. I just want to run away from it all. I even want to run away from you. You brought her into my life. You called me to be her spiritual mother. But all I do is come up short. I'm so intolerant with Christine, and I know my attitude toward Ruthie is all wrong. But I don't know how to change anything. I don't know how to change me. I just want to run away from it all. I just want it all to go away. I can't do this for another day.* From the depths of my being, a cry arose within me. *Help me!*

My gaze went to the cross at the front of the church. The cross. The symbol of Christ's suffering. My eyes were fixed on it. Once again, I prayed. *Part of me wants to run away from all this and from you. But to whom else can I go? Only you have the words of eternal life.* I recalled these words of the apostle Peter[11] and mulled them over in my mind. *God, you are my only hope. I need to trust that you will get me through. There is nowhere else to go.*

---

[11] John 6:68.

I took a deep breath and prepared to reenter the battle.

*****

Fall came early that year. The warm colors of the fall foliage were especially magnificent. With the sunlight glistening off the golds and yellows and oranges, I felt wrapped in a warm blanket of color, secure and comforting. I tried to let the beauty surrounding me calm my inner turmoil.

I wondered how the view from my old office window looked. I no longer worked with Dr. Kirkly. He had left the practice, and for various reasons, I moved on too. My new office had a large window, but the only view was of the parking lot. But as I drove about town, I tried to stay focused on the surrounding beauty. I kept reminding myself this was God's love being expressed to me.

I reassured myself that the group was not getting Lucinda very often. Ruthie was keeping a hawk's eye on her at night. Occasionally, they would have her during the day, but I was well aware it was often a week or more between these times. For this, I was deeply grateful.

*****

With the group's interference decreasing, Christine found herself with more time on her hands. She was home a great deal and was beginning to detect an uneasiness in Kurt. He seemed to avoid her, and on several different occasions, he mumbled something about having to check in on his mother, who was now living in a senior high-rise apartment.

One chilly November Saturday, he grabbed his car keys and headed out the door mumbling something about taking his mother for groceries and then to visit her other children. "Not sure when I'll be back."

Christine cocked her head as he headed out the door. Spending time with his mother was new for him. She wondered if her health was okay. She had already had a bout with cancer, though the doctors had declared her to be in remission.

Kurt was gone all that afternoon and into the early evening. When he returned, Christine was waiting for Ruthie to pick her up. "You sure were gone a long time. Is everything okay with your mother?"

Kurt breezed past her. "She's fine, but she's getting older and needs more help."

Christine followed him into the kitchen. "There's leftover spaghetti in the fridge."

Kurt kept his back toward her. "And I suppose you're going to be with Ruthie. You're always with them women."

Christine could tell that Kurt was uneasy, but she didn't respond. She headed back to the front door. Just then, Ruthie's car pulled up. "I'm leavin' now," she yelled.

There was no response.

She could not quite put her finger on it, but something seemed out of kilter with him.

*****

Several nights later, Christine woke up suddenly from a sound sleep. Kurt's side of the bed was empty. She checked the clock. It was shortly after one in the morning. She wondered why she had woken up so suddenly. She hoped the boys were all right.

To settle her fears, she slid out of bed to check on them. First, she checked on Michael, whose room was just down the hall. He was sleeping soundly. Then she headed up to the third floor to check on Matthew and Mark. They, too, were sound asleep.

Why wasn't Kurt in bed?

As she headed back toward her bedroom, she heard a muffled sound downstairs. She quietly made her way down. Sometimes when Kurt couldn't sleep, he would sit at the kitchen table and drink milk or hot chocolate. She checked the kitchen. He wasn't there. She was about to leave the kitchen when she saw a slight sliver of light from under the door to the basement.

Why would Kurt be in the basement? Very quietly, she pulled the door open, and trying not to make a sound, she stealthily made her way down the stairs. A dim light came from across the basement.

About two-thirds of the way down, she stooped to see the expanse of the basement. She could make out Kurt's silhouette in front of his computer screen. He was talking in low tones.

Christine craned her neck to get a different angle, trying to see what was on the computer screen. Then Kurt started to laugh and leaned to the side, giving her a full view of the screen. She clearly saw the face of a middle-aged woman with light-colored hair and a very round face. She was smiling coyly. Kurt was chuckling.

Christine's heart pounded. She was not surprised at what she saw. In many ways, she was relieved. Now she knew why Kurt seemed so uneasy.

Not sure what to do next, Christine decided to let him know she was there and had seen him in conversation with this woman. She coughed.

Kurt swung his head around and saw his wife's form on the stairs. He snapped off the computer. "Sh-sh-sh-she's -j-j-just a fr-fr-fr-friend."

Christine knew there was more here than a friendship. She turned around and went back to bed.

*****

It was a Thursday night in early November when the inevitable finally happened. Michael had a home wrestling match that evening. Joby had been a high school wrestler and was interested in the sport, so he planned to attend. Christine was in the kitchen when she mentioned this to Kurt.

Much to her surprise, he erupted.

She watched as he ranted on and on about what he was going to do to Joby.

In his fury, Kurt lunged at her and threw her against the wall. He grabbed her by the throat and began to choke her.

Christine kicked at his legs, jamming her sneaker into his shins.

He released her neck and threw her onto the floor. Then he stormed out of the house, slamming the front door behind him.

Christine slowly got to her feet, taking several deep breaths. It felt good to breathe again. She leaned against the wall. Then it hit her; a swirl of wild emotions seemed to be crashing over her from every angle. She wanted to strangle Kurt, but she also knew she must protect Joby. She grabbed the phone.

*****

I was in the midst of throwing a quick dinner together so we could eat before going to the match. The phone rang.

The instant I answered, Christine screamed, "Don't let him come to the wrestling match!"

"Why, what's wrong?"

"Don't let him come. Kurt is really mad. Said he was gonna go up to that match, and when he saw Joby, he was gonna choke the shit out of 'im."

"What did Joby ever do to him?"

"Nothin'. I just wanted him to know that you was gonna be there. And then he went on and on about beatin' the shit out of Joby."

"Well, if you think it's best, we'll stay home, but personally, I doubt he'd do anything. He'd look pretty lame going after a man twenty years older than he is."

"No, you'd better stay home. When he's mad, he's not right. He could do anything."

"Okay, we'll stay home."

*****

Christine hung up and stood in her kitchen as all those emotions assailed her from every angle. She felt unbridled rage toward

Kurt. She felt self-hatred for the turmoil she had brought into our lives. She felt panicked fear for what Kurt might actually do.

The emotions were strong—overwhelming. Her ability to think clearly was eclipsed. No light could penetrate her tormented psyche.

"I'm done with his shit," she screamed. She grabbed some old newspapers and shoved them into her gas oven. When the oven was crammed full, she ran throughout the house to make sure her boys were not home.

Then she waited for Kurt to return. As soon as he came in the door, she would turn the stove on and burn the house down with both of them in it. She would put an end to Kurt and to her own torment.

As she waited, her emotions continued to swirl, rage and hatred, self-loathing and fear. She waited and waited. Christine assumed Kurt went out to cool down and would be back shortly. Instead, he had headed up to the wrestling match. It would be several hours before he returned.

Tired of waiting, Christine decided that she could at least get rid of her own torment. She turned the oven on, opened the oven door, and waited. The papers began to burn.

In that moment, a ray of light came into her mind. Why was she killing herself? Kurt was the one she wanted dead; and besides, her boys needed a mom.

She turned the oven off and watched as the flames burned out and ashes smoldered.

*****

For the second time that evening, she called me. This time she was crying copiously. "I need help. I tried to burn the house down. I wanted to kill me and Kurt. I can't do this no more. I might hurt somebody. I've got to get out of here." She sounded truly wretched as she ranted and raved about wanting to kill Kurt, about wanting her own misery to end, about needing help.

I listened, wondering what to do next. Did I need to hospitalize her? It had been many years since she had a mental health hospitalization. I truly did not want to do that. But she had tried to burn their house down. Obviously, she was decompensating. What to do next?

The clear, calm, rational voice of Cinda came across the phone. "You have to get her out of here. Call Ruthie and move her out. It is too dangerous for her to stay."

"I can't do this no more!" Christine was back. The toughness was gone, and she was a broken cacophony of sobs and tears and wails, unrestrained emotion pouring out and meeting my ears on the other end of the phone. But at least I had a plan now.

"Christine, I am going to call Ruthie, and we are coming to get you. Pack up what you want to take with you. We need to get you out of the house. You are a danger to yourself and Kurt, and maybe even your boys.

"Where will I go?" she wailed.

"You can stay with Ruthie until we have a clear plan."

"What about all my dolls? Kurt might destroy 'em when he finds out I'm gone."

"Pack up what you want to take. We'll bring as many cars as we can."

So that night, with the help of my two sons, we removed Christine from her home.

When we arrived, she was carefully placing her expensive, collector dolls in their original boxes, which were then placed in their shipping boxes. Having this to occupy her mind and hands gave her a focus and helped allay the emotions that had overwhelmed her earlier.

Just as we were making our last trips to the cars, Kurt arrived home from the wrestling match. He said nothing as he watched us fill our cars with his wife's belongings.

"She tried to burn the house down. It isn't safe for her to stay here." I offered this as my explanation.

Kurt said nothing. But as we made our final exit out the door, I saw him standing in the kitchen. He looked very forlorn, like he was brooding over what was happening.

I felt bad for him, but in many ways, it was surprising this had not happened sooner. Their marriage had been on a collision course for a long time.

*****

After Christine left and moved in with Ruthie, her main concern was for her boys. She tried her best to maintain a relationship with each of them, but the upheaval affected them as well. Matthew, now attending a local college, had discovered the intoxicating and numbing effects of alcohol. Mark had retreated into a cocoon of depression, and Michael seemed a seething ball of anger.

Christine's heart ached as she tried to figure out how to be a mom for her boys when she didn't live with them. Ruthie lived in a small apartment—not a place where her boys could hang out. "I just want to be their mom, and I don't know how I can do it. That's all I really care about."

I could see the sincerity of her concerns.

Her second son, Mark, was the one most likely to share his heart with her. She saw the pain in his eyes and longed to make it easier for him. She tried to explain that her relationship with his dad had been dead for a long time.

"Well, you know, Mom. Dad has been seeing someone else."

"You mean that fathead on the computer?"

Mark chuckled. "She is kind of a fathead, isn't she? But it's not just on the computer. She lives at the shore and sends him all these lighthouses. He has a whole collection of them. And he's been going down to see her."

"How do you know all this?"

"Well, the lighthouses he had hidden in the basement, but now he has 'em displayed in the living room. Some of them arrived while I was home. I saw her return address, so I know where she lives. Maybe

I'm a snoop, but I keep my eyes and ears open. I heard him calling off work early in the morning, then taking off and being gone all day. I think he's been seeing her for about six months."

Christine's heart skipped a beat. Six months? She didn't know that.

"One other thing, Mom."

"What's that?"

"She's a pastor."

"What? Fathead is a pastor?"

"Yeah, she has a church at the shore."

For a second, Christine was speechless. When the words finally came, they spilled out of her. "How dare she? She stands for God, and she's having an affair with my husband?" The fighting instincts that ran deep in Lucinda's psyche rose to the surface as she described in detail what she planned to do to this woman.

"Mom, you can't do those things. You'll end up in jail."

Mark was right. Somehow she had to curb her anger. She took a deep breath. "Mark, the only reason I stayed with your dad as long as I did was to be with you boys. As far as I'm concerned, this marriage is over."

"I know, Mom. I know he hurt you a lot. "

"I'm sorry it's come to this, Mark. But I'm still your mom, and I still love my boys."

Mark gave her a glimmer of a smile. "Even in your worst moments, I always knew you loved us."

*****

Finding out about Kurt's six-month-long affair with a pastor did not sit well with Christine. Inwardly, she seethed with anger. She harbored no jealousy toward this woman. From Christine's perspective, he was no prize package; she could have him. But she did care that her family was torn apart and that she no longer lived with her boys.

Now she understood why Kurt had become so distant. She suspected his own uneasy conscience was behind much of his recent erratic behavior, like his threats to beat up Joby and his attack against her.

Adding to her indignation was that fact that this woman pastored a church. Did she not even care that this family was torn apart? How could she stand before her church each week, knowing she was in the middle of all this? The more Christine brooded on this, the more despondent she became.

I understood her anger. I was angry too. I was also fearful that she might do something rash. She had prodded Mark to tell her this woman's name and address. The address he had seen was the address of her church. Fortunately, she didn't drive, so that made it difficult for her to get to a town several hours away, but I also knew she was checking out bus schedules.

I tried to process this with her in our sessions. "Christine, what do you hope to accomplish by confronting her?"

"I want her to know she destroyed a family."

"But you know that sooner or later, with or without her, your marriage was going to end."

"But maybe I coulda made it last until the boys were all out on their own."

"Do you think you could confront her without getting violent? If you lay a hand on her, it will not go well for you."

"I think I could, but if them parts came out, it could be the end of her."

I knew all too well that some of Christine's alters were violent. Lucinda had a long history of fighting. Indeed, she had been expelled from school in ninth grade for that very reason. "Well then, I think it's best you don't try to confront her."

Christine nodded.

*****

The holidays came and went. Christine was devastated that she couldn't be with her boys on Christmas morning. Her anger at the woman on the computer continued to simmer. As she tried to manage this anger by repressing it, she became deeply depressed. I was concerned for her emotional well-being. She was convinced the only solution was confronting this woman.

We were at a deliverance session with Paul and Adele, discussing the matter, when Cinda popped out. "She needs to confront her. And this woman needs to be confronted. What she is doing is wrong. I will be close to Christine, preventing any violent alters from coming out. It will be just Christine. She is going to do what none of them was ever able to do: stand up to a woman Kurt was involved with. She will represent all of them, and it will be healing for all of them. You are all to go with her, to encourage and support her."

I gulped. This confrontation sounded scary. I looked at the others—Paul and Adele, Ruthie, and my dear husband, Joby. No one said anything.

Finally, Paul broke the silence. "It looks like we're going to the shore."

*****

The day arrived for the planned outing. Christine was subdued on the ride down. We offered up prayers for an effective confrontation, that Christine would be able to say what she needed to say, and that this woman would be convicted of the error of her ways.

We drove to her church and parked in the parking lot. *What do we do now?*

"Why don't I go in and get her, tell her why we're here and see if she will come out to the car?" Paul suggested. We all agreed to this plan.

Paul headed down a slope to the church. We sat in silence. After a short time, we saw Paul emerge from the church…alone. He came back up the incline. He opened the car door and poked his head inside. "Well, I talked to her. But she refuses to come out."

"Well, you tell her that if she ain't comin' out, I'm comin' in." Christine's voice was loud and filled with anger.

Paul was silent for a minute. "Well, let me give it a try."

Once more, Paul walked down the slope to the church. We watched from the car. When he finally emerged from the church, he was alone, again. When he got back to the car, he shook his head. "She still won't come."

"Then I'm goin' in." Christine lunged for the door. She was halfway out when a round-faced, light-haired woman emerged from the church.

Ruthie and I scrambled out of the car and stood on either side of Christine. Paul went down to meet her. We watched as he escorted this middle-aged, somewhat overweight woman up the incline. She wore a dark skirt and blouse with a clerical collar.

I silently prayed this would go well.

When Paul and the pastor reached the car, there was an awkward silence.

The pastor spoke first. Never in a million years would I have guessed her opening words. "I was expecting you."

I wondered why she would expect this visit.

Christine straightened up, looked her in the eye, and blurted out, "Are you having an affair with my husband?"

The woman lowered her eyes and bit her lower lip. In a barely audible voice, she said, "Yes, I am."

I was grateful for her honesty. Lying would not have gone well with Christine.

"How long has this been going on?" Christine's voice was loud and accusatory.

Again, her voice was quiet, her eyes downcast. "About six months."

"Six months? You've been having an affair with my husband for six months? And you call yourself a pastor? You know I have three boys who are seeing their family fall apart because of you."

"Well, I didn't plan for this to happen. I was counseling him online. Then he came down to see me so we could have an in-person session. And it just happened."

"Just happened? These things don't *just happen*!" Christine lunged toward her.

Ruthie and I grabbed her and pulled her back.

Christine screamed. "You call yourself a pastor? You stand for God? Look at you. What does he see in you?"

I cringed when she said this.

I have no recollection of how the conversation ended. I do remember the relief of being back in the car. It was a long ride home.

Christine cried most of the way. "Now I know for sure this marriage is over. There's no pretendin' nothin' else. He cheated on me with that pathetic woman."

The next day, Christine called the church. When she got an answering machine, she left a lengthy message for whoever would check the church's messages. She explained that their pastor was having an affair with her husband and the church should know about it. I'm sure she used absolutely no tact and held nothing back. We have no idea who heard that message or how it might have affected the pastor's status with the church. I do know that Christine relished the opportunity to expose this woman.

So the final nail was in the coffin. Lucinda's marriage was not just dead but buried. Now she just had to figure out how to move forward.

CHAPTER 32

Good News

In the weeks that followed, Christine was consumed with wanting to be a mom for her boys. She tried to spend time with them, but they were busy teenagers trying to find their own way through their family's breakup. Hanging around Mom was not high on their priority list. She wondered what she could do to draw them to her. In her eagerness to please them, she would spend money on them, buying Michael a new bicycle or Mark a guitar, but that did not work. She thought that if she just had a nice place where they could visit her, they might come around. Ruthie's little apartment was just too small to accommodate them.

One day, Ruthie and Christine dropped in on me at home unexpectedly. For the first time in quite a while, Christine was smiling. Ruthie seemed almost giddy.

Ruthie was the first to speak. "We're just so excited. You know, for a long time, I've been saving to buy a house. But then, I'd think that being by myself, I didn't want all that responsibility. But now that it looks like Christine is going to be with me long-term, I think it's the right time. So we've been looking at houses, and I think we found one I can afford. We're just so excited. I think the owner is pretty desperate to sell, so the price is very reasonable."

Christine jumped in. "It's in the country, has a lotta land, and a swimming pool!"

"And it's only about fifteen minutes from my work."

"And there are four bedrooms, so there will be a lot of room for the boys when they visit."

Their excitement was palpable. I smiled and congratulated them.

"Oh, don't congratulate us yet. We're going to put in a bid tomorrow. Just pray we can get it." Ruthie put her arm around Christine. "It will be our own home, a place where I can help my daughter to grow up because we all know that under that tough exterior, she's just a broken child."

When Ruthie called Christine her daughter, it felt like a gut punch. I said nothing, but once again, I wondered where I fit in. Ruthie seemed convinced she was her mother. They were going to move to the country and have this idyllic mother-daughter relationship. They would have a life together.

Who was I? Her therapist? Her spiritual mother? How did I fit in? Was it time for me to just back away and let them have their life together?

If either Ruthie or Christine detected my unsettledness, they said nothing. They bubbled on about the new house and left with smiles and laughter, talking about who would get which bedroom.

I stood in the middle of my kitchen, trying to reason my way through this. It was, of course, a wonderful opportunity for Ruthie. The property sounded like a great place for Christine to entertain her boys. I reassured myself that there was still room for me.

Indeed, I was the only one with a relationship with child Lucinda. Cinda had made it very clear to Ruthie that she was not to have Lucinda out, and Ruthie had complied with that.

For the two of them to live together in this house was wonderful for both of them. In many ways, they needed each other. Ruthie was quite alone in the world. Her marriage had failed. She had no children and no close family connections. And Christine, of course, needed a home. This was perfect for both of them.

I told myself these things, and I believed them to be true, but it did not allay the raw jealousy I felt. It had been smoldering for a long time, but now it was right on the surface, raw and ugly. Ruthie had waltzed into the picture and walked away with the prize, leaving me empty-handed.

I looked upward, raised my fist, and shouted, "I don't get it. I have poured myself into her for over fifteen years, and now I am left out. Where do I fit in?"

This kind of jealousy was new for me. I was stunned by the intensity of the feeling. It was wrong, but I had no way of controlling it. Anger rolled over me in waves.

I got down on my knees and sobbed uncontrollably. When the tears finally subsided, I knew I needed help. I did not like the person I was. I wanted to be free of all this intense emotion. I wanted to be at peace again. I had become consumed with this triangle of Christine, Ruthie, and me. Something had to be done.

The next day, first thing in the morning, I made an appointment with a psychologist.

*****

My counseling sessions with Christine were becoming more sporadic. The intense work with alter personalities that had characterized so much of our work together had ceased.

Christine, as the host personality, the one who was out and in control of the body most of the time, was very different from the Lucinda who had first come to see me. From the beginning, Lucinda had been willing to show me her soft and pliable side. Christine, on the other hand, was invested in remaining tough and impenetrable. I attributed much of this to her history with the group. They had split her off and groomed her to be this way.

Every once in a while, I would catch a glimpse of her softer side, of the broken child within, but I was sorely aware that she was much more likely to let Ruthie see this child side of her. That did not help with my jealousy. I told myself it was good she had this trust in Ruthie. I truly believed that to be so. But it did not help allay my intense emotions.

I was also keenly aware that Christine felt I preferred child Lucinda over her. In deference to Christine, I chose not to have Lucinda out with me very often. At one session, while Christine and Ruthie were waiting to hear if they got the new house, I asked Christine if it would be okay if I had Lucinda out for a little while. It had been weeks since I had seen her. When Christine assented, I called her out.

"NanNan!" Lucinda threw her arms around me. As always, she was filled with life and light. "I missed you. It's nice and warm inside in the light, but I like being out here with you. Let's color."

I opened my desk drawer and pulled out paper and crayons. She grabbed the brightest color crayons and filled a paper with color and stick figures, and of course, her signature bumblebee angel. Her exuberance was contagious, and we laughed together. She was completely uninhibited, a child in every sense of the word, except, of course, her body. It was good to be with her.

Then we sat on the couch while I read her a story. She snuggled in close while I read to her about animals in the woods. After I closed the book, she laid her head on my chest and listened to my heartbeat. "Bump, bump. Bump, bump," she whispered.

I thought of all the child alters who had been healed of their traumas by listening to my heartbeat. Slowly, Lucinda drifted off to sleep. When I knew she was sleeping soundly, I quietly called Christine back. Little did I know that it would be over a decade before I would see child Lucinda again. It is best I didn't know. I am certain it would have added to my emotional turmoil.

*****

Drawing by Lucinda, complete with her bumblebee angel.

The psychologist I chose to see was well schooled in dissociative identity disorder. He was also a committed Christian. I spent the first session giving him the history of my relationship with Lucinda. I tried to hold nothing back, including the battle with the group and my conviction that Cinda was an angel from God. We discussed this at length, considering all possibilities of what she might be.

He suggested that perhaps she was just an alter personality who truly believed she was an angel from God. I considered this but objected that her understanding of spiritual matters was far beyond that of Lucinda or any of her alters. Where could she have gotten that knowledge and understanding?

He suggested that for now we put the question of Cinda's true identity to the side. It was not a question that would be easily answered. I was a bit uncomfortable knowing he questioned my assessment of Cinda's identity, but otherwise, I could tell that Dr. Learner was tracking with me. I left that session feeling hopeful. Perhaps Dr. Learner would be able to help me with my inner turmoil.

At our second session, I carefully explained how Ruthie had come into the picture. I tried to be as objective as possible, explaining the positive ways she had affected Christine and helped me with the struggles of battling the group. But…I hesitated before I proceeded. I did not want to be unfair in my portrayal of Ruthie.

I explained to Dr. Learner that her way of being with Christine was to hover over her protectively. When she was there, it was as if there was no room for me, or anyone else. Once she was involved, it was as if she took over everything. She had a hawk's eye for anyone who might hurt Christine, and if someone did, she would rise up with indignation against that person. There were times I had been the object of her mother-bear ire.

Now that she and Christine were planning to live together in an idyllic setting in the country, I found myself seething with a jealousy that I did not want. "I should be glad for both of them. They need each other."

Dr. Learner listened carefully. He did not say much, but I could tell he was pondering the things I said. Finally, he concluded our session by asking me to be in prayer before we met again. "I believe there are few things we need to address."

Again, I left feeling hopeful.

*****

It wasn't long before Ruthie received word that her bid had been accepted. Settlement was just a month away. She and Christine began to make plans for the move. Ruthie did not have enough furniture to fill the house, so they tried to figure out where they could find some inexpensive furniture.

Christine could be very resourceful, and I watched as she set about finding furniture for their new home. She knew Kurt had an extra couch stored in their basement, so she approached him.

"You want that old thing? You must really be desperate. You can have it, but I want it out of here by this weekend."

Christine was elated he was cooperating. She knew my husband had access to a pick-up truck from his work, so she asked him to help her move it. And she had one more request: could they store this couch in the second floor of our garage until they moved to the new house?

Joby saw no problem helping her with the couch, so on a cold March night, he drove off to meet her at Kurt's house. When he arrived home and parked in front of our garage, he had a solidly built, sightly tattered, full-length couch edged into the bed of the pick-up truck.

I went out to greet him and eyed the couch.

"It's a heavy sucker," Joby said. "It took both of us and two of her sons to get it onto the truck."

"And how to you plan to get it up those stairs to the second floor of our garage?" I eyed the steep, narrow stairs.

Ruthie and Christine drove up at that moment. Christine popped out of the car, obviously pleased with her find. "It'll be perfect until we can afford something nicer. Thanks so much for helping."

Joby lowered the tailgate and climbed onto the bed of the truck. I watched as he and Christine pushed and shoved and heaved. Finally, with Ruthie and me helping, the couch was lowered onto the pavement.

Christine was a very strong woman, much stronger than most, but I saw no way they were going to get it up those stairs. The stairs were so narrow there would only be room for Joby and Christine. Ruthie and I could only stand and watch. They had the couch positioned at the base of the stairs and began to creep it up the stairs.

To make the task much more difficult, a hand railing protruded from the wall. They had to lift the couch above that railing to fit it up the stairs.

Ruthie and I shivered in the cold March air as we listened to Joby shouting instructions to Christine. "Okay, now lift." We heard grunts and groans, and then Joby was shouting, "Lift it higher."

I shook my head. There was no way they were going to be able to get that couch up those stairs.

"Good, that's high enough. Now step up."

That was last I heard from Joby, but a short three minutes later, Joby and Christine emerged from the garage, laughing.

He shook his head. "Where did you get that strength? It felt like there was a team of wild horses at your end of the couch. It just lifted into the air, above the railing, and over the half wall at the top of the stairs. I've never seen anything like it."

Christine was not often at a loss for words, but she was silent awhile. "I wish that had been my strength, but it wasn't. I felt Cinda draw very close to me. Then I felt her strength pulsing through me. She gave me the strength to lift it. Or she lifted it using my body. I'm not sure how it worked."

We all shook our heads in amazement. Joby, ever the science guy, said, "I have no natural explanation for what just happened. Even with a huge adrenaline rush, I don't believe she could have that much strength. She lifted it like it was a toothpick."

I marveled at what had transpired. *How do I explain this if Cinda is just an alter personality who thinks she's an angel?*

*****

I arrived for my next session with Dr. Learner a little nervous, but very hopeful. I had been in prayer that morning, asking God for an open heart for whatever Dr. Learner had to tell me. After we exchanged pleasantries, I jumped right in. "You left me hanging last week. What is it that you feel we need to address?"

"As I listened to you last week, I realized that you feel your problem is with Ruthie."

I nodded.

"I don't think Ruthie is your problem."

I cocked my head, wondering where he was going with this.

"I believe your problem is with Lucinda."

"Well, there is a problem with Lucinda. At least there is with Christine. Her abrasiveness so often rubs me the wrong way."

"That may be true, but it's not what I'm talking about. I believe you have become so invested in helping Lucinda that you have formed an unhealthy soul tie with her."

I had heard of soul ties before, but usually in the context of sexual relationships.

Dr. Learner elaborated. "A soul tie is a connection to another person through our mind, will, or emotions. With all that you have been through with Lucinda, you have formed a very deep connection with her."

I nodded. Of course, he was right.

"This connection is also spiritual. But you have allowed the connection to become unhealthy. You want more from her than is healthy. What is it that you want from her?"

I considered his question. Inwardly, what he was saying rung true, that my connection with Lucinda was unhealthy. So, what did I want from Lucinda?

Finally, I spoke. "I want her to be healed, to be whole."

"And if she gets healed and whole, what will that mean for you?"

"It will mean that I've succeeded." As soon as the words were out of my mouth, I realized I was invested in Lucinda's healing because I wanted a success story. That's why it drove me crazy when Christine's hardened exterior kept me out. That's why Ruthie's success with Christine was such an obstacle for me. *I* wanted to be the one with the success story.

My jaw dropped. I looked at Dr. Learner. "I see it now. I wanted the success story for me. How self-centered. What do I do now?"

"Remember I told you soul ties are spiritual. We can pray together and break this soul tie in the spirit. Then it should filter down and affect you on the natural level."

"Then let's do it. Now. I don't want this soul tie any longer."

Together we prayed. I confessed that I had let Lucinda become an idol in my life. Her healing became the way I was going to be a success. I asked God to beak any unhealthy ties I had with Lucinda or any of her alters. I asked him to forgive my selfishness and my intolerance of Ruthie. I wept quietly, as Dr. Learner commanded that this tie be broken in the name of Jesus.

When we had finished, I felt lighter and greatly relieved. I was confident that something significant had happened.

That was a turning point for me. I was no longer consumed with the triangle of Christine, Ruthie, and myself. My resentment toward Ruthie gradually began to lessen. Christine's abrasiveness… well, there were still times when that was a struggle for me, but my reactions to it were less extreme.

I needed to trust God with Lucinda's healing. That was in his hands. I did not need her to be whole to feel I was a successful person. I hoped to find peace with Ruthie and Lucinda having a life together in the country. It did not mean there was no room for me. Ruthie might consider herself Christine's mother, but I was still her spiritual mother. That was the role God gave me. And no one, even Ruthie, could take that away.

*****

Christine and Ruthie moved into their new home on a lovely weekend in April.

Joby and I were out of town for a wedding. I was able to stay focused and enjoy the festivities, reconnecting with old friends and celebrating the occasion. I barely gave a thought to the move happening back home.

That smoldering jealousy was receding, and I was able to have a realistic assessment of what was happening. Ruthie and Christine having a life together was not going to be all flowers and candy. Christine still had significant mental health issues. The excitement of the move had distracted her from the depression that haunted her, but she still was deeply depressed over losing her life with her boys.

And Ruthie, like me, had feet of clay. Sooner or later, conflict would arise. I wondered how long Christine would tolerate Ruthie's style of hovering over her. Ruthie thrived in the role of the doting mother, but realistically, I knew Christine, with her strong personality, needed space of her own.

The weekend after the move, Joby and I, along with Paul and Adele, were invited over to see the new house. We arrived in the late afternoon. We traversed a steep driveway with a switchback. Mature trees lined the driveway. We arrived at a split-level house nestled into the side of a hill. A lawn ran along one side of the driveway. The other side was a wooded drop-off. This was not so much a house in the country as a house on a wooded hillside.

Paul and Adele pulled up right behind us. Christine burst out of the door, anxious to give us a full tour of the property. As dusk settled in, she showed us the lawn, then took us around the back of the house. Ruthie came out the back door and joined us as we climbed about a dozen stairs that led to a gate.

Christine opened the gate and ushered us into the pool area. A small, covered, in-ground pool was surrounded by cement walks and a patio. The chain-link fence surrounding the pool area backed right up to the woods. The way the pool seemed to nestle into the woods did indeed seem idyllic. I tried to imagine what it would look like in the summer when the trees were decked in their finest green and sunlight filtered through them.

"This seems so secluded," I observed. "It will be absolutely lovely in the summer."

Christine beamed. "I can't wait to have the boys over for a swim party. Next month we're gonna to take the cover off the pool. Hopefully what's underneath isn't in too bad a shape."

Ruthie led us into the house. We made our way through unpacked boxes and partially assembled rooms. In many ways, the house was laid out like a standard split-level, but the previous owners had added an addition, which increased the living area. Christine had already chosen an extra bedroom as a doll room. She hoped to buy several large glass cabinets so her collector dolls could be handsomely displayed. She envisioned a pool table in the back room of the addition. "Then the boys will have something to do in the winter."

I excused myself for a minute and went out to the car. I brought in a cake with *Congratulations* sprawled across it. I also brought some plastic stemmed glasses and sparkling grape juice. We toasted their new home.

Remnants of jealousy tried to surface as I looked about the house and realized they truly were going to make a life together in the country. *No, I'm not going to let their happiness destroy my peace.*

"This is a happy occasion."

I instantly recognized the voice of Cinda. We all did. Five heads turned toward her.

"I have something more for you to celebrate. I have some very good news."

"I don't know how much better things can get," Ruthie said.

"Oh, it can get better. The good news is that the group will never again have Christine." Her words hung in the air.

I couldn't believe what I was hearing. "Never again?"

"No, never again. Your battle with them is over. They plan to move out of the area. They are afraid Christine knows too much about them, that perhaps she will go to the authorities."

The moment felt surreal. I felt light, like I was floating. No more broken children to hold. No more late-night phone calls. No more strategizing with Ruthie to make sure Christine was safe. I felt as if a thousand-pound weight had been lifted from me.

Cinda looked right at me. "God has seen your faithfulness through this ordeal. He has heard your cries for your spiritual daughter. He knows this has not been easy for you. It is all behind you now."

I sat down on a packing box. I watched as Ruthie and Joby and Paul and Adele hugged each other, rejoicing over this good news.

Paul came over to me and put his arm around me. "Celebrate with us."

"I've dreamed of this day. Now that it's here, it feels too good to be true."

Cinda looked at me. "Oh, it's true. Now call Christine and let her know the good news."

"Christine, come back. We have some great news for you."

Instantly, Christine was in the body, looking at us with questioning eyes.

"Christine, we have wonderful news from Cinda." I choked back tears as I relayed all Cinda had said.

Christine was speechless, most unusual for her.

I threw my arms around her. "It's over. This horrible, awful nightmare is over. Never again will they torture you." We hung onto each other for a few minutes. Then each one hugged her.

Paul spoke next. "I think a prayer of thanksgiving is in order."

We stood in a circle holding hands, each of us offering heartfelt prayers, thanking God for this wonderful news.

The battle with the group was over.

*****

I slept like a baby that night. When I awoke, my first awareness was a sense of relief. For the first time in over three years, I did not have to concern myself with Lucinda's well-being. She was safe in her new home in the country.

In the weeks that followed, Ruthie decided Christine needed to learn to drive so she wouldn't be stranded while Ruthie was at work. Christine was eager to learn, so driving lessons began. They speculated that once she had her license, she might be able to find work. I was pleasantly surprised that Ruthie seemed eager to help her spread her wings.

Her boys did come to see her in her new home, but Christine was disappointed they did not make it a regular hangout spot. But for the first time since she left Kurt, she felt she had a place where she could be a mom to her boys.

These were all new beginnings. For Christine, split off and groomed for evil purposes by the group, this new life stretched before her with endless possibilities.

As I watched Christine taking the first steps in her new life, I was excited for her. In many ways, Kurt had kept her stunted. He had never wanted her to drive or to find work outside the home. Now she was starting to spread her wings.

But I also knew that mental illness was still a significant concern for her. All the broken parts within were still there. Depression was a constant battle. Ruthie would have her hands full.

And one question plagued me as I watched Christine's new life unfold. If Christine was going to live in the country with Ruthie, how would she ever be a trophy for the city? *A trophy for the city.* That phrase had hung with me since it was first pronounced over Lucinda. It had given me hope and strength and encouragement. But now I wondered how that would ever unfold. Could she be a trophy for the city while living in the country?

But it was not mine to orchestrate or figure out. I needed only to do my part in this journey, which had already taken me to places I never could have imagined. I wondered what more lay ahead, but I had an abiding confidence that God would be with us no matter the mountains, rivers, deserts, or lush valleys we had to traverse.

I was her spiritual mother, and she was my spiritual daughter. I could rest in that.

One more volume to come.

About the Author

Photograph by Julie Soisson

Nancee Soisson is a retired mental health counselor. She spent thirty years in the field, specializing in the treatment of women who were traumatized by sexual and ritual abuse. She is now retired and enjoying her ten grandchildren, her Scottish terrier, world travel with her beloved husband, and of course, writing Lucinda's ongoing story. (One more volume to come.) She is active in her ethnically diverse inner-city church, leading a recovery ministry with her husband for the past fifteen years. She never tires of seeing God at work in people's lives, including her own.

She is very grateful for the incredible journey she has shared with Lucinda.

To God be the glory!

www.ingramcontent.com/pod-product-compliance
Lightning Source LLC
La Vergne TN
LVHW051103210926
848486LV00023B/416/J
* 9 7 9 8 8 9 3 4 5 4 3 4 5 *